THREE WISE MEN
OF THE EAST

THE EMPEROR CH'IEN LUNG MOU

, BY CASTIGLIONE AND T'ANG TAI

*The University of North Carolina Press, Chapel Hill,
N. C.; The Baker and Taylor Company, New York;
Oxford University Press, London; Maruzen-Kabushiki-
Kaisha, Tokyo; Edward Evans & Sons, Ltd., Shanghai.*

乾隆大皇帝
TCHIEN LUNG TA WHANG TEE
TCHIEN LUNG, THE GREAT EMPEROR.

THREE WISE MEN
OF THE EAST

By ELIZABETH BISLAND, AUTHOR OF
The Life and Letters of Lafcadio Hearn,
The Truth About Men, etc.

CHAPEL HILL
THE UNIVERSITY OF NORTH CAROLINA PRESS
1930

COPYRIGHT, 1930, BY
THE UNIVERSITY OF NORTH CAROLINA PRESS

PREFACE

Walt Whitman, with a poet's insight, suggested two generations since that "As soon as history is properly told there will be no more need of romances":—perceiving that man's actions have ever been more astonishing and romantic than his fictions.

The greater popularity of fables has doubtless been due to their pleasanter presentation. The older school of historians, prone to distrust the temptation of imaginative sympathy, have conventionalized the past into a siccated mummy, wound tightly in the stiff bandages of formal phrases. Buried under mounds of dates and labouriously accumulated *disjecta membra* of facts, heaped over with dusty cairns of dull words, the men and women who clanged and sounded full-bloodedly through those vanished days become mere grey heaps of ashes, to be yawned at absent-mindedly — thin, gibbering ghosts of unrealizable tenuity; touching our interest but vaguely; bearing but phantasmal relation to our vivid present.

To strip from the dead these tedious accumulations, to blow upon their ashes until the extinguished fire of their passionate lives wakes and glows, relates them once more to ourselves and renews, in the now dead and pallid past, the burning present that it was in other days. Not lightly, however, may such resurrection be undertaken. The industrious gatherer of fragments, who jealously proclaims his task the only one worthy of a scholar, who pins all his faith upon "documentation," is impatient with those who would cause these vanished folk to walk again pulsating and viable. He resents, even as an entomologist might, one who disturbs his carefully labelled and ticketed butterflies, his soft-hued moths, his sharded coleoptera ranged in air-tight cases, and by the magic of imagination teaches those glittering vans and rainbowed pinions to flutter once more in the sunlight of actuality. The old-fashioned historian hotly declares such sorcery suspect and ridiculous, proving his point by showing that the thaumaturge has fallen into the absurd blunder of mentioning a battle as occurring on Monday, the 27th, when careful investigation proves it probably could not have taken place until the morning of Tuesday, the 28th. To such as these it seems in a manner indecent that the dead should again grow quick; that out of the dust of the past a living being should be re-created; that graves should be opened to liberate spirits, instead of mere bones and ashes arranged in museums to be casually gaped at by bored and hurried tourists.

Not by catalogues of dates are the dead called forth from the tombs. It requires some *Ephphatha;* some magic phrase of evocation. More than in all the assiduous searchings of mousing scholars, Caesar lives for us in the record that while he was still but a dissipated and magnificent young idler, one more observing than his fellows warned the powers it were wise to keep an eye upon "that young Patrician with the loose girdle"; a sudden door is opened upon the Roman scene, a door through which we catch the glimpse of a man instead of a faint and voiceless ghost. We become in a moment aware of a languid young leader of fashion moving in a world of decaying politics, pondering great dreams of change ... regarding too, with nascent distaste and growing attention, another young dandy by the name of Pompey, beloved of the light ladies who declared him "the sweetest smelling man in Rome."...

A new conception of the true task of the historian has been evolved of late, and the success of these efforts to make the past alive has verified Whitman's prophecy.

To find the necromantic word which shall revive the dead of the East is a task not facilely achieved, their records being buried in annals accessible only to the skilled Orientalist. Some curious and interesting volumes by early European travellers are, nevertheless, available. Preëminently the tales of Marco Polo, the chronicles of the wandering French physician, Bernier, of Tavernier, the jeweller, of Van Braam Houckgeest, of the first missionaries, Protestant and Catholic, and reports of such pioneer embassies as those of Sir Thomas Roe or Lord Macartney; but these cast a dim light upon the great personalities of the Oriental scene. It is probable their intercourse with distinguished persons was less intimate than the writers are inclined to suggest. Their revelations are so chill and vague as to arouse the suspicion that their portraits are the result more of hearsay than of actual observation. It must be taken into consideration also that the mind is aware only of such things as its quality fits it to observe. Religion and trade being, for the most part, the prepossession of these earlier travellers, many significances escaped their vision. An added limitation lay in their ignorance of matters coming under their eyes, an ignorance at the root of many misinterpretations. Occidental orgulousness led them often to speak with scorn or condescension of conditions they were incapable of appreciating or even comprehending.

Modern Western historians of Eastern lands are sufficiently numerous, but they usually follow the beaten, arid track of the old method, too much concerned over meticulous records of those wearisome, gory scufflings with which humanity has ever defaced its progress. They have been more occupied with now negligible and unimportant defeats and conquests, dates and dynasties, than with the achievements, mental and moral, of those labouring lands and folk, rarely attempting to vivify the men who led the races in the past along the upward slopes from the mire of mere bloody struggle. Certain of these leaders have left such poignant echoes and moving memories of their existence as to wake an irresistible desire to cause them once more to

> "Stand up bold
> To a magic of old
> And walk to a muttered charm—
> Life-like, without alarm."

PREFACE

A wish to discover some incantation which should call them back from the devouring past to move again in their real likeness as they lived.

Three Wise Men of the East—in India, China, and Japan—seem preëminently to deserve such resurrection for Western eyes, since each is the archetype of his respective race. Each embodied the culmination of an epoch and wrought greatly at his task. Each had other and nobler purposes than the destructive and futile conquests which so dazzle and absorb the attention of the historian.

Shah Jahan of India, flower and consummation of the Mogul Dynasty, that most romantic episode of kingship in all history. The greatest lover woman has known. A Master Builder whose constructions have never been rivalled in pure majesty and beauty. Most splendid and sumptuous of princes, beyond even fairy-tale imagining. Toppled from the dizziest height of human splendour by the fruit of his own loins. An Indian Lear—not wanting his tender and faithful Cordelia.

Chien Lung, wise, humourous, politic devotee of learning, of beauty, of administration. Magnificent Emperor of China, who gathered into one personality all the most admirable characteristics of that strange, tremendous, paradoxical people over which he ruled.

Hideyoshi, . . . not porphyrogene as were the other two, but the most delightful and engaging of parvenus—bold, subtle, exquisite, the representative of his Japanese race. Rich with life, endless of resource, bubbling with wit, entranced with every form of beauty, he carried under the silken wrapping of this colourful externality a core of stern, high, patriotic purpose, firm and unyielding as a stone.

To comprehend the meaning and quality of these three great personalities it is necessary to understand somewhat the history of the lands over which they ruled; to learn the roots from which they grew; to see the scenes in which they moved, the influences—psychologic and material—that shaped their minds. No pictures would be clear which did not visualize for the beholder India, China, and Japan. Against these backgrounds one sees their implications—a supreme artist given unlimited power to realize his dreams; an autocrat who remained always a man, giving his land peace, beauty, and prosperity, rising above all the temptations of autocracy; a plebeian who welded his broken people into a close-knit nation and laid the foundations of one of the great modern powers.

These three historical studies are an endeavour to present to Western readers three of the noblest and wisest men of the Asian scene.

CONTENTS

Preface

I
SHAH JAHAN
THE GREAT LOVER, 1

II
CHIEN LUNG
THE MAGNIFICENT EMPEROR, 93

III
HIDEYOSHI
THE DELIGHTFUL PARVENU, 177

I
SHAH JAHAN
THE GREAT LOVER

SHAH JAHAN

Let us consider first the storied and splendid India of Shah Jahan; consider those puissant Mogul and Rajput sires from whom stemmed that exceptional and noble figure whose great outlines have been shrouded in strange miscomprehensions. Only by knowing the world in which he moved, by understanding his inheritance, can the man be discerned.

India has ever been the Desired of the Nations—a Helen, sought not so much for her dark beauty as for her dazzling dower of gold and gems, a dower so inexhaustible that even yet, though greedy lovers have through millenniums, plunged their rapacious hands deep into its riches, untold treasures still remain in the secret hoards of the temples, in the strong-boxes of the Maharajas, in the hidden depths of the earth, to tempt the lust of sworded men. Over and over again have strong-armed reivers grasped at her possessions, and still that fountain of splendour, "the wealth of Ormuzd and of Ind," is not exhausted. For some unexplained reason gold seems inevitably to drift back to and remain with her. Genghis and Timurlane wooed her with hands of steel; Turk and Mogul went down to her again and again; but always the great heiress, while yielding her riches, wrapped her wooers in dusky arms, made them her slaves, and slowly but surely plucked from their hearts ferocity and courage, brain and will, like Circe degrading them by her magic to swine wallowing futilely in the luxury she gave.

While the Caliphs were reigning at Damascus, the Arabs gnawed at India's southern coasts but never made their way far into the interior. Her worst scourges came out of the North. From the great Asian plateau—inexhaustible well-spring through the ages of a prodigious stream of strenuous humanity— an Aryan inundation poured over the Indian peninsula in the days before recorded history, overwhelming and possessing the land. But although the conquerors strove, by rigid laws of caste and ferocious religious taboos, to keep their blood pure, yet insensibly interbreeding, climate, and environment moulded succeeding generations into a new people, softer and suppler, less savagely aggressive, more civilized, a people who at length took definite shape as the fixed type of Hindu. Except for internecine strife, this gradual process continued unhindered for many centuries. A Grecian raid from the West, under Alexander, swept across the land like a brief cyclone but soon passed, leaving small trace.

Meanwhile that Northern plateau was once more brimming over with fighting men, and irresistibly they began to flow downward to the lure of Indian wealth.

The first of these invaders to linger for more than a flying raid was Mahmud of Ghazni, who came in 1001 with an army of Turkish horsemen as far as Peshawar and ravaged down the passes far into the interior. He made in all twelve plundering expeditions, carrying back to Ghazni vast booty of gold and gems and a multitude of women and slaves. Though he annexed the Punjab, he preferred his own high altitudes and so established no permanent capital in the subjugated country.

It is related of Mahmud that having heard rumours of treasures in the temple of Somnath in Guzerat, he organized a foray to the South and seized this sacred place where the Hindus, for thousands of years, had worshipped before the great pillar that stood in the shrine of the temple. The priests yielded a considerable tribute, but, not satisfied that all had been revealed, he determined upon the temple's complete destruction. . . . The attendants cowered helplessly until the demolition approached the sacred pillar; then, in a vain attempt to protect it, they flung themselves passionately before the huge battering rams. Sweeping them from his path like a swarm of flies and breaching the great column, Mahmud with malignant triumph discovered it to be full to the brim of the gold and jewels that many generations of the devout had offered to their deity. Master of an almost incredible booty, he rode laughing away.

A century or more later Mohammed Ghori, the Afghan, conquered Delhi and plundered as far to the South as Benares, establishing a capital and a dynasty. Kutub-ud-din, his slave, succeeding him, founded the dynasty of the Slave Kings and built another capital in the long succession of Delhi's.

The only portion of his city which now remains untouched is the famous Kutub Minar, one of the tallest and most beautiful towers in the world. Tughluk, the Turk, came later, ousted the Slave Kings, and built still a new capital, an hour's drive from the old one, a city now but a mass of stark cyclopean ruins in whose grim immensities flocks of wild peacocks feed and scream.

The Moguls first appeared in 1399, Timurlane, that terrible "Great Wind of the World," leading his hordes of Tartars and Mongols to fall like a tornado upon India and her treasures. His army was the most ruthless and fierce in all fierce and ruthless human history; as animal and savage as a herd of baboons; yellow-skinned, flat-nosed, high cheekboned; riding with their rations of raw meat fastened under their saddles; whirling and banging behind them the rough carts that held the women and children as cruel and wild as themselves. When they turned again to the North, these carts held an enormous plunder of riches, as well as many women ravished from the homes left smouldering in ruins and drenched with blood. So terrible were these incursions of Timur, marked by such hideous and wanton brutalities, that for a thousand years the cry "The Toorkh! The Toorkh!" sent the Indian flying madly for his life.

The whirlwind spent itself at last. Timur did not choose to establish himself in India, for although the richest of his conquests, it was but a small portion of them. He had carried his victorious arms on one side from the Irtish and the Volga to the Persian Gulf, and on the other from the Hellespont to the Ganges. Samarkand was his favourite capital, and when he died in 1405, this ferocious destroyer

THE GREAT LOVER 5

of his kind was embalmed in musk and attar of roses, wrapped in fine linen, laid in an ebony coffin, and entombed at Samarkand. Wherever he had passed he had left in great mounds the skulls of his victims, the Mongol fashion of celebrating conquests.

In the century following his death India had respite from Northern incursions, while far away in the distant Western seas the rumours of her wealth were stirring the imaginations of other adventurers. Drawn by appetizing lure of plunder, Vasco de Gama rounded the Cape and landed on the Malabar coast in 1497. The next year he founded a factory for trading at Goa, and thereafter, for two hundred years, the Portuguese struggled with the Arabs for mastery of the enormous wealth of Indian commerce. As when a vulture stoops towards his quarry, and the seemingly empty sky suddenly shows black wings of rivals coming from every quarter to contest his find, so the Dutch and the English followed hard on the Portuguese, longing to share in the opportunity.

While the Westerners approached from the South, a new storm gathered on the Northern border. The Mongols came again, this time led by Baber. But they were now called Moguls, a modified version of the old scourges. In the prodigious loot which the predecessors of these Moguls had carried away with them, there was one element more potent than the gold, the silver, and the jewels which they had so greatly valued. Women always seemed to them mere cattle to be driven along with their other herds —materials of pleasure and luxury. The seraglios of the Indian rulers had been ravished of their fairest; the raiding chiefs and soldiers had torn from the wealthy merchants their wives and daughters, little guessing how great a change these slaves were gradually to effect in their own rough wild race. Sons were born to them who inherited not only the savage ichor of their father's veins but also a mellowing stream from their more civilized and delicately bred mothers—blood that carried with it inherited instincts for beauty, learning, and refinement.

Historians pass over in silence the lives of captive women. Nothing is ever said of the fate of these unhappy victims; and yet their voiceless history very potently moulds the future of the victors. All the Northern races have been but brute fighters, beasts and birds of prey, until ameliorated by the influences of Southern civilizations. The Tartars and the Mongols, the Vikings, the European Crusaders, even the blond hordes of the Greeks and the Assyrian conquerors of Babylon have all learned their civilization from the Southern races upon whom they have fallen, and with whom they have interbred.

In the five hundred years between the coming of Mahmud of Ghazni and the descent of Baber, there had been a constant plunder of women carried North. In the interval, these semi-human fighters had been modified, not only by the blood within their veins but by the teachings that the children had received from the captive mothers—teachings of things higher and more to be desired than mere eating, warring, and lust. Baber was but fifth in descent from Timur and seventh from Genghis Khan; yet that short time had sufficed to change the physique of the flat-nosed, yellow-faced Mongol into the fair skin and aquiline features that characterized the new Moguls. Baber himself was an interesting mixture, mentally and spiritually, of the two streams of blood. The enormous vitality and passion for war inherited from his Northern ancestors was curiously interblended with a thousand Southern subtleties and graces of mind and nature.

Could the history of the world be written, not as it always has been from the masculine viewpoint of the ravishings and adventures of the restless sex, but as the secret story of the lives of women, how new the tale might seem! It would tell of long hours of desperate patience; of slow, timid attempts at a softening culture; of subtle adjustments and influences in the push toward gentler conditions. Where shall be found an adequate record of that gradual pressure which, during five hundred years, had been brought to bear by the infiltration of gentler blood? No epic has been written of the efforts of captive women to soften the minds and manners of their rude masters; of their small tentatives here and there to instill into the children, before they were snatched from their mothers' arms to join the fighting hordes, some delicacies of spirit and behaviour—the love of the bath; the charm of the garden with its graces of colour and perfume; the gradual touches of luxury and refinement which the captives inevitably gathered around themselves in faint, far-off imitation of the magnificence which they had known in the seraglios of Persian Shah and Indian Sultan; the old songs and stories of chivalry sung in the twilight to the child drowsing in its mother's arms. A difficult task this of the women and perhaps an impossible one had it not been that these children had inherited the predispositions of the finer races.

The results of this slow, secret struggle between two conceptions of life made themselves manifest in Zahir-ud-din Mahommed, or Baber. He was born near Kabul on the fourteenth of February, 1483, and was destined to be the fifth Mohammedan conqueror of India, and the founder of that Mogul Empire which endured for three hundred and twenty-five years—an Empire whose annals are more vivid and splendid that any other of which we have record. They are more like a colourful and imaginative fairy story than the usual pedestrian narrative of human events, a tale of high romance, through which amazing figures move amid incredible adventures.

Zahir received, like all of his family, a special title supposed to signify special qualities. Oriental history suffers constant confusion from this practice. A man's or a woman's own name was always so overlaid by the assumed title (which might be changed from time to time, according to individual fancy, to signalize some innate quality or special achievement), that the student of their records has to keep several names in mind. He has also to decide which one of many spellings is correct, since most of the Western writers follow their phonetic instincts. Zahir suffers less than most in this respect, his title name of Baber, The Tiger, being simple and giving small range for phonetic variation.

Stanley Lane-Poole in the Introduction to his *Life of Baber* says:

"Baber is the link between Central Asia and India, between predatory hordes and imperial government, between Tamerlane and Akbar. The blood of the two great Scourges of Asia, Genghis and Timur, was mingled in his veins, and to the daring and restlessness of the nomad Tartar he joined the culture and urbanity of the Persian. He brought the energy of the Mongol, the courage and capacity of the Turk to the listless Hindu; and, himself a soldier of fortune and no architect of empire, he yet laid the first stone of the splendid fabric which his grandson Akbar achieved."

This crossing of blood produced one of the strangest, and in some respects the most delightful, characters imaginable, whose qualities we know perhaps better than those of anyone else in history except the immortal Pepys, since he had Pepys' passion for setting down his intimate thoughts and feelings and his own view of his actions. The *Memoirs of Baber* is one of the great classics of literature. Of this autobiography an authority says, "It is one of those priceless records which are for all time and is fit to rank with the Confessions of St. Augustine and Rousseau, and the Memoirs of Gibbon and Newton." Indeed, to some readers it seems much more admirable than any of the aforementioned, with the exception of Pepys, for none of the other four have Baber's quality of gaiety, his shrewd humour, his frank ingenuous revelations of his own faults, or his minute observations of a thousand matters which, for the most part, lay outside the cognizance of the most famous of the solemn and egotistic self-confessors.

Life to Baber was forever a delicious and exciting adventure. Discomforts, defeats, and disappointments had as much savour as triumphs. They were all parts of the thrilling drama of being alive. Every one of his senses was widely awake to his surroundings. Whatever was, was violently interesting. A flower enchanted him. A beautiful landscape made a day worth while. Every person amused or interested him. Wine he loved, but again and again he dwells upon the joy of a drink from a pure cold spring.

The Memoirs begin: "In the month of Ramazan of the year eight hundred and ninety-nine [June, 1494], I became King of Ferghana," and this eleven-year-old monarch continues thereafter the gay recital of his amazing and stirring career. He was betrothed at the age of five, a king at eleven, a father at fifteen; and he died in his forty-eighth year, having been a fugitive three or four times, often with scarce a single follower, and having made himself master of two other thrones and finally, Emperor of India. He had starved and feasted; hunted and been hunted; achieved incredible feats of arms; had never known discouragement; and had never ceased throughout his brief and strenuous life to enjoy every instant of it. Wherever Baber went he noticed with interest and pleasure the wild flowers and the plants along his tempestuous path. He observed the social and political conditions of the people he conquered; he jotted down reflections upon the best military methods, made exact records of his battles and the causes of his defeats or his victories, and sketched vivid portraits of his friends and opponents.

Interspersed with these are relishing accounts of the beauty of the scenery, the deliciousness of the fruits he ate, and of frolicsome parties with his officers and companions when they competed with one another in song and story and, lamentable to say, frequently became profoundly intoxicated. The last, of course, was strictly forbidden to Mohammedans, and we hear nothing of Baber's drinking until he was nearly thirty years old, although drunkenness was common enough in the Moslem armies. But the same man who would carefully note down that he had counted thirty-three species of tulips in one place, who knew every animal and bird of his country, and who was a passionate lover of gardens, of Persian poetry, and of the best music, yet frankly tells us that for some years he was almost constantly, and sometimes violently, intoxicated.

At the approach of his fortieth birthday he made up his mind that he would abandon the wine cup, and in 1519 he notes roguishly in his Memoirs, "As I now wanted something less than a year of that age I drank wine most copiously." He found, however, that this overcoming of bad habits was easier said than done, and he frequently fell from grace. In December of 1525 he had the serious warning of a violent fever and dysentery, and he made new virtuous resolutions. "I knew," the Memoirs record, "whence this illness proceeded and what conduct brought on this chastisement," and he quotes verses in Arabic to prove the sure penalty of breaking a vow. "I now once more composed myself to penitence and self-control; I resolved to abstain from all idle thoughts and unseemly pleasures, to break my pen in contrition for all the frivolous verses I had scribbled," but two or three days later, when he was well again, he was so charmed with the view of the flickering campfires in the valley that he must celebrate his pleasure by taking a drink.

Yet that prodigious vigour which had enabled him to endure so many hardships and to accomplish so many amazing feats, seemed for long to remain unimpaired. It is on record that he had been known to take up a man under each arm and run with them around the battlements of a fortress, leaping the embrasures.

In March, 1529, Baber notes, "I swam across the river Ganges for amusement. I counted my strokes and found that I swam over with thirty-three of them. I then took breath and swam back to the other side. I had already crossed by swimming every river I had met except the Ganges." He was equally hardy in the saddle and thought nothing of riding eighty miles a day. On the eve of his final great battle with the Rajputs of Kanwaha, he made himself master of his own weakness as he was the next day to master the last great Hindu confederation: he broke all the wine cups, poured out all the wines, and from that day never again relapsed into his favourite vice, though he frequently sets down how severe the struggle was to keep his promises to himself.

The story of his battles has been told many times and by many people, but on the whole they vary little from all the oft told bloody struggles of human history. What is more interesting and far more individual is the self-revelation of one of the most contradictory, and in many ways the most engaging, of men. He could be as cruel and bloody as any other Oriental conqueror; after the siege of Bajaur, for example, he had no hesitation in putting to the sword man, woman, and child. Of the skulls of the three thousand killed he built a pyramid, after the old Mongol fashion. Later in India when an attempt was made to poison him, the taster was cut to pieces, the cook flayed alive, and a woman supposed to be implicated was trampled under the feet of elephants. On the other hand, he frequently forgave the treacheries of his family, and in one case the chief traitor's son himself has set down what happened:

"The Emperor in conformity with his affectionate nature, without ceremony, and without a sign of bitterness—nay with the utmost cheerfulness and good humour—came into the presence of his stepgrandmother, who had withdrawn her affection from him and set up her grandson in his stead. Shah Begum was confounded and abashed, and knew not what to say. The Emperor going down on his knees, embraced her with great affection and said, 'What right has one child to be vexed because the motherly bounty descends upon another? The mother's authority over her children is in all respects absolute.' He added, 'I have not slept all night and have made a long journey.' So saying, he laid his head on Shah Begum's breast and tried to sleep; he acting thus in order to reassure the Begum. He had scarcely fallen asleep when his maternal aunt, Mir Nigar Khanum (daughter of Yunus, and widow of Sultan Ahmed, and herself apparently in the plot), entered. The Emperor leaped up and embraced his beloved aunt with every manifestation of affection. The Khanum said to him, 'Your children, wives, and household are longing to see you. I give thanks that I have been permitted to behold you once again. Rise up and go to your family in the castle. I, too, am going thither.'

"So he went to the castle, and on his arrival all the Amirs and people began to thank God for His mercy. They made the dust of the feet of that loving king kohl for their eyes. Then the Khanum conducted Khan Mirza and my father [the treacherous uncle] before the Emperor. As they approached, the Emperor came out to meet them. The Khanum then said, 'O soul of your mother! I have also brought the guilty grandson and the unfortunate brother to you. What have you to say to them?' And she pointed out my father. When the Emperor saw my father, he instantly came forward with his wonted courtesy, and smiling openly, embraced him, made many kind inquiries, and showed him marked affection. He then embraced Khan Mirza in like manner, and displayed a hundred proofs of love and good feeling. He conducted the whole ceremony with the utmost gentleness of manner, bearing himself, in all his actions and words, in such a way that no trace of constraint or artifice was to be seen in them. But, however much the Emperor might try to wear away the rust of shame with the polish of mildness and humanity, he was unable to wipe out the dimness of ignominy which had covered the mirror of their hopes."

There are many other records of his chivalry, and his devotion to his own family never failed. Coming to Agra to take up his residence, after he had solidified his conquest of India, he brought with him ninety-six of his women relations from Kabul, and he made a point of going to pay his respects to them every Friday when at Agra. Lane-Poole says that when his wife remonstrated with him for going out in the heat to see them, he replied that his aunts had neither father nor brother, and there was none but him to comfort them.
Among Baber's many wives, most of whom he had married for political reasons, the only one for whom he seems to have felt a special affection was the mother of his son, Humayun, and of three little daughters named Rose-blush, Rose-face, and Rose-body. For the son he had a passionate affection. He writes to him in terms of the greatest tenderness constantly urging him to good behaviour and pausing to criticize the prince's indifferent handwriting. Baber himself was extremely proud of his own beautiful calligraphy and even invented a special script called the "Babery hand." He scolds the boy for bad spelling and careless phraseology. He says, "Write unaffectedly, clearly, with plain words, which saves

THE GREAT LOVER

trouble to both writer and reader. The language of kings is the king of languages." In the Memoirs the father speaks of the arrival of his son at Agra:

"I was just talking with his mother about him when in he came. His presence opened our hearts like rosebuds, and made our eyes shine like torches. It was my rule to keep open table every day, but on this occasion I gave feasts in his honour, and showed him every kind of distinction. We lived together for some time in the greatest intimacy. The truth is that his conversation had an inexpressible charm and he realized absolutely the ideal of perfect manhood."

How complete was this devotion to his heir he proved shortly after when the young man became desperately ill of fever, and priests and doctors declared he could be saved only by a supreme sacrifice. Baber, catching at this hope, resolved to lay down his own life for that of his son. To the remonstrances of his court that he should offer instead the great diamond of the Rajahs he replied, "Is there any stone that can be weighed against my son? Rather shall I pay his ransom myself, for he is in grievous case and my strength must bear his weakness." Pacing thrice around the bed of the dying man he repeated many times, "On me be all thy sufferings." After a time crying out, "I have prevailed, I have taken it," he sank down apparently overcome by illness, and the son immediately began to recover.

Baber called for all his chief officers and, directing them to put their hands into Humayun's in token of investiture, he solemnly proclaimed him his successor and resigned him the throne. Shortly afterwards he passed away in his garden-palace at

Kabul, the palace which he had built, the gardens of which he had laid out with so much delight.

This story of Baber's death was, until very recent times, looked upon as a mere tale of Oriental superstition. But cock-sureness in rejecting the claim to credibility of recitals which seem to contradict the accepted course of human events, has been shaken by more recent knowledge. We have grown aware how potent are ideas in producing physical results, and how cures may be effected by the influence of suggestion. Also, how the same power of suggestion might react to cause a man's death. Much more was this true at the period in which this event took place. Baber himself was not without his share of superstition, though the wholesome quality of his mind and the vitality of his nature made him constantly question his own credulity. His diary relates that before one of his battles he was anxious to engage the enemy on a certain day because on that day, the "eight stars" were exactly between the two armies. Yet he laughs at his feeling in the matter and says, "these observations are all nonsense," and still, because he did not act upon his superstition, he admits that later on he gnaws his hands with the the teeth of regret. "If on that same Saturday I had fought, it is probable that I could have won." Many times in his Memoirs he shows himself swinging back and forth between the impulse to believe and an equal tendency toward doubt. When, however, the deepest passion of his life was stirred by the danger to his son, he did not hesitate to throw aside all incredulity, and fling himself before the beloved one with an appeal to the invisible powers. Of the nature and method of their action he had no conception save the deep-seated instinct of the

THE GREAT LOVER

human race that these invisible forces may be deflected from their purpose by a vicarious sacrifice, and without hesitation he demonstrated that greater love has no man than this, that he lay down his life for his beloved.

But forty-eight years old when he died, yet a king for thirty-six of those years, he rejoiced in every moment of his tumultuous career. As much, apparently, when he was an exile hiding among the snows of the mountains, as when he was capping verses with his boon companions under the flowering boughs of the tamarisks in his palace gardens, or leading his wild horsemen against the armies of India. For wealth he cared nothing. The enormous plunder after the Battle of Panipat he distributed among his troops, his friends, and relations. He sent to every person in Kabul, young and old, slave and free, a silver coin in celebration of the victory. Humayun brought to him the great diamond which was said, with Indian imagery, to be worth "half the daily expenditure of the whole world," and which had been taken from the Rajah Bikramagit. Baber tossed it back to him with scarcely a glance. He cared more for the jonquils and the apple blossoms of his Northern home than for all the jewels of India.

Out of this virile stem, out of this contradictory and yet fascinating personality grew up the great Mogul Empire, bearing always the impress of the qualities that made Baber. Tartar ferocity, a genius for arms, and the element of richness and beauty were curiously commingled in Baber the Conqueror. Later, in his great-great-grandson, Shah Jahan, the Tartar element had been largely subdued. The instinct for beauty had grown more and more dominant, flowering in the supreme creativeness of that great artist whose works still remain unrivalled by any later successor in the whole world.

Humayun, for whom Baber had laid down his joyous, lusty, puissant existence, proved hardly worth the sacrifice. To reverse the Biblical image, his loins were not so thick as his father's little finger. At one time driven into exile from his throne in India, he regained it only through the activity and skill of his adherents. He reigned for twenty-six years, and the Mogul power became more firmly consolidated under his rule, though he seems, according to chronicles, to have done nothing spectacular. The two most striking results of his administration were his magnificent tomb, which he built upon the plains of Delhi, and his admirable son, Jelladin Mohammed, known to history as Akbar, signifying The Great. Proper title indeed for this large, sanguine man, imaginative and yet practical, both idealist and realist.

Akbar was a grandson worthy of his famous ancestor, Baber, of the same restless and active mind ranging widely through the realm of ideas; inheriting his grandfather's streak of ruthlessness, his love of beauty, and his dominant personality. Less of a warrior but more of an administrator, he enacted many wise laws and reformed the confused land tenures, so that the revenues and prosperity of the Empire greatly increased. Realizing the need of reconciling the conquering race with the native inhabitants, he admitted the Hindus to all positions of trust and power and actively curbed the intolerance of his Mohammedan subjects. His patience with the bigotry of the Moslem priests was small. So strongly did he feel that narrowness of creeds was one of the most fruitful sources of human struggle and disorder, that he formed the idea of discovering some universal religion by which to reconcile all conflicting beliefs. Fired by this magnificent but thoroughly impractical idea he admitted the Jesuits to Agra and listened with intelligent attention to Christian missionaries sent from Goa. He likewise permitted the Parsees from Persia, the native Brahmans, and the Buddhist Lamas from Thibet to discuss with him their various cults. From these studies he gradually worked out for himself a synthetic creed of pure Deism, and a ritual based upon the system of Zoroaster, which he endeavoured to impose upon his people. There is something naïvely boyish in this touching conviction of his that the pietists really wished for peace; that they were really searching for fundamental truths, rather than fumbling along the lines of their own instincts towards the solution of the mysteries of life and death. While he lived his strong hand controlled any overt struggles, but each sect held fanatically to its own dogmas, and the only point upon which they cheerfully united was the conviction that Akbar was the prince of heresiarchs, all combining to spread abroad the usual libel of his desiring to be himself worshipped as a god.

Forty-nine years Akbar maintained his wise and powerful sway, keeping his Empire for the most part peaceful and contented. He ruled with wisdom and moderation, finding time beside his public duties for a thousand activities and amusements, for he too possessed his grandfather's tireless energy and interest in life. Still in Agra towers his great fortress of red sandstone, a mile and a half in circumference, perhaps the most perfect and imposing mediaeval fortress in existence. Still, after the lapse of more than three hundred years, stands that glorious whim—a carved jewel—the city of Fatteh-pur-Sikri, scarce touched by the tooth of Time.

There is no record of what prompted Akbar to abandon Agra and build this new capital twenty-three miles away—possibly merely a gratification of the building instinct or a desire to create a magnificent monument to his own reign. Upon a lofty eminence called Bahund-darwaza, commanding the plain, an ant-like horde of labourers was loosed by a magnificent gesture of empiry, out of which rose a palace and a mosque approached by the famous Gate of Victory, one of the most imposing and perfect portals in the world. This superb arch, rising a hundred and thirty feet, gave entrance to a great quadrangle four hundred feet square, surrounded on every side by buildings of the same glowing red sandstone, of which the whole city and its gateway were constructed. From the quadrangle broad streets led in four directions, bordered by the façades, the balconies, and towers of the palaces, the zenanas, and the dwellings of the imperial officers and the multitude of attendants required by the court. As if by magic there appeared baths and gardens, pleasure pavilions, and buildings for every possible need which the luxury of an Oriental ruler demanded.

It is said that the Moguls "built like giants and finished like goldsmiths." All the surfaces of these noble constructions are covered with incised work as delicate as the carvings upon a gem. The effect of such fine and simple outlines with the exquisite finish of intricate flat carving is indescribably noble and delightful. Akbar, with his eclectic turn of mind, was endeavouring to fuse the simplicity of the Moslem architecture with the richness and beauty of Indian adornment, but where the Indian taste overloaded its construction with superfluity of sculptured figures, the tenets of the Koran prevented this vulgarity of excess and confusion. The decoration, because of Moslem law against the picturing of life, was obliged to confine itself to geometrical designs with conventionalized patterns of fruit and flower, resulting in a magnificent purity of outline combined with sumptuous delicacy of adornment.

In Fatteh-pur, Akbar was at his happiest. He surrounded himself with poets, artists, musicians, and philosophers, and was free to make a thousand intellectual experiments and excursions, indulging his vivid curiosity concerning every phase of the mind and the spirit. He held constant courts of discussion where he sat as moderator and umpire during passionate controversy between the representatives of the various religions. Long night sessions were held in gardens perfumed by jasmines and roses, under the dark star-spangled skies of the splendid Indian night. There musicians interpreted with pipe and string all the varying modes of music, or metaphysicians and philosophers discoursed of the mysteries of life and death until the dawn shone palely through the orange and tamarisk trees. Even learned women were honoured by the Emperor, who as a liberal spirit refused to be bound by the old masculine egotisms. One of the most beautiful small palaces within the city was the private residence created by Akbar for the learned Lady Miriam, whose intelligence he so reverenced and whose advice he constantly sought on matters of public policy.

Suddenly the whole thing is cast aside. Fatteh-pur-Sikri is evacuated—left to bats and owls. The staring sunlight looks down on a beauteous deserted city. The stars wheel above silence as the centuries go softly by, leaving the carvings as clear and fine as when made, towers and superb doorways as truly plumb as when the great Emperor created them; an empty and echoing monument to the memory of a great man.

Historians have guessed as a reason for this desertion the discovery that the water supply was inadequate and unwholesome. The Moguls, able to bring water by great aqueducts a hundred and twenty miles to Delhi, would have found the task of conveying it twenty-three miles from Agra but a trifle; and also, as Akbar's new town must have taken years to achieve, the want of water at Fatteh-pur would have been obvious long before he took up his residence there. Some other and more compelling motive there must have been for throwing aside this rose-red city—possibly some passion of disappointment. When in that great quadrangle he attempted to preach and expound his majestic dream of the reconciliation of humanity's warring beliefs, he only excited more violent assertions on the part of those who believed they alone possessed the truth. "To Akbar's open eyes there was truth in all Faith; no one creed could hold the master-key of the Infinite."

Abdul-Fazl, the Emperor's favourite poet, the man he had chosen to conduct the arguments held on Thursday evenings between the various sects in the moonlit courts of the great Mosque of Fatteh-pur-Sikri, has crystallized in verse his master's views on this subject:

> "O God, in every temple I see those who see Thee
>   and in every tongue that is spoken, Thou art
>   praised.
> Polytheism and Islam grope after Thee.

Each religion says, 'Thou art one, without equal.'
Be it Mosque, men murmur holy prayer; or church, the bells ring for love of Thee.
Awhile I frequent the Christian Cloister, anon the Mosque
But Thee only I seek from fane to fane.
Thine elect know naught of heresy or orthodoxy, whereof neither stands behind the screen of Thy truth.
Heresy to the heretic,—dogma to the orthodox,—
But the dust of the rose-petal belongs to the heart of the perfume-seller."

It is said that at one of these Thursday evening disputes, the Emperor listened in silence and displeasure to the bitterness and fanaticism growing ever more violent. Finally he rose, shrugged his shoulders disdainfully, and calling for his horse rode back through the night to Agra, never to return to the city where he dreamed of the possible growth of man's wisdom and tolerance.

The court was summoned to follow him the next day. Gradually the whole city was evacuated and has never since been occupied. Yet it remains a greater monument to the great heart that conceived it, than even the famous tomb in which he lies at Sikandra. After the Mogul fashion Akbar had prepared his own last resting place. Their manner was to enclose a garden with high walls, entered by splendid gateways, and in the centre to build a tomb crowned by a dome. The tomb was mounted on a lofty square terrace from which radiated four broad alleys, generally cloven by marble-paved canals and ornamented with fountains. The spaces between were planted with cypresses and other evergreens and with flowering trees to make a formal and beautiful pleasance. Many hold this tomb of Akbar's, in which, after his usual taste, he combined the Moslem and the Hindu styles, to be the most perfect achievement of Mogul architecture. The custom of the great men of that period was to use these garden tombs as pleasure grounds until their death, after which, feasts and music were excluded and the place assumed a sacred character, being opened only once a year for memorial services by the descendants of the man who lay within, or for interment in the crypt of members of his immediate family.

Jehangir, father of Shah Jahan and the son and successor of Akbar, showed few of the great qualities of his predecessor or of his heir. It is not uncommon in a famous line to find these intervals of comparative obscurity between a grandfather and a grandson. Neither Akbar's intellect nor his personality seems to have been transmitted to Jehangir, though we have more intimate knowledge of him through Western observation than of any of his forerunners.

Hawkins, an English sea captain, sent out by the East India Company in 1608, was the first English delegate to the court of Delhi, the object of his mission being to combat the influence which the Dutch and the Portuguese had acquired in the rich Eastern trade, a trade for which all the Western Powers were avid. According to Hawkins' account, Jehangir received him with great kindness, welcomed him to drinking parties, and was not only a rather uproarious drunkard but was also lacking in dignity and self-respect. The English delegate has left some curious records of the loose manners of the Emperor. He also notes that the government, so skillfully administered by the firm hands of Akbar, was falling into disorder and that the people were becoming impoverished and discontented. Despite the intimacies which Hawkins asserts were accorded to him, he was unable to make any substantial progress towards his ends and finally retired in disgust.

Eight years later Sir Thomas Roe was sent by the English Government as a formal ambassador. It had no doubt reached the ears of the British, that the Dutch and Portuguese were suggesting to the court of Delhi that the sending of a simple sailor like Hawkins to make requests was a mark of contempt and discourtesy. It is interesting to note that one of these Dutch critics had said to the Emperor, "Beware of opening any door to the English; once they have put their foot well over the sill they will end by pushing you out."

The new ambassador, though coming with an imposing train and bearing gifts, made no great progress in gaining privileges for his countrymen. He was forced to content himself with some few minor indulgences for the English trading company. The real door was to be opened later, and in a most curious manner. The Ambassador, however, returned to England to make elaborate reports of the conditions of the country and the manners and the customs of the people, and to remark upon the extraordinary imitative talent of the Indian handicraftsmen. One of the presents brought by Roe from England was a magnificent gilded coach. He reports that, at the desire of the Emperor, in a very short time several coaches were built by his own people far superior in materials and fully equal in workmanship to the foreign models. He also gave a painting of the English King to the Mogul, and was soon after presented with several copies which he was unable to distinguish from the original. Roe notes as to this, that at his surprise "the Great Mogul was very merry and joyful, and craked like a Northern man."

Sir Thomas himself seems to have been a most excellent, God-fearing individual, who was both perplexed and distressed at the attitude of the heathen towards his own faith. He writes,

"I found it impossible to convince them that the Christian faith was designed for the whole world, and that theirs was mere fable and gross superstition. Their answer was amusing enough. 'We pretend not,' they replied, 'that our law is of universal application. God intended it only for us. We do not even say that yours is a false religion; it may be adapted to your wants and circumstances, God having, no doubt, appointed many different ways of going to Heaven.'"

Of the name of Jehangir's first wife, the mother of Shah Jahan, there is no record. We are told only that she was a Rajput princess, the daughter of the Rana of Marwar. The Rajputs were the proudest, the most potent race in India, and one may guess, from the qualities she passed on to her son, that hers was a nature of beauty and power. Perhaps the haughty princess found in the boy's budding instincts some consolation for an enforced marriage to a foolish and self-indulgent mate, some compensation for being unloved and set aside for the famous Nur Mahal. Possibly it was she, in the impressionable years of his infancy and first youth, when the mother in the Indian harem so moulds the mind and character entrusted to her hands, who instilled the great ideas and spiritual impulses which manifested themselves later in her remarkable son. The Rajput blood in his veins was a great inheritance and would account for much.

THE GREAT LOVER

The boy can be pictured leaning against his mother's knee, his large dark eyes upon her wistful face as she tells him tales of her own people, whose pedigrees go back for millenniums to the ancient India of the Golden Age, the listening child faintly conscious, meanwhile, of the odour of rose leaves amid her silk and silver tissues—that odour so beloved of the House of Baber. He would hear in her stories all the noblest names of India's spiritual history: Rama, the Wandering Prince of endless adventures; Krishna, whom every woman loved; Siddartha the Buddha, the Enlightened, Friend of all the World. All Rajputs. From her he would learn, too, the sonorous measures of the Upanishads, in which the Rajputs found the core of their faith.

Though so little is told of Jehangir's wife it is not to be supposed that his life was without other feminine influences. As with his son, a woman was the centre around which his deepest emotions oriented.

The tale of this rival and supplanter of Shah Jahan's mother is as romantic as every other episode in the Mogul royal epic. The story runs that a Persian noble in Teheran, accused of treachery, snatches his wife and babies out of their beds and flees with them into the desert night. There follow long wanderings in thirst and hunger, till, in desperation, their youngest child, a tiny daughter, is laid by the side of the caravan route in the blind hope that her innocent beauty may touch the heart of some passer-by, and she at least may survive. As in all proper fairy tales, appears at once upon the horizon a train of camels laden with Persian carpets for the Court of Delhi. It is hardly to be expected that a travelling merchant so far from home will be inclined to burden himself with a weeping infant, but this is no common child; all her life men are to do her bidding. Seeing the girl taken up and clumsy masculine efforts made to console her, the rest of the family creep from their hiding and are convoyed in honour to the Mogul Court along with the carpets.

In the Emperor's harem the small bit of feminine loveliness rescued from the desert becomes a pet and plaything. Jehangir, a rough, wild youngling, heir to Akbar, but still juvenile enough to be free of the women's quarters, leaves his sports to carry in his arms the tiny charmer around the fountained and flowery courts. They dabble together in the cooling waters, pick the blossoms, romp shrieking and laughing through the chambers. The boy remains always the girl's slave and playmate. Nur Mahal ripens to womanhood at last, and Akbar's heir insists that she alone shall be his wife. But the Emperor has other and more ambitious plans; a mate from among the proud and restless Rajput princes will be a means of solidifying the hold of the Mogul house on India.

Nur Mahal's father, now risen to place and power, receives a hint from Akbar, and blandly replies that never having looked so high for his child he has, indeed, already affianced her to her cousin, Sher Afkan, a young Persian officer in the Emperor's service. Jehangir rages in vain. The girl is wedded. Sher Afkan, with his beautiful wife, is sent to serve under the Viceroy Bedeang in the distant South. The Rajput princess is found. Unconsulted as to her desires —a mere pawn shoved about by masculine ambition—she is thrust into the arms of a sullen and resentful husband, no one guessing how splendid a flower is to bloom from this loveless union.

Years passed. Four sons, among them Shah Jahan, were born to Jehangir from his marriage to the Raj-

THE GREAT LOVER

put princess. Still his thoughts turned ever to the woman who had been his baby playmate. Still he hated his father for the ruthless destruction of his life's romance. Akbar magnificently ignored this spleen, but the gulf between him and his son ever widened and deepened as Jehangir grew ever more rough, drunken, and unroyal, jeering at his father's new religion, scoffing at his conscientious efforts to rule the Empire wisely and well. From Jehangir's point of view, the kingdom was the Monarch's possession to be exploited as he liked: the people existed for his use and pleasure and must adapt their needs and desires to that fact.

With ever deepening displeasure Akbar began to consider that he had the right and privilege of appointing his own successor, since primogeniture was not the law of the land. Khusru, Jehangir's eldest son, gave some promise; the other three were still children. It might be wise to set aside Jehangir and devise the throne to Khusru.

This was to reckon without due consideration of his own son's character. Not again was Jehangir to be balked of his desire. Gathering a following of the discontented and restive, he broke into open rebellion, in the midst of which Akbar died suddenly, rumour murmured from poison administered by a minion of his son.

Seated on the throne, Jehangir cast his own son Khusru into prison and at once set about securing the woman he loved.

Unwilling to incur the odium of robbing a well known nobleman of his wife, he caused her to be abducted secretly along with her only child, a daughter. The husband, infuriated over the disappearance of his wife and child, and suspecting the Viceroy of being cognizant of their whereabouts, attacked his superior officer sword in hand, and was immediately cut in pieces by the Viceroy's guards.

Nur Mahal, now no longer young but still beautiful and brilliant, resented this violent wooing and, perhaps secretly preferring her Persian mate, resisted all Jehangir's advances, declaring she would never marry her husband's murderer. Months elapsed before the Emperor could persuade her that Sher Afkan had rushed upon his own fate. Once the doting Emperor had induced her to accept his tenderness, he became, and remained as long as he lived, her complete slave. Her renowned beauty, her wit and accomplishments, and vivid temperament enchanted him, and soon her talent for public affairs made her the real ruler of the Empire as well as of the dissipated and idle Emperor. Consulted on every matter of importance, her face and name associated with his own upon the coins, she was treated with the honours of a co-sovereign. Her father was raised to the rank of a grand vizier, and her brother, Afzul Khan, became a high officer of the court. Gradually the self-indulgent and frivolous Jehangir allowed all his powers to drift into the hands of the Empress and her family. Searching always for new methods of domination, she at last hit upon the idea of wedding her own niece with Khurram, Jehangir's second son, who was to be known to history as Shah Jahan.

This girl, Arjamand Banu, seems to have been the noblest and most beautiful of all that remarkable Persian family which had so nearly perished in the desert. Where and how she met Shah Jahan, the chronicle does not tell. Only it is certain that these two unusual young people each conceived for the other a deathless passion—a passion out of which grew an immortal treasure of beauty. The grave, slender, starry-eyed youth, who had been nourished by his mother on legends of Rajput chivalry, found in this Persian girl the realization of all his high dreams and imaginings. Theirs is the most serene and exquisite of love tales, a clean white flame beside which the ardours of Antony and Cleopatra, of Launcelot and Guinevere, of Paolo and Francesca seem but lurid and destructive fires. To Arjamand Shah Jahan repaid, in part, the monstrous debt to helpless women that masculine ruthlessness has, through the ages, incurred.

How much blame may be attached to Nur Mahal herself for the gradual disorder and disorganization which marked Jehangir's reign is not now plain. It is certain that under the administration of her father as grand vizier, the prosperity the country had known under Akbar's strenuous and efficient rule began swiftly to decline. After her father's death she built for him one of the most beautiful tombs in India, still a delight and a place of pilgrimage for travellers, but she kept all the reins of power within her own hands, and as Jehangir's health began to fail, she looked about for means to maintain her dominance even after the Emperor's death.

Of the possible heirs, Prince Khusru, for so many years a prisoner by his father's orders, had small wits and powers. The second son, Khurram, though related to Nur Mahal through his marriage to her niece, was far too dominant a character to control if he ascended the throne, nor had she any confidence in Arjamand Banu's submission to herself. The third son, Parwiz, was a drunken waster not to be seriously considered. There was left a fourth possible heir, Shah Ryar, the youngest son of the Emperor, and to him she married her only daughter, the child of her first husband, Sher Afkan. No fruit had come of Nur

Mahal's union with Jehangir, and her daughter she regarded as a pawn to be used in her great game for power. There remained then only Khurram between Shah Ryar and the throne. Nur Mahal reasoned that if she could eliminate Khurram she might, by influencing her daughter, continue to govern the empire. In the power she so loved, the Empress probably found consolation for the death of her handsome Persian husband and for the long years of wifehood with a weak and foolish despot. The Emperor possessed neither dignity nor force and was stained by all the vices, his one good quality being an unswerving, unquestioning devotion to his first love.

For the few remaining years of Jehangir's ignoble existence the court was a maelstrom of intrigue; everyone distrusted everyone else; spies listened and peeped at every corner, babbling all they knew and a thousand things which were only suspected. Practically where all was secrecy there were no secrets. Every movement, every word was reported; and every plot, no matter how carefully guarded, was known sooner or later to the one against whom it was directed.

Khurram of course became aware that his stepmother intended his disappearance. He saw the Empire falling into ever increasing disorder, and her whom he blamed for this condition, planning to maintain the government which had been so ineffective. Being at that time in command of certain forces which his father had given him to assist in the subduing of an outbreak in the Deccan, he decided to take definite action before it was too late. Seizing some of the royal treasure, he openly declared his intention of putting an end to the conditions at the court. Jehangir sent an army against him, commanded by Mohabet. Obliged to submit, Khurram

THE GREAT LOVER

forwarded his two little sons to Agra as hostages for his future behaviour.

After this, the situation clouds into one of those maddening tangles which seem to involve despotic Eastern governments whenever the ruler, nearing his end, grows too feeble to exercise his terrific power. The chronicler finds himself confused in a maze of murders, poisonings, rebellions, conflicting records. Eventually, hopeless of making head or tail of the situation or of being able to give any clear narrative, he cuts his way abruptly through to the story of a new reign.

We see for an instant the dead, distorted face of the wretched Khusru, strangled, some say, by his brother .... Parwiz is swept away vaguely into darkness .... Shah Ryar and his wife disappear, fugitives at the Court of Persia .... Mohabet, the Emperor's chief of staff, infuriated by some move in the intrigues, turns his arms against Jehangir and captures him and Nur Mahal, the latter boldly fighting from the back of her elephant. Later the Empress has Jehangir once more on the throne, and while he is dying she snatches in her desperation at the young son of Khusru and declares him Emperor. But the indomitable beauty who has ruled for so long is finally overcome. Jehangir is under ground. The boy puppet disappears. Mohabet summons Khurram to assume the crown. That clement Emperor, in spite of his stepmother's long struggle against him, treats the broken and disgraced lady with high distinction. She is provided with a palace and an income suitable to her rank. One catches faint glimpses of her through the long years as a tall and beautiful figure, dressed always in the mourning white of Indian widows, concerning herself only in constructing a great tomb, which she finally occupies. That romantic figure vanishes; the rest is silence....

At last the mists enshrouding his childhood and early youth melt away, and there emerges into the light one of the least understood and most exceptional figures with which Asian history has ever concerned itself. Prince Khurram becomes Shah Jahan (signifying King of the World) and is known thereafter only by that name.

One says "emerges," but the light of history which falls upon this man is so broken and confused, so full of empty shadows in which there is no light at all, that only by the use of imaginative understanding, by fitting together detached glimpses, is it possible to discern the real nature of this Fairy Prince upon whom fortune had lavished all her gifts. Because of his unusual personality, Shah Jahan has been strangely misrepresented. Western chroniclers have universally treated him with cold depreciation. One of them says roughly, "The reign of Shah Jahan was unimportant and without anything especial to record." Sir Thomas Roe, at the court of Delhi while the succession was still uncertain, says that Khusru was a good man, inclined to the Christians, while Khurram was a very objectionable person with no inclination to Western religions and "likely to be of little interest to the English." Sir Thomas thought him cold and repellent, though always stately and magnificent. "I never saw so settled a countenance," he wrote, "nor any man keep so constant a gravity, never smiling nor showing any difference of mien." He also mentions that this sternness on the part of his son greatly discomposed Jehangir, who confided to Sir Thomas that he regretted Shah Jahan's temperance and self-control and wished that he would

THE GREAT LOVER 35

drink wine to "promote good spirits." Others, in speaking of him, are careful to set down all the ugliest and lowest of bazaar gossip and to repeat, as if substantiated, every accusation made by the Emperor's detestable son Aurengzebe—accusations circulated in order to justify his own treacheries and rebellions. Encyclopedias and most Indian histories written by Western men reëcho this attitude of mingled indifference and dislike. Baber, Akbar, and Aurengzebe have had their doings set down at length. Their battles have been analyzed; their conquests carefully recorded in lengthy volumes, while a few fleering phrases have been considered sufficient to express Occidental contempt for a character the writers instinctively disliked and misunderstood.

Universal is the herd's distrust of those unmoved by herd desires. That one should conquer by whatever means, should grasp, should waste, should indulge all the herd passions—all this the herd can comprehend and appreciate. The noisy destructions, the bloody footsteps that mark the mounting to great place are but means, forgotten and condoned by the herd in view of the great ends attained. But to be apart, to desire things not commonly desired, to be possessed by a dream or by purposes remote from those of the multitude, renders the herd uneasy and distrustful. Such uneasiness and distrust arise, it may be surmised, from a subconscious feeling that these different aims impugn the validity of what the herd itself has sought.

Only some such explanation as this can account for the almost universal attitude of contempt and depreciation of the great descendant of the line of Baber. Here was a man, raised to the very pinnacle of human power and splendour, who desired to use those potencies for aims not conceived by the type of ruler to which the herd was accustomed.

Dryden in his poem "Aureng-zebe" expressed the Occidental attitude toward a man who had the power to make war and yet desired other things. Contrasting Shah Jahan with his bloody son, who by his continuous military enterprises wrecked the Empire which his father had left so peaceful and prosperous, the poet says, referring to the father's youthful feats in the Deccan:

> "O! had he still that character maintained
> Of valour which in blooming Youth he gain'd!
> He promised in his East a glorious Race;
> Now, sunk from his Meridian, sets apace.
> But as the Sun, when he from Noon declines,
> And with abated heat less fiercely shines,
> Seems to grow milder, as he goes away,
> Pleasing himself with the remains of day:
> So he who in his Youth for Glory strove
> Would recompense his Age with Ease and Love."

As if war and destruction of life were alone glorious and worthy of admiration!

Of the boy and young man Khurram, few details are obtainable save only that his portraits show him in his early youth as a figure unusual and beautiful. From these portraits and from some few references by visitors to the Court, it can be gathered that he was tall and slight, with fine aquiline features and large eyes, brilliant, very heavily lashed, and surmounted by sweeping brows like the outstretched wings of a bird. His complexion is darkly olive, and his hands and feet are peculiarly small and aristocratic. In him there remains nothing of the yellow-skinned, slant-eyed Mongol. He is the haughty Rajput of long descent, the essential patrician. Yet it is obvious that in him the savage powerful line from which he came has not yet degenerated into feebleness. The broad-axe has gradually been fined into a rapier—no longer a weapon to crush and destroy but still with deadly possibilities in case of need.

Of what he thought, of what he felt, of his hopes, his studies, his ambitions, his desires in the formative period, we get no hint whatever. We hear that he was greatly devoted to his grandfather, Akbar, and carefully studied his methods of administration; also, that when his father endeavoured to draw him away from Akbar's deathbed he haughtily refused, saying that his father might do as he chose but that he would watch by the Emperor till his last breath.

Certain it is, that in the quiet years of Shah Jahan's youth he must have been maturing the splendid dream which in the days of his power he was to realize; such things are the fruit of long reveries. Beyond doubt he must also have been pondering the duties of a ruler, studying the details of administration and the essential secrets of government, rejecting the facile and surface seductions of power and violence, studying the arts, meditating profoundly upon thoughts and emotions which might be embodied in lovely forms of architecture. Most of all, it would seem, he must have been considering the possibilities of man's relation to woman— not as the brief, brutal crises and intoxications of physical lust, but as a high and beautiful relation of creature to creature which should lift the alliance to the most exquisite and permanent of human joys.

These movements of his mind can be guessed at by the results achieved during his years of power. We know only that during the military mission in the Deccan his actions were swift, brilliant, and along lines wholly unforeseen by either his enemies or his advisers. It is obvious, however, that the passion of conquest was never in him. In his long reign of forty years, from 1627 to 1666, but three wars took place: one to repel an attack by the Persians, and two to suppress Hindu revolts in distant provinces.

Plainly he was neither a bigot nor an experimenter with religions. He was content to accept the Moslem faith without much question but had no will to impose it upon his Hindu subjects. He swept out all the disputing sects which had lingered on from the reign of Akbar, and even the Jesuits abandoned their hopes of achieving his conversion. He gathered the machinery of power quietly into his own hand. There are no records of favourites or aggressive viziers who could sell their influence over the monarch to the highest bidder.

A silent man, it seemed, with few confidantes, going his own way toward his own ends. The only suggestion we get of a possible influence helping to shape his life is again a matter of inference: Arjamand Banu, his wife, must be supposed to have affected his life profoundly. Not that we have any record in words. One hears nothing of any public action of hers. She does not appear to have attempted any such seizure of power in public matters as did her famous aunt; her head was not upon the coins struck in Shah Jahan's reign. We get only the most fleeting glimpses of a lovely figure, enshrined like a jewel in a marvellous setting of splendour.

A portrait of the Empress reveals an unusual beauty, delicate, romantic, poetic; and tradition bears out this impression. Tradition tells also that her wit and accomplishments, her learning and her grace, made her the consummate flower of her gifted family. If she made use of all these potent charms to bend her great husband to her will, it was done with such entire art that the world had no vision of the process. From the story of their lives, however, we may deduce the belief that this woman was a strong factor in the life of this man. It is to be remembered that practically no restraint existed either in law or public opinion to control the sexual impulses of a Mogul Emperor. There was no woman, no matter how highly placed in the Asian world, who would not have willingly entered his harem as a consort, even though others already preceded her. He was absolutely free to take women where he would and use them as he willed; yet never, save in the slanders set about in his later years by his rebellious son (slanders which have no confirmation), is there a suggestion that Shah Jahan gave his wife a rival. So far as is known his fidelity and devotion to her as long as she lived were complete, and after her death he made for her the most magnificent testimonial of tenderness that man has ever made for woman.

It is to be supposed, then, that this lovely and abiding influence was in full sympathy with the great purposes of his life, since in Arjamand Banu he found his only real intimate, and from her alone—could that delicate spirit return and become articulate—might we learn to understand the inner life of the taciturn Emperor who made so slight a use of words.

It is no doubt because of his indifference to this form of expression that he has been so little understood. It was a characteristic unusual in Baber's line. He and all of his descendants had loved to record their feelings and actions. Even Jehangir kept to his family's custom of writing memoirs. Of all his house, Shah Jahan alone lacked this engaging and revealing loquacity, and without verbal expression humanity finds it difficult to give him comprehension and sympathy. Nor was the great Emperor fortunate in finding an admirer who possessed the gift in which he was deficient. It was pointed out long since by Lafcadio Hearn that a man's fame depended largely upon his finding a bard to celebrate his deeds. The tremendous outlines of Achilles and Hector, Priam, Agamemnon, and Ulysses would be smothered in forgotten dust, were it not for the voice of a blind singer who dowered them with immortality. It is part of the strange fate of this strange grandson of Akbar that no one should have arisen to interpret him to his fellows. Not that he was without power of self-interpretation, unrivalled in its line by any one figure in history. Carefully studying the manner in which he expressed himself through his great creations, it would seem as if no other artist had so completely revealed the quality of his spirit. Possibly this was because no other has ever had placed in his hands such opportunity and power to embody his ideal in the actual and the permanent.

Probably not another man of whom we have record has held such unchallenged rule, such incredible riches. Princes of fairy tales were but poor by comparison. Reference has been made to the tendency of gold to drift inevitably towards India. Despite all the plundering, looting, and draining away of precious metals and jewels in the three hundred years since Shah Jahan's day, Clairmont Daniel, a student of the subject, estimated that in 1889 there existed in India gold bullion valued at not less than two hundred and seventy million pounds sterling, and this was increasing at the rate of three million pounds annually, in addition to an almost unbelievable wealth of jewels. In the city of Amritsar alone there were said to be in private hands precious stones worth more than two million pounds. Yet this is but a fragment of the treasure of India in the days when the Mogul rulers had been able to prevent all alien plundering for several centuries.

It is not to be forgotten that the Emperor was not only the ruler but the actual owner of the entire country. All land and all wealth were held simply by his permission. At the death of a noble his property automatically escheated to the crown, the family retaining such portion as the ruler permitted. Not only were the fixed revenues, as estimated by Bernier, six scores of rupees monthly, but the tribute of gifts which flowed into the Emperor's coffers made the taxes seem small by comparison. Bernier asserts that in the crypts supported by great marble pillars under the palace of Delhi there was deposited a huge store of gold and silver, cast into pieces so large that no thief could carry them away unobserved. The same French physician says that at all times more than two thousand horses, nine hundred elephants, and a great number of camels, as well as sumpter mules, were maintained in the Imperial stables, along with a full supply of magnificent harness, trappings, and jewelled howdahs.

In estimating the Emperor's wealth Bernier attempted no figures in regard to his seraglio, but considered almost beyond computing the precious stones worn by the women, the luxurious vessels of their toilet and table use, also the value of their garments, so many of which were woven of threads of pure gold and silver. As for the Emperor's own store of jewels he believed no man, not even the owner himself, had a clear idea of their value. In his hands at that time were most of the famous gems of the world, since dispersed among the royal treasuries of Europe. The Koh-i-noor and the dazzling ruby wine cup were among them.

Some idea of the extent of this jewel-treasure may be gained from the following description of the famous peacock throne made by Shah Jahan's order: according to Bernier it was

". . . . six feet long and four feet wide. Upon the four feet which are very massive, and from twenty to twenty-five inches high, are fixed the four bars which support the base of the throne, and upon these bars are arranged twelve columns which sustain the canopy on three sides, there not being any on that which faces the Court. Both the feet and the bars, which are more than eighteen inches long, are covered with gold, inlaid and enriched with numerous diamonds, rubies, and emeralds. In the middle of each bar is a large balass ruby, cut *en cabuchon*, with four emeralds around it, which forms a square cross. Next in succession from one side to the other along the length of the bars there are similar crosses, arranged so that in one the ruby is in the middle of the four emeralds, and in another the emerald is in the middle and four balass rubies around it. The emeralds are table cut, and the intervals between the rubies and emeralds are covered with diamonds the largest of which do not exceed ten or twelve carats in weight all being showy stones but very flat. There are also in some parts pearls set in gold and upon the longer sides of the throne there are four steps to ascend it. Of the three cushions which are upon the throne that which is placed behind the King's back is large and round like one of our bolsters, and the others that are placed at his sides are flat. There is to be seen moreover a sword suspended from this throne, a mace, a round shield, a bow and quiver with arrows; and all these weapons, as also the cushions and steps both of this throne and the other six, are covered over with stones which match those with which each of the thrones is respectively enriched.

"There are a hundred and eight balass rubies, weighing a hundred carats, and some two hundred and more. The emeralds have plenty of colour but have flaws; the largest may weigh sixty carats and the least thirty carats; there are about a hundred and sixteen emeralds.

"The underside of the canopy is covered with diamonds and pearls with a fringe of pearls all around, and above the canopy which is a quadrangular shaped dome, there is to be seen a peacock with elevated tail made of blue sapphires and other coloured stones, the body being of gold inlaid with precious stones, having a large ruby in front of the breast, from whence hangs a pear-shaped pearl of fifty carats and of a somewhat yellow water. On both sides of the peacock there is a large bouquet of the same height as the bird and consisting of many kinds of flowers made of gold inlaid with precious stones. On the side of the throne which is opposite the court there is to be seen a jewel consisting of a diamond of from eighty to ninety carats weight, with rubies and emeralds round it, and when the King is seated he has this jewel in full view. The twelve columns supporting the canopy are surrounded with beautiful rows of pearls which are round and of fine water, weighing from six to ten carats. At four feet distance from the throne there are fixed on either side two umbrellas the sticks of which for seven or eight feet in height are covered with diamonds, rubies and pearls, the umbrellas are of red velvet and are embroidered and fringed all round with pearls.

"Its cost is one hundred sixty million five hundred thousand French livres" (about six million pounds sterling). There is also, he adds, a smaller throne, oval in shape, seven feet long and five feet wide; the outside covered with diamonds and pearls, but with no canopy.

When the young prince Khurram mounted to this gorgeous eminence it seemed natural enough that the court should have chosen for him such a name as Shah Jahan—King of the World. Coming of a race so lusty of life, inheriting untrammelled power, young, beautiful, and brilliant, the nation must have tingled with desire to know what he would do with his tremendous opportunity. Was it to be a plunge into the sea of war, spreading his dominion still further? Would he sink into the sloth and debauchery to which his father had been seduced by the allurements surrounding wealthy and despotic rulers, or would he attempt the wide and disturbing religious experiments of Akbar the Great? Was it possible that upon so dizzy a pinnacle a human being could preserve his equilibrium, could resist the thousand temptations which beset such an eminence?

None of all these temptations appears to have held any enticement for the strange Fairy Prince. With the opportunity of being a magnificent fool he bored everybody by behaving with complete good sense. Quietly gathering into his control all the details of the administration, without noise or display, he eliminated the unwholesome parasites who had collected about his predecessor. Akbar's wise land laws were reënacted. The religious controversies were allowed to die. The Moslems maintained their dominance, but were not permitted to meddle with the religious observances of the Hindus. With a strong hand the balance was kept in the racial rivalry, and so successful was this policy that only once in his long reign was there an outbreak among the Indians, the cause of this rebellion being political rather than either racial or religious, and it was quickly subdued. The revenues which had declined and the trade which had languished under his father's administration soon became greater than at any other period of Mogul rule.

The inducements to spectacular action were so great, that in all chronicles of the period there is sensed a certain impatience with the quiet dignity of the Emperor's life and government. With such unrivalled opportunities to create tremendous dramas, to dazzle with startling experiments, it was felt that he scarcely had the right to be reasonable, to be wise, to create rather than to destroy. Happy, it is said, is the country that has no history. According to the historians' usual vision of what makes history, the Mogul Empire may be said for the larger part of this man's reign to have been a happy country. Public affairs flowed so smoothly that chroniclers find no episodes of blood or violence to record, and therefore pass over his reign with a more or less annoyed indifference. Perhaps this makes plain the reason for their inclination to depreciate the individual and his period. He supplied no material for burning pages; for details of battles, no stories of intrigue and the clash of human passion and ambition, no pictures of Sardanapalian orgies, no tales of favourites plundering and oppressing the people. Historians have never been able to forgive him for this smooth quietude, and in their hurried passing on to his successor, the reign of Shah Jahan, with its true significance, has been ignored and misunderstood.

Yet it had significance more real, more vital than all the tumult and the shouting of those who preceded and who followed him. Of all the Mogul emperors, save Akbar, he alone put a seal upon India, conferred upon her splendid gifts. The tumult of the other rulers has died into mere ghostly echoes; the blood they shed is now but dried dust. Nothing is left of their dominance. The wealth they accumulated is scattered like leaves before the winter winds. That "worldly hope men set their hearts upon" has

> "Like snow upon the desert's dusty face
> Lingered a little hour or two and gone"

But the deeds of Shah Jahan stand today fair and firm, among the greatest jewels of our planet. Today, two hundred and fifty years since he and his dream vanished from our ken, human beings stream from all the nations of the earth to stand before his creations in wonder and amazement. The Taj, the Jamma Musjid, the Mosque of Pearl, the Jasmine Tower, the gardens of Chah-limar, and his Delhi Palace remain to tell what images passed through that quiet head for which the recorders of his day showed so little reverence. Nothing the hand of man has so far fashioned presents quite such perfection, such significance. And so well did he build that, save where violence and stupidity have attacked them, they stand as unmoved and flawless as when they rose at his command. Even time seems to turn aside its cruelties from these realized visions. They remain stainless, beautiful, and complete as the years lapse by.

THE GREAT LOVER

It is part of the curious fate which has followed this man, the fate of being always minimized and depreciated, that Western commentators constantly strive to lessen the value of the creator while reluctantly admitting the beauty of his creations. Efforts have been made to ascribe these conceptions to supposed Venetian architects and decorators, but it is interesting to observe that nowhere else and under no other circumstances did these mythical Venetians achieve an equal beauty. When Shah Jahan had passed, no other hand produced rivals of his works. That he used his tools where he found them is to be understood, but that the conception and the inspiration were his own can hardly be denied, since, with his going, such tools never again wrought the realization of such tremendous visions. Moreover, as in the work of every great artist, an innate style and expression of individuality characterizes all he achieved. A certain calm splendour, a proud, grave spirituality is set like a seal upon whatsoever he created, not to be mistaken for the work of any other builder.

Of the man himself we can catch but vague glimpses, for he could never express himself save in stone, and of his daily life there are but few anecdotes. One of these few relates to the aforementioned law that upon the death of a subject his property automatically escheated to the sovereign. The record says:

"Some years after the death of a wealthy banyane or Gentile merchant, who had always been employed in the King's service and like the generality of his countrymen had been a notorious usurer, the son became clamourous for a certain portion of the money. The widow refusing to comply with the young man's request on account of his profligacy and extravagance, he had the baseness and folly to make Shah Jahan acquainted with the real amount of the property left by his father, about two hundred thousand crowns. The Mogul immediately summoned the old lady and in the presence of the assembled Omrahs commanded her to send him immediately one hundred thousand rupees and to put her son in possession of fifty thousand. Then he ordered the attendants to turn the widow out of the hall. She did not lose her presence of mind; she struggled with the servants and exclaimed that she had something further to say to the King.

" 'Let us hear what she has to say,' cried Shah Jahan.

" 'Hazret-Salamet (Heaven preserve your Majesty). It is not without some reason that my son claims the property of his father; he is our son and consequently our heir. But I would humbly inquire what kinship there may have been between your Majesty and my deceased husband to warrant the demand of one hundred thousand rupees?'

"Shah Jahan was so pleased with this bold speech and with the idea of a King being related to a tradesman that he burst into laughter and commanded that the widow should be left in the enjoyment of her husband's money."

Out of this mist of silence which surrounds him, we get but these vague flashes here and there by which to build up some conception of the man. We learn that he loved magnificence for his person as well as for his surroundings. A door opens for a moment: in his Audience Hall certain emissaries have been wrangling with the Emperor's officers, sending to him in his retirement many messages and petitions, conflicting, abusive, passionate. The chronicler says:

"Shah Jahan appeared suddenly before his visitors. He was tired of their intrigues. He wore a turban brocaded with gold, decorated with a topaz without price, dressed in a costume of white velvet, embroidered with silk, his feet in white slippers. He seated himself on the Peacock Throne."

The glimpse is but momentary. The narrative thereafter flows on into matters political. We can see, however, by this flash of light a white-clad figure seated beneath the great jewelled Peacock shimmering with a thousand hues; the "priceless topaz" shining like gold above the dark brow and the large impenetrable eyes. What has he to do with these little questions, momentary and teasing, of conflicting policies? Yet never does he let the great thought which possesses him obtrude itself to the damage of his realm. The government is always his own; no favourites, no spoiled viziers thrust themselves between him and his public duties.

The very smoothness of the course of events in this reign mislead the observer with the idea that nothing is happening, but such smoothness never exists unless some force, silent but effective, ensures it. Never has India since the days of the great Asoka known such freedom from foreign invasion, such peace within her borders, such prosperity and order. That very tranquillity which his skilled and wise administration made possible, has robbed the great flower of the Mogul race of his reputation for genius in government. That a man should deal effectively with disorder is much; that he should prevent disorder is still more. Such a ruler must have laboured enormously since he committed so few of his duties to other hands. Shah Jahan's extremely successful foreign policy, too, seems to have been all his own, along with his domestic jurisdiction.

Like other Indian sovereigns he held a daily Durbar, or court, to which every subject was supposed to have access to present petitions and make complaint of any oppression or injustice. The despotism of the ruler was modified by the democratic nature of these daily audiences where the humblest could demand redress from the Monarch himself. Unlike China and Japan, India did not surround her Emperors with seclusion and mystery. No doubt doorkeepers and officials exacted bribes before the plaintiff secured access to the Presence, but in those gorgeous Halls of Audience in Agra and Delhi, thousands of all classes saw and spoke with Shah Jahan face to face. The handsome, dark-eyed sovereign, with his impassive countenance and his jewelled garments, listened to a multitude of dissensions and petitions, giving swift decisions and learning much of the condition and needs of his people. A stenographic report of the proceedings of one of these morning courts would be of far more value and interest now than all the dull and elaborate stories handed down to us of Aurengzebe's endless battles.

Another record recovered is that every Monday—that having been the day of the week on which the Emperor ascended the throne—soup kitchens at both capitals provided a meal for five hundred poor persons.

There is a charming glimpse of a curious ceremony held yearly in honour of Shah Jahan's birthday in the great courtyard of the Palace. On a large pair of silver scales he was weighed against a counterpoise, first in grain, afterwards in bread and other forms of food, and this was distributed among

THE GREAT LOVER

the people. Again he was weighed against gold and silver, to be given as a perquisite to his nobles; and lastly against a great mass of rose leaves and jasmine blossoms, used by the harem later to distill perfumes or to make flower conserves.

Of what the harem consisted we have no record. No woman in this Emperor's life was of sufficient importance to deserve even a passing mention by the chronicler, saving only that best beloved, his wife, whose "palace name" was Mumtaz Mahal. Impossible to make any picture of this man apart from this woman. So closely were their lives interlaced, so supremely does she appear to have been his inspiration that it is necessary in imagination to outline one profile next the other as were Jehangir's and Nur Mahal's upon the pieces of money struck during their reign. Beautiful miniatures of this lady still exist. Edwin Arnold thus describes her:

> "I have two pictures of Queen Arjamand
> In the Persian manner. Oh, a lady fair!
> Everywhere beautiful, and born for love;
> A face to win worship of hearts, once seen.
> No vain voluptuous Odalisque, with orbs
> Set bold under low brow, but kind, but good,
> More woman than Sultana; yet with air
> Of majesty, as fitted great Princess;
> And in her high-bred nostrils, habit of rule.
> Complexion like the shell of ostrich-egg,
> A tinted ivory; hair midnight black,
> Braided in seven bright tresses; dark brown eyes
> Splendidly lambent under eyebrows arched
> Like edge of swallow's wing;—love-lighted eyes
> Curtained with long, fine, sweeping eyelashes;
> Cheeks hardly touched by palest rose-colour;
> Chin delicately moulded; sweetest mouth

Flower-soft and sensitive, with curves to make
The smile divine—a mouth of rose and pearl—
Mouth to give orders to an Emperor:
The neck an alabaster pillar; hand
Perfect and small; but stained upon the palms
With henna's russet-red, the Persian way,
Holding a blossom of the pomegranate
Flower of true Faith! Upon the proud smooth head
A Persian cap of state sewn thick with pearls;
Necklet and ear-rings pearl; a ruby clasps
The scarlet silken choli laced with gold
Binding her high-girt breasts; a shawl of blue
Sits on her comely shoulders, stiff with gold,
Letting a dagger's jewelled handle peer;
And cloth of gold, clasping a slender waist,
Droops to the feet, slippered in silver, gemmed.
Arjamand Banu Begam—such she was."

It is the strangest part of the history of these two highly placed and gifted persons, that in spite of their great position they managed always to maintain so much privacy. Through the mists of the past you can discern Shah Jahan and Arjamand Banu only as luminous shadows. You grasp at their outlines and the shadows melt between your fingers. So much regarding them is implicit in what has not been said. We know that the wife of the Emperor was born in 1594 and that she married him in 1612 at the age of eighteen; somewhat late for an Oriental woman of noble birth to enter matrimony. We know that eight children were born of the marriage, and the husband's fidelity is still further attested by the fact that there is no mention anywhere that he had other children than these.

Like the Emperor's, Arjamand Banu's garments were sumptuous, her jewels splendid. A sari, still to be seen in India, is a tissue of rose silk embroidered with golden peacocks and cypress trees—favourite pattern of both Emperor and Empress. There are copies also of her famous necklace, pictured in the best known of her miniatures, a long collar of the gems which were called the "nine lucky stones of India"; squares of virgin gold into which are sunk diamonds, rubies, emeralds, sapphires, opals, turquoise, cats' eyes, chrysoprase, and moonstones. The undersides of these squares were beautifully enamelled with flowers, and all were strung together by three strings of fine pearls, the large pendant at the end being thickly set with flat table diamonds, and the reverse enamelled in glowing red.

Of her eight children, fruit of tender love between two such beautiful and gifted mates, only Jahanara, the youngest, had the qualities to be expected from such a union. This is one of those strange perversities of heredity which baffle the speculations of the eugenists. The eldest son, Dara, was the only one of the family inheriting Baber's and Akbar's love of verse and literature. He gained renown by his translation of the Upanishads into Persian, and the Latin translation of his version first brought those mystical scriptures to the knowledge of the Western world. Happily Arjamand never knew her family tragedy.

At last with relief one pushes aside the cloudy inferences and implications obscuring the efforts to know this reticent Emperor. Something sure and definite emerges. His immortal creations limn the real Shah Jahan. Solid in the enormous sunlight of India stand the expressions of his spirit—dreams which long before his reign began must have taken definite shape in his mind. He must have been meditating profoundly the work he intended to do. His soul was a soul that walked alone in the high places of beauty.

Firmly settled upon the throne and with vast resources to his hand, he could bring out of nothingness his visions and make them reality. But first he must set himself to reorganize and reëstablish his realm, to give it that peace and prosperity which were the first of his gifts to his subjects. When this was accomplished, he turned to his capital to begin there the true work of his life.

Agra had been the favourite residence of the Moguls, and Akbar had done much for it. Mandelslo, a native of Mecklenburg, who was a visitor there in the first days of Shah Jahan's reign, describes it as the noblest city of Hindustan. He says it was as much as a horseman could do to ride around the city in a day.

"Its streets are fair and spacious, and there are some of them vaulted, which are above a quarter of a league in length, where the Merchants and Tradesmen have their Shops, distinguished by their Trades and Merchandizes which are there sold; every Trade and every Merchant having a particular Street and Quarter assigned to him. There were eighty caravanserais for foreign merchants, most of them three Stories high, with very noble lodgings, Store-houses, Vaults, and Stables belonging to them."

He counted seventy great mosques and estimated the number of public baths or "hothouses" at above eight hundred, the tax on which brought in a considerable revenue to the state. In and outside the city he saw numerous palaces of the rajahs and lords, and chiefest of all the imperial palace, fortified with a moat and drawbridge. The treasure there jealously guarded was estimated on credible authority at above fifteen hundred millions of crowns, or over three hundred million pounds.

Shah Jahan determined, however, to build a city for himself. The plain of Delhi was strewn with capitals. Each conqueror, sweeping aside as unworthy of him the seat of his predecessors and moving a little further on, had begun a new monument to his own greatness, leaving the abandoned city to fall into neglect and decay. Tuglukhabad was the fifth, Indrapat the sixth. So far the Moguls had done nothing important for the place of their government, and the new Emperor began the erection of a city to be called after himself, Shahjahannabad, the seventh Delhi capital. His first work was to bring clear water from the sources of the Jumna by an aqueduct one hundred and twenty-six miles long to supply the needs of Shahjahannabad. This great aqueduct carried sufficient water not only for a large canal and for the many gardens of the new city, but also for the uses of the people.

The new capital was laid out on a noble plan—a plan which has since been much obscured by the lack of intelligence of Shah Jahan's successors, but which at the time was spoken of with unstinted admiration by Western travellers. Two great avenues, thirty-five yards wide, crossed the city in opposite directions, lined with arcades of the shops and dwellings of the industrial classes. The whole was surrounded by high walls with towers interspersed and with four great gateways giving access to the avenues. The walls enclosed a space ten miles by six, but Bernier says that the thatched dwellings of the poorer classes clustered outside the walls, greatly increased the city's size. In the centre of the town the surface of a rocky height was levelled, and around it was cleared a great square, upon which the four long streets gave, each through a magnificent gateway. Some thirty steps mounted to the top of the rock, and here Shah Jahan began the erection of the famous Jamma Musjid, the greatest mosque in the world.

It was said of Augustus that he found Rome built of brick and left it built of marble. Akbar, in all of his constructions, had utilized the warm, lovely, red sandstone native to the country, and one sees in the first attempts of Shah Jahan a mingling of this material with white marble. Later everything he built tended more and more to the exclusive use of marble, until it finally became the sole material of his magnificent conceptions. Also a gradual transformation took place in both plan and decoration. The rich Indian ornament and the square Hindu construction were abandoned, and a peculiar elegance and simplicity replaced them. The incised ornament gave way to inlay, often of precious stones, in the form of flat decorations of flowers and vines in jasper, carnelian, onyx, agate, and bloodstone.

The great mosque, Jamma Musjid, accommodating more than a thousand worshippers, showed the early combination of sandstone and marble in the smooth and splendid façade which gave upon a courtyard three hundred and ten feet square, and in the three domes of marble and the minarets a hundred and thirty feet high. Even today, despite all the vicissitudes through which it has passed, the calm splendour of outline and proportion revealed here, demonstrates a Master Builder whose mind could conceive and whose power and will could create a triumph of architecture. As always in the constructions of Shah Jahan, the work is so well done that time seems to have had no effect upon it. Within, all is cool, dim shadow and gracious line, calm

THE GREAT LOVER

purity of space. By contrast with this simplicity and grandeur, Christian fanes seem almost tawdry. The Moslem faith requires no image or other reminder to stir religious impulse or fix the intention of the worshipper.

Slowly year by year foundations were laid; walls arose; the lofty domes rounded between the delicate spires of the minarets. Always the hand of this quiet ruler guided and directed the realization of his great imagination. He needed no words, had no desire for those wild enterprises which the historian loves to analyze and relate. Here was the speech, here the actions in which he revealed himself, in which he embodied his aspirations. Because the eloquence of the man, his self revelation, was so massive and enduring, the human personality behind this solid splendour grew vague to the average mind. The builder was obscured by the architectural utterances of his spirit.

While the city was being created, while the greatest temple of his faith in all the world was rising, Shah Jahan was also creating his own palace, which Fergusson, the historian of architecture, thinks the most magnificent ever constructed. He says:

"The fort on which it stands is about a mile and a half in circuit, the massive walls rising sixty feet above the river, and higher still on the moated side towards the land. Within was a vast series of public and private halls and apartments, with a Mosque, bathhouse, and gardens; the whole permeated by a marble channel bringing in the bright and wholesome water of the canal. It was situated close to the river Jumna and measured sixteen hundred feet East and West by three thousand two hundred feet North and South, surrounded on all sides by very noble walls relieved at intervals by towers, which overlooked a wide moat."

The Diwan-i-khass, or special audience hall, was three hundred and seventy feet in length, and Fergusson says of this:

". . . . this great vaulted chamber forms the noblest entrance known to belong to any existing palace. The entire hall is of white marble with superb mosaics of birds and flowers done in precious stones. Frescoes of fine wood are set into the marble and with its Moorish arches it is one of the most beautiful rooms imaginable. At one end, separating the principal part from the Woman's Hall, is an exquisite white marble fretwork screen as delicate as lace. When the peacock throne stood in its midst it must have looked like a realization of the Arabian Nights. Above the rich columns holding up the ceiling, in beautiful Persian script in pure gold, is the famous inscription: 'If there is a Heaven on earth, it is this, it is this, it is this.' The place is indeed so beautiful with the exquisite outer vistas of courts, full of trees and flowers, that even an Occidental is fain to confess it an elysium."

The whole palace was a mass of glorious chambers opening on green and flowering courts watered and cooled by pools and springing fountains. But perhaps the most beautiful portion of this fairy residence was the harem to the South and East; it was about a thousand feet in length, more than twice the area of the Escurial or, in fact, of any palace in Europe. Here indeed the Emperor allowed his fancy full sway in making a home for his beloved wife and her attendants. The harem had three large garden courts and some fourteen other smaller ones, all filled with trees, vines, fountains, and many-coloured roses always the special joy of Baber's descendants. Every lovely fantasy was employed to give grace to this home of his love, and yet all was wrought with such fine reserve that the effect is of extreme purity and simplicity. The burning light was softened by passing through delicate veils of marble so exquisitely pierced and wrought that one could almost feel as if they might be swept aside by a slender hand, and yet of so durable a material that centuries have left no flaw upon them. Here and there low archways opened through the screens to frame a picture of green-shaded fountains springing among the roses. The sunlight filtering in through marble veils lit the rooms with pale golden rays, tempered by the opaline shadows, blue and purple, of the softly curved marble ceilings. One of these chambers was devoted to the bath, a wide pool sunk in the floor, fed by runnels damascened with delicate lines of onyx and silver, over which the clear waters flowed with an effect as of shining ripples:

> "—Full conduits streaming
> Where fair bathers lie."

No foreign eye ever saw this secret place of joy and love until after the fall of Delhi and of the last of the Moguls, when the English signalized their conquest by using it as barracks for their soldiers and afterwards pulled down a large portion of it to erect a rough building to serve for the housing of troops. During Shah Jahan's life it was probably the most perfect dwelling place that man had ever made for himself.

To this refuge the Emperor came for refreshment at the end of labourious days: days full of the busy details of administration; days of poring over the multitudinous maps and plans of his many constructions, sketching, correcting, studying the subtle intricacies of line and form, of spacing, of stresses and strains, of the rhythm of ornament—all tested by an ever-growing purity of taste. Here was his place of relaxation in the presence of his beloved amid the pretty playthings of the laughing children. Here came the merchants of stuffs and jewels and the sellers of perfumes. In the cool of the evening, poets and story-tellers recited their verses and romances in the moonlit courts, while lute and vina breathed their music and the dancers wove rhythmic measures—pleasures of a fairy palace for a fairy prince and princess.

Even with such housing, however, the heat of summer in Delhi was so great that the members of the court frequently sought other quarters, although nothing was spared to provide them with every luxury. There was even a chain of couriers who passed to and fro between the capital and the western coast of India to secure those famous mangoes not to be had in the plains, as well as other rare fruits for the royal table. But when Grishma, "season of heat," arrived, the royal household usually removed to the Vale of Kashmir.

Akbar had seized upon that mountain paradise, always famous in the annals of India for its charm, but his constant activities left him small time to enjoy it. Jehangir, however, had visited it occasionally in his youth, and after his marriage to Nur Mahal, she induced him to make frequent residence there. That the journey might not be too unpleasant, a great avenue of trees was planted, at her command, between Delhi and Lahore and from there on to the foothills. Perhaps nothing gives so complete an idea of the wealth and power of the Mogul rulers as this amazing road prepared for their summer pilgrimage. Through the hot plains, it is bordered by trees that make an over-arching shade, and it mounts six thousand feet in about thirty miles, winding by the edges of great precipices, by rushing rivers, through forests and passes; while far below, cloud masses roll about the flanks of the deodar-clad mountains. At last it opens out upon a watered and flower-bestrewn plain — a lofty Paradise, famed through the centuries.

Along this famous road, made practical and comfortable for the transportation of the numerous court with its necessary impedimenta of luxury, passed the Emperor and his train. A great colourful caravan, this. The Emperor and the Empress and the high officers of the Court were mounted on elephants especially trained to roll their huge bulk along with swift smoothness—elephants washed and oiled, with blue circles of paint around their eyes, with gilded devices upon their brows, and with every toenail painted a coral red; the housings were cloth of gold hung with bells, and the gold-plated and jewelled howdahs were made soft with cushions of flowered silks. Even the ankus, with which the mahouts pricked forward these mammoth steeds, was of precious metals set with gems. Followed the mounted Royal Guard of turbaned, bannered Moslems in gold and silver mail so finely woven of metal links that it gave as supply as silk to every movement. The Rajput light-horse came next, with turbans of every tint wound at dashing angles; with upturned moustaches and braided beards dyed turquoise blue or scarlet. The manes and tails of their snow-white horses were tinted vividly with yellow, crimson, or rose. The children, women of the court, dancers, and musicians trailed behind in brilliant palanquins, armies of attendants bringing up the rear. The pauses for rest were made at magnificent pavilions already pitched, carpeted, cushioned, where were served delicate food and snow-cooled sherbets.

Bernier, the French physician, who was in India in the latter part of Shah Jahan's reign, has given us perhaps the most delightful and detailed description of that famous summer retreat of the Mogul court. He says:

"Kashmir is a beautiful country, diversified by a great many low hills; about thirty leagues in length, and from ten to twelve in breadth. It is situated at the extremity of Hindustan, to the north of Lahore; enclosed by mountains at the foot of the Caucasus....

"The numberless streams which issue from the mountains maintain the valley and the hillocks in the most delightful verdure. The whole kingdom wears the appearance of a fertile and highly cultivated garden. Villages and hamlets are frequently seen through the luxuriant foliage. Meadows and vineyards, fields of rice, wheat, hemp, saffron, and many sorts of vegetables among which are intermingled trenches filled with water; rivulets, canals, and several small lakes vary the enchanting scene. The whole ground is enamelled with our European flowers and plants, and covered with our apple, pear, plum, apricot, and walnut trees, all bearing fruit in great abundance. The private gardens are full of melons, pateques, or water melons, water parsnips, red beet, radishes, most of our potherbs, and others with which we are unacquainted.

"The capital of Kashmir bears the same name as the kingdom. It is without walls and is not less than three quarters of a league in length and half a league in breadth. It is situated in a plain, distant about two leagues from the mountains, which seem to describe a semicircle, and is built on the banks of a fresh-water lake, whose circumference is from four to five leagues. This lake is formed of live springs and of streams descending from the mountains, and communicates with the river, which runs through the town, by means of a canal sufficiently large to admit boats. . . .

"The lake is full of islands, which are so many pleasure-grounds. They look beautiful and green in the midst of the water, being covered with fruit trees, and laid out with regular trellised walks. In general, they are surrounded by the large-leafed aspen, planted at intervals of two feet. The largest of these trees may be clasped in a man's arms, but they are as high as the mast of a ship, and have only a tuft of branches at the top like palm trees.

"The declivities of the mountains beyond the lake are crowded with houses and flower-gardens. The air is healthful, and the situation considered most desirable. . . .

"The most beautiful of all these gardens is one belonging to the King, called Chah-limar. The entrance from the lake is through a spacious canal bordered with green turf, and running between two rows of poplars. Its length is about five hundred paces, and it leads to a large summerhouse placed in the middle of the garden. A second canal, still finer than the first, then conducts you to another summerhouse, at the end of the garden. This canal is paved with large blocks of freestone, and its sloping sides are covered with the same. In the middle is a long row of fountains, fifteen paces asunder; besides which there are here and there large circular basins, or reservoirs, out of which arise other fountains, formed into a variety of shapes and figures.

"The summerhouses are placed in the midst of the canal, consequently surrounded by water, and between the two rows of large poplars planted on either side. They are built in the form of a dome, and encircled by a gallery, into which four doors open; two looking up, or down, the canal, and two leading to bridges that connect the buildings with both banks. The houses consist of a large room in the centre, and of four smaller apartments, one at each corner. The whole of the interior is painted and gilt, and on the walls of the chambers are inscribed certain sentences, written in large and beautiful Persian characters. The four doors are extremely valuable; being composed of large stones, and supported by two beautiful pillars. The doors and pillars were found in some of the idol temples demolished by Shah-Jahan, and it is impossible to estimate their value. I can not describe the nature of the stone, but it is far superior to porphyry."

Later and ruder generations are probably unfamiliar with that delight of their grandmothers, Moore's *Lalla Rookh,* as light in texture, as fluently ornamented, and as sugary in flavour as an old-fashioned bride cake. Moore spent his most convoluted decoration of sweetness upon Chah-limar and the Vale of Kashmir. Only the most stolid of that generation when *Lalla Rookh* lay on every marble-topped centre-table, failed to memorize part or all of "The Light of the Harem," beginning:

"Who has not heard of the Vale of Cashmere,
 With its roses, the brightest that earth ever gave,
 Its temples and grottoes, and fountains as clear
 As the love-lighted eyes that hang over their wave?"

or were unfamiliar with all the charms of Chah-limar and the delights of that summer villegiature of the Mogul court.

Everyone who affected verse knew of the Feast of Roses; of the musical parties in the moonlit nights upon the lake; of the illuminations at the dances; of the singing of the goldfinches brought from Tonkin, which had voices so melodious that they were known as the Celestial Birds. They had all read of the anemones that starred the fields, of those great sweeps of Hemasagare flowers called the Sea of Gold, of the white moonflowers, and of that tree having blossoms with so delicious an odour that the Hindus entitled them the arrows of Kamadeva, the God of Love. They also knew how the pools of the gardens contained numbers of tame goldfish, each one adorned with a little collar of gold wire, which came flocking to feed from the Empress's fingers.

To this beautiful Vale of Kashmir, until the death of his wife—that wife of whom the poet says:

> "He preferred in his heart the least ringlet that curled
> Down her exquisite neck to the throne of the world!"

Shah Jahan came every year for rest from the cares of government and the enormous labours of administration. Time and neglect have robbed the famous resort of many of its glories, and motor-cars now climb the passes over which Mumtaz Mahal was borne in a jewelled howdah upon a painted elephant; but still many traces remain to show that the Emperor's taste never failed, and that, more perhaps than any other man, he knew how to live, and help others to live, beautifully.

Even while Delhi was building, Shah Jahan did not spare to adorn the city of Agra. To the great frowning red fortress of Akbar he added a splendid Hall of Audience, beautiful chambers for the residence of his household, and the marble crowned Jasmine Tower, with its pavilion overlooking the Jumna and adorned with carvings of his favourite flower, where he was so long to live as an unhappy prisoner and where he drew his last breath.

In Agra, too, the Emperor built Moti Musjid, the Mosque of Pearl, with the exception of the Taj the crown of his genius. Always as time passed his inspiration cleared and refined itself. One notes that his work, instead of growing more sumptuous, becomes more firm and clean in outline. An inclination toward utilizing the innate beauty of material and the subtlety of form to achieve the effects of colour, is perceptible. In the Moti Musjid, reflections of light fill the white arches with an infinite play of tints like the shimmer of colour upon the shifting surface of a bubble, giving a sense as of music moving through those ivory spaces with the soft interplay of voiceless harmonies.

Meanwhile the years slipped quietly by—years seeming to have had no interest for the historian, though in them the Emperor was creating slowly and surely the most perfect jewels of architecture ever wrought or conceived by one man.

Under his strong hand the empire had passed through a long period of almost unbroken peace and prosperity. His four sons were growing up about him tall, handsome, and talented. His three daughters gave promise of succeeding to the beauty of their mother's famous Persian family. Between himself and his beloved consort there seemed no shadow of chill or ending of their perfect affection. But the gods, who had given so much, began, as is their wont, to consider that gifts from them are but temporary loans and may at any moment be required again from the one who enjoys their indulgence. Their first move was to stretch out ruthless hands and take suddenly the one jewel valued more than all of his possessions. In camp at Barhanpur where the queen had accompanied him, although she was

THE GREAT LOVER

in near expectation of the birth of her eighth child, the blow fell. From an old Persian manuscript is gleaned a strange account of the event:

"Shah Jahan, Emperor, Conqueror of the World, Protector of the Poor, Sustainer of the unhappy, very learned and illustrious, had four sons by the Empress and four beautiful daughters. The last one, Jahanara Begum, cried out before she was born and caused the death of the Empress. The day that the infant cried the Empress became much alarmed, and all the women of the palace, and the children who heard the sound were greatly frightened, and the memory of it remained with them during all the days of their lives. They said that such a thing had never happened before. It was a terrible prodigy and they began to say 'O great God let not this turn to evil!' and went at once to inform the Emperor. They said that the Empress was suffering terribly from birth pangs and he ordered at once all the most skillful doctors and experienced midwives to assist, and the women began to pray saying: 'Without the will of God not a leaf moves.' They tried all sorts of remedies without success. The priest came and read prayers and the women rubbed the hands and feet of the poor Empress. The child continued to cry without having yet seen the light. The Empress gave up all hope and calling the Emperor to her side and weeping said: 'Oh King, these sufferings and this strange event leave my mind troubled and oppressed and I know not how it will finish.' The Emperor hearing these words was astonished and afflicted. He put his finger upon her lips and tried to find words that would comfort and console the Begum. She made them bring all her jewels and gave them to the Emperor and prayed him to be good to her children. The Empress said:

'Pardon me all my faults and every angry word I ever said. After that I shall be ready for the supreme journey.' The Emperor hearing these words wept bitterly because of the great love he bore her and one would have said that the stars fell in heaven and the rain upon earth. The Empress weeping said: 'Oh King, I have lived with you in joy and also in sorrow. God has made you a great Emperor, and given you worlds to govern; at the moment of parting I give you two counsels, Almighty God has given you four sons and four daughters to perpetuate your name, do not take another wife to make discord among them, and build me a tomb to make my name remembered.' Shah Jahan promised to observe her wishes and the child was born.

"Her women continued to pray for her life and say: 'Oh God let us die but save the life of the Begum' and all was done according to the usage of a day of birth. Soon after the Empress began to tremble and her limbs became cold and such lamentation arose in the palace, that one would have said the day of judgment had arrived. The Emperor weeping and striking his breast repeated the language of the poet Saadi: 'Gold will not rest in the hands of a prodigal nor patience in the heart of a lover more than water in a sieve.' Then the Empress left this world and went to live in Heaven with the Peris."

Of Mumtaz-i-Mahal—"The Exalted One"—the Emperor, after his manner, spoke no word, but grief stirred his genius to its supreme accomplishment. He resolved that upon the grave of that sweetest of ladies should be laid Love's perfect crown. Wandering lonely through the fair chambers, now empty of her presence, he pondered long and deeply. . . .

THE GREAT LOVER

The great buildings of the world have been monuments to the pomp and pride of kings, temples to the gods, or records of the power of rich and haughty cities. He, in the white comeliness of marble, would for the first time give utterance to man's love of woman. Not physical desire—of which there had been expression more than enough in all the arts—but that mating of spirit with spirit from which was born the human soul, which brought by slow gestation out of brute slime, the birth of intellect, of art, of ecstasy and aspiration.

During solitary nights in the Palace courts—from which music and merriment had been banished, and where only the voice of fountains broke the silence, the vision came to him. Here at last he found the work he was meant to do. For this he had been given supreme power, well nigh limitless wealth, and the dower of art. All his sex's cruelties to women should have an exquisite expiation in the supreme homage of a man to his mate. All she had been at her best should find embodiment in this sublimated purity and tender beauty. No man should be able to look upon the tomb of Arjamand without a cleansing of the heart; no woman, without a new stirring of nobleness and loyalty. None who had suffered but should find solace in the presence of this record of a lofty and unforgetting sorrow. He would give to the world a majestic and unmatched gift.

Command was issued for drawings and pictures of the most famous tombs to be assembled. The Emperor sent for his favourite architect, Isa-Mahmoud-Effendi. In consultation with him the plan of the Taj Mahal was completed. No pains were spared to bring to perfection the last dwelling of his beloved Queen. Twenty thousand labourers toiled upon it for seventeen years. Winter and summer, ox wains creaked across the plains. Red sandstone for the gateway came from Fatteh-pur, marble from Mukrani in Jeypore—marble chosen for its exquisite shadowings of rose within the grain, toning coldness from the white purity. Across deserts and mountains, from Balkh, Iran, and far Khorasan came camel caravans bearing precious bales of jewels to serve for fine inlays of flower and leaf, inlays so sumptuous yet so restrainedly used, so admirably spaced that the final impression is one of austerity.

It is part of Shah Jahan's great good fortune that he was allowed to complete this last crown and flower of his life's labours, for almost immediately upon its accomplishment disaster overtook him; yet of the cruel wrongs he suffered none could have touched him so deeply as the failure to finish this ultimate expression of himself and his love. To so supreme an artist, the loss of empire, imprisonment, and humiliation were but minor afflictions when weighed against the frustration of opportunity to fulfill his ideal.

The intention of the Emperor was to have made for himself another tomb immediately opposite the Taj upon the further bank. It was to have been of black marble with a bridge of silver to connect the two. How beautiful such a monument would have been, how supreme a splendour, can now only be imagined. Had the plan been realized even the angels would have been tempted to lean over the bar of Heaven to admire and to envy what man had accomplished. The foundations for this second tomb were being laid when the rebellion of his sons put an end for all time to his labours. One of the charges brought by Aurengzebe against his father was that he wasted the country's revenues in these costly constructions; but Aurengzebe himself spent far more in the eternal wars by which he ruined the Empire, leaving nothing to show for them but wretchedness and a broken realm.

Happily the Taj had been achieved, a building said to have been modelled and painted more frequently than any other in the world. Word pictures of it are numberless. Bernier, who saw it when it was almost new, gives an elaborate description in his *Letters from Agra*, and though the little doctor was rather inclined to apologize for admiration of anything so unlike the ornate architectural taste of France at that epoch, he cannot wholly restrain his enthusiasm. He says:

"Nothing offends the eye; on the contrary it is delighted with every part and never tired of looking. The last time I visited the Tage Mehales mausoleum I was in the company of a French merchant who, as well as myself, thought that this extraordinary fabric could not be sufficiently admired. I did not venture to express my opinion, fearing that my taste might have become corrupted by my long residence in the Indies; and as my companion was come recently from France it was quite a relief to my mind to hear him say, that he had seen nothing in Europe so bold and majestic . . . . It is possible that I have imbibed an Indian taste but I decidedly think that this monument deserves much more to be numbered among the wonders of the world than the pyramids of Egypt; those unshapen masses which when I had seen twice yielded me no satisfaction, and which are nothing on the outside but heaps of large stones piled in the form of steps one upon another."

Which demonstrates that his Eastern travels were inspiring Bernier with a little of the courage of his own taste and opinions.

Fergusson, the great historian of the world's architecture, who writes always with much restraint and with reserve of adjectives says:

"The Taj stands in a garden court of more than a thousand feet square. The mausoleum itself is a square of a hundred and eighty-six feet and the principal dome is fifty-eight feet in diameter and eighty feet high, immediately under which is an enclosure formed by a screen of marble trellis work. Within this enclosure stand the tombs of Mumtaz-i-Mahal and Shah Jahan. She is in the centre and he a little on one side. The light to the central apartment is admitted only through double screens of marble trellis work of the most exquisite design, one on the outer face and one on the inner face of the wall. In any other climate this would produce nearly complete darkness but in India and in a building entirely of white marble this was required to temper the light. As it is, no words can express the chastened beauty of that central chamber, seen in the soft gloom of the subdued light that reaches it through the distant and half-closed openings to what must always have been the coolest and the loveliest of garden retreats, and now that it is sacred to the dead it is the most graceful and the most impressive of the sepulchres of the world. Not less exquisite was the inlaying with precious stones such as agates, bloodstones, jaspers and the like. These are combined in wreaths, scrolls, and frets as exquisite in design as beautiful in colour, and, relieved by the pure white marble in which they are inlaid, they form the most beautiful and precious style of ornament ever adopted in architecture."

Lord Roberts, the soldier, said of it: "Neither words nor pencil can give to the most imaginative,

THE GREAT LOVER

the slightest idea of the all satisfying beauty and purity of this glorious conception"; and Baxter, a recent traveller, has this to say:

"I had expected great things, but found that I had formed no conception of the reality. Anything so fairy-like, so spotless, so gracefully gigantic, so totally unlike other creations of man, I did not imagine had existence on earth. I have now seen it from various points of view—from the gateway, from under the shade of the forest trees in the garden, from a distance, from the top of one of the minarets, from the lofty platform overlooking the Jumna; and each time that I shut my eyes and opened them again it seemed like a heavenly vision, a something utterly superhuman dropped down by the celestials to astonish man."

This from a Russian traveller:

"The real tombs of the two lovers lie in a subterranean chamber immediately beneath the tombstones above. They are covered with silken stuffs, and always with flowers, and sprinkled with essences of sandal, of rose, and jasmin. . . . Neither time, nor weather, nor wars have left a stain upon this perfect thing. It is as if the elements and even man himself have respected it."

Mrs. Steel in *India Through the Ages* says: "The Taj remains ever a thing apart. Something the world can not speak of with either praise or blame—something elusive, beyond criticism in three dimensional terms."

A few dissenting voices there have been, some fleering comments; but there will always be spirits who find an uneasy sense of an implicit criticism of themselves in all expression of nobility, purity, and beauty.

Edwin Arnold says:

"He hath not eyes to see whose eyes have seen
  That glory of the beauty of the Taj,
Nor knew and felt—at seeing—how man's hand
Comes nearest God's herein, touching His charm
Of rounded silvery clouds in that poised Dome
Which hangs between the sky's blue and the
  stream's—
Fixing the fleeting structures of His snow
In those piled pilasters and stainless flats
Which mount and mount—delicate, drifted, still;—
Simple, yet subtle, as the curves and shades
Of the white breasts of her it celebrates,
Arjamand Banu, Queen of Love and Death:
A passion, and a worship, and a faith
Writ fast in alabaster, so that Earth
Hath nothing anywhere of mortal toil
So fine-wrought, so consummate, so supreme—
So, beyond praise, Love's loveliest monument—
As what in Agra, upon Jumna's bank,
Shah Jahan builded for his Lady's grave."

Seeing this tomb for the first time, standing in the shadow of the magnificent deep portal that leads to the garden and upon which is inscribed "Only the pure of heart enter the gates; enter God's garden!" one perceives that this is:

". . . . not masonry!
Not architecture: as all others are,
But the proud passion of an Emperor's love
Wrought into living stone, which gleams and soars
With body of beauty shrining soul and thought."

THE GREAT LOVER 75

Later there swims upon the attention the long avenue of dark, century-old trees of thuja and cypress—cypress which they both loved—bordering the white paved paths that lead to the great mounting terraces on which the tomb stands. Between these paths flows the crystal water of the tanks; from which the thin streams of the fountains spring into the sunlight. Always the impression is of a delicate austerity, even within the large tomb chamber with its lace-like lattices of marble, its great domed roof, and those fair, delicious fancies of wreath and vine and flower.

"All done in cunning finished jewellry
  Of precious gems—jasper and lazulite,
  Sardonyx, onyx, blood-stone, golden-stone,
  Carnelian, jade, crystal, and chalcedony,
  Turkis, and agate; and the berries and fruits
  Heightened with coral-points and nacre-lights
  (One single spray set here with five-score stones)
  So that this place of death is made a bower
  With beauteous grace of blossoms overspread;
  And she who loved her garden, lieth now
  Lapped in a garden."

Also by way of adornment the architraves bear in beautiful Arabic script in the Toghra text verses from the Koran such as the famous fatihah, "In the name of God most High, the Clement, the Compassionate!" and other inscriptions such as, "Jesus said (on Whom be peace!) 'This world a Bridge is; pass thou over it, but build no house of Hope there,'" and "His Majesty, Shadow of God, Mujtahid of the age, built this for Resting Place of Arjamand." This beautiful flowing lettering has all the effect of decoration. The jewel-work in no way mars the whole impression of white purity. The actual resting place of the dead is marked only by two low slabs. That of the Empress is slightly raised above the level of the other and is seen through a surrounding screen of lace-like alabaster; a milk-white marvel of Jaliwork tracery.

Perhaps the Taj echo is the most moving wonder of the whole place. Whether this was an accident of construction or was carefully arranged for, no one knows; but Shah Jahan, who had built so much in marble, must have been well aware of the magic music which lies within that special stone, a harmony more celestial than can be produced by any instrument made by men's hands.

The Pazzi chapel in Florence is an example of this strange quality in marble, but lovely as are the echoes there called out by the notes of a violoncello, nothing in all the world is comparable to the aërial tones which reverberate from the great dome of the Taj Mahal. If one with a sweet and resonant voice standing by the tomb cries: "Arjamand Banu! Shah Jahan!" there comes from above a sublimated clear response of unearthly loveliness pronouncing the two names, as if those who lay below, from somewhere in another dimension, were wistfully calling athwart great spaces, seeking through the deeps of Time to find again one loved and lost. Fainter and fainter, higher and higher breathe the lovely syllables in melting antiphons, never blurred or confused, of an undying yearning quest across the worlds, passing away at last by minor murmurs into a fainting silence. A music to melt the heart with its ethereal tenderness.

That he who created all this should have been ignored, passed over with half-contemptuous in-

THE GREAT LOVER

difference by historians is one of those strange phantasies of human fate and fame seen so startlingly often in the long story of the human race. So many lesser figures have been analyzed and anatomized with endless industry and patience. So many vulgar souls have been pursued to their uttermost intimacies. Such elaborate and relishing descriptions have been set forth, in so many ponderous volumes, of all the blood and dirt and horror, of the grief and wretchedness following the pathway and adventures of conquerors; while silence and indifference have fallen like dust upon the memory of this artist and poet, this tenderest and most expressive of all lovers. It would seem as if the average mind found its only real pleasure and interest in violence, wickedness, and excitement.

One must gather up here and there with the greatest difficulty the records of Shah Jahan in those years when he was ruling his empire with such wisdom, was creating all this treasure of beauty for the world. Only after disaster began to cloud and shadow him do we see any sign of interest in the historian.

During the seventeen years while the Taj was in process of construction, that daughter who had cried out before her birth and who had cost her mother's life, had been ripening to womanhood, inheriting the dead Empress's beauty and charm. In spite of the fact that her coming had robbed Shah Jahan of his companion, he transferred to her much of that complete devotion which had been given to his wife. He hardly let the child out of his sight, surrounding her with every tenderness and care, and apparently finding in return the same sympathy and understanding which he had never had from anyone but his wife.

When in her fifteenth year, Jahanara through an accident was badly burned, and for long her life was despaired of. The native doctors seeming unable to effect a cure, the unhappy father in his search for help heard of a certain English physician, by name Gabriel Broughton. Miraculous cures were attributed to his skill. He was found at the little factory on the Hooghly which was almost the only footing which England up to that time had been able to obtain in India. Messengers were sent to bring him with all honours to Agra. He succeeded in saving the child's life, though her great promise of beauty remained deeply marred. The joy of the Emperor and his gratitude for the cure of his daughter knew no bounds. The physician was offered what payment he might choose. The modest but shrewd Englishman replied that the only reward he desired was a sufficient amount of land for his company's factories, and the permission to trade on equal terms with the Dutch and the Portuguese. The camel had at last got his head into the tent!

England has never fitly acknowledged in any memorial what she has owed to the daughter of the Emperor and to Broughton's skillful choice of fee.

By the time the Taj was completed Shah Jahan was becoming an old man. His four sons had reached maturity and already among themselves were intriguing for the succession to the throne. Dara, the eldest, most resembled his father in character and was his favourite, though he had succeeded to no touch of wisdom or genius. He had, however, much of his mother's beauty, with a generous, careless, impetuous temperament. The two youngest appear to have been merely the average type of the self-indulgent Oriental prince. It was the second son,

THE GREAT LOVER

Aurengzebe, who was to be the undoing of all his family. It would be incredible, had not the same thing been seen before and since, that out of the mating of genius, beauty, and goodness could come a son who, like a monstrous serpent, was to crush all of his immediate blood.

The Emperor, old and weary and full of grief, absorbed in the building of the great mausoleum, had delegated much of the task of administration to his sons, only turning angrily now and then to reprove their abuses of the powers he had delegated, or to discipline them when their mutual wrangles became unendurable. Aurengzebe had frequently to be checked, although his father was unaware of his darkest intrigues and ignorant of how profoundly he was scheming to be rid of all those who stood between himself and his magnificent prize.

Probably no despotic ruler has ever had the courage and intelligence to abandon a portion of his own power for the purpose of creating laws which would be superior to himself. The Emperor seemed not to realize, despite the confusion he had experienced at the time of his own accession, that a definite settlement of the succession to the crown was necessary to avoid the inevitable conflicts which began as soon as it was seen that the end of the ruler was approaching. Shah Jahan was not a creative political genius, it is plain, though as an administrator he has had few rivals. The genius of the East has never tended towards organization. There is some quality in the Oriental mind which renders it antipathetic to methodizing. In Eastern lands laws have always been more a matter of custom and habit and the will of the ruler than a matter of any thought-out system or constitution.

This fluidity or flexibility has permeated all Oriental life, more especially that of India. There has never been any real organization in her military forces, and this fact, rather than any want of courage or fighting capacity, has made the Peninsula lamentably subject to conquest through its whole history. No people has ever known how to fight more bravely or to die more nobly. The great story of the siege of Chandari, with its tremendous and passionate sacrifice, its chivalry and self-devotion, is characteristic of the manhood of India. Baber, the Tiger of the North, here came to hand-grips with the great Rana Sanga, head of the Rajputs, whom he had defeated in a pitched battle at Kanwaha; and the remnants of the Indian forces made their last stand at Chandari. When they finally realized that all was lost, the Rajputs killed their women and children, and fighting their way to the ramparts, threw themselves naked upon the spears below. The few who remained, said Baber in his Memoirs, who had gathered in Medini Rao's house, when they found they could not escape, slew each other with enthusiasm. "One man took his stand with the sword, and the others came pressing on one by one stretching out their necks eager to die." The Tiger adds cheerfully, "In this way they all went to Hell," and records that he piled up the heads of these heroic self-slaughterers upon a tower on a hilltop. He has no word of admiration for their heroic end.

But all their heroism was futile because of the great weakness inherent in their lack of coördination. Bernier, commenting upon one of the battles won by Aurengzebe, says rather scornfully that the enormous multitudes of fighting men could win only by the mere weight of their onslaught. Once they were checked or confused, they got into one another's way and added to the general disorder. He remarks contemptuously that a very small body of the trained soldiers of France, with their compact order and obedient discipline, could easily have dispersed an Indian force of ten times their own size. It was the strength of Baber and the Northern conquerors that they had a closer organization and a sharper discipline than the foe they subdued, though they themselves had never perfected the deadly mechanism of a highly organized European army.

The success of the political rule of the Mogul Empire, also, was due in large part to its more rigid structure. The Hindus were divided into mutually jealous principalities, capable at times of combining into loose confederations but never accepting a central overlord to whom they owed a superior fealty. The Mogul Emperors, on the other hand, were strong through their centralized government, though neither Akbar nor Shah Jahan realized that such government must rest eventually upon the support of fundamental laws controlling the individual will even of the Emperor himself. It is perhaps too much to expect that even so wise an administrator as Shah Jahan, who during his maturity balanced with infinite skill the conflicting desires of his Hindu and Moslem subjects, should have seen this truth, since the genius of Asia has never grasped the secret of continuous power.

Again we are plunged into those tenebrous turmoils which so often marked the passing of the Mogul succession. Aurengzebe was secretly plotting to make himself master of a sufficient force to insure his ends when the time was ripe. Jemla, vizier of the King of Golconda, who had made himself rich and powerful by his administration of the famous jewel mines, was the first foolish fly drawn into Aurengzebe's wide-flung web. He allowed himself to be seduced into a treacherous assault against his master, the King of Golconda. When the news of this attack upon one of his suzerains came to Shah Jahan, he sternly repressed it, and Jemla, hoping to placate him, sent as a gift the famous Koh-i-noor.

This great diamond has had a confused and contradictory history. Some chroniclers pretend to trace its story back to 1500 B.C. Others declare that Jemla privately seized it when it was discovered during his administration of the Golconda mines. It is even uncertain whether or not there were two stones which have been confused with one another. A renowned gem of this character was in the treasury of the Rajahs of Malwa in the fourteenth century, and there is the story of Humayun's getting possession of it at the time of Baber's conquest and presenting it to his father, only to have it carelessly returned. There seems to be no special mention of it again, and it is possible that by some means this historic stone had fallen into the hands of Jemla and that it was the diamond presented by him, instead of a new find.

Tavernier gives a description of this gem, affirming that it exceeded all others in existence both in size and worth. He speaks of it as a rose in form, like half an egg, and says that in its rough state it had weighed over seven hundred and ninety-three carats, but that bad cutting had greatly reduced it. It remained in the treasury of the Mogul dynasty in Delhi until the time of Mahmud Shah, the great-grandson of Aurengzebe. He valued it so much that he always wore it hidden in his turban. When the

Persian conqueror, Nadir Shah, took possession of Delhi, he grasped all the Mogul jewels, including the Peacock Throne, but could find no trace of the Koh-i-noor. It is said that one of the women of Mahmud's harem betrayed its whereabouts to the Persian. As peace had already been signed, Nadir Shah was a little embarrassed for the means of possessing himself of this last most splendid piece of loot. The solution of his difficulty was characteristically Oriental. Giving a great feast to celebrate the signing of the peace, and formally swearing love and friendship for the conquered monarch, he proposed to exchange turbans—an old Eastern mark of amity. Before Mahmud had time to protest, Nadir Shah snatched off his own turban and exchanged it for that of his friend. Mahmud managed to conceal what this meant to him and was so self-controlled that the Persian began to suspect he had been deceived by the woman; but as soon as he was alone he untwisted the turban and found the packet containing the diamond.

After the death of Nadir it passed by some mysterious shuffling to Armid Shah, the founder of the Kabul dynasty, and thence to his descendant, Shah Shugar, whose life was as wild and romantic as the adventures of the stone. When Shah Shugar was driven from Kabul the diamond was his only companion. In spite of his blindness he managed to carry this dangerous treasure with him through his wanderings until he fell into the hands of Ranjit Singh, who robbed him of all he possessed, but was unable to discover the whereabouts of the desired gem. He cheerfully set about starving his prisoner by way of putting pressure upon him, and Shah Shugar's wife, unable to bear the sight of her husband's suffering, promised to reveal the hiding place of the jewel in return for her husband's liberty. Shugar, having been allowed to return to his home, soon received a formal visit from Ranjit Singh, who brought with him some testers of gems. When the guests arrived, they were greeted and seated in the place of honour. An hour passed in dead silence until Ranjit, becoming restless, ventured to remind his host of the reason for the visit. The Shah then beckoned to a slave who brought a packet, which was placed on the carpet midway between the two men. When it was opened it was found to contain what the judges declared to be the Koh-i-noor. Ranjit asked at what price it was valued, and Shah Shugar replied bitterly: "Good fortune, and that is always the property of those who vanquish their enemies."

On Ranjit's death the priest made an attempt to induce him to bequeath the stone to the idol, Juggernaut, but it remained in the Kingdom's treasury until the Punjab was conquered by the English, when it passed to the crown jewels of Britain, being recut at Amsterdam into its present shape. For three quarters of a century it has led a quiet existence in the Tower of London, but this is only a brief moment in its tumultuous career. As long as the human race sets so enormous a value upon these special pieces of bright stone, it is not impossible that it may be again dipped in blood, may again become the cause of ruthless crime.

The Koh-i-noor brought no good fortune to Shah Jahan. Though the Emperor strained every nerve to reconcile his sons and to oblige them to be content with such power as he had given them, the fatal Oriental system of leaving the crown open as a possible prize among the brothers produced the usual mad result. Each played for the position of vantage and endeavoured to build up a powerful partizanship. Thus, when the Emperor was seized with a violent illness which seemed likely to be his last, all four of the sons set out for Delhi, each bent upon seizing the throne. Dara, who reached Delhi first, proclaimed himself Emperor, and Aurengzebe, thinking himself hardly strong enough to oppose the other three—for both Shah Riyar and Murad had put themselves into the field against Dara—employed his usual sinuous and serpentine tactics. Flinging himself on his knees before his youngest brother, he declared that Murad was his choice of the aspirants for the crown.

"For myself," he averred, "I have no ambition for power. You know that my whole life has been devoted to the Faith. Dara, like our late lamented father, is but lukewarm and indifferent to the doctrines of the Prophet. Shah Riyar is a drunkard and a sensualist. You alone are fitted to preserve the empire and properly enforce the teachings of the Koran. Will you allow me to use upon your behalf such forces as I control? When once I have seen you seated upon the throne of our ancestors, I desire nothing more than to be allowed to go upon a pilgrimage to Mecca, and spend my life as a teacher of truths of our Faith."

The foolish young prince, wishing to believe this, did believe it, gladly allowing Aurengzebe with his army to join his own forces and, as the more experienced commander, to place himself in virtual control of the troops.

That Shah Jahan quickly recovered and indignantly repudiated the action of Dara in proclaiming himself ruler did not give Aurengzebe pause. To Shah Jahan's envoy, sent to announce the recovery of the Emperor's health, and conveying orders that his sons should return to their respective provinces, Aurengzebe replied that he suspected these messages were merely a ruse on Dara's part to prevent his coming to the capital; that he proposed to see for himself if the Emperor still lived and, if so, to demonstrate his own immense joy at the continuation of his father's life. He also declared his determination to punish Dara for his insolence in seizing upon the crown before making certain that it was vacant. Remorselessly, persistently, he pursued his plan.

The aged and disease-broken Emperor found himself no longer able to control these passionate contestants for the throne he still occupied. Exhausting in vain every effort to force his children not to engage in a fratricidal strife for that to which as yet none of them had a right, he unwisely shrank from using his great military power against his own children. Doubtless to draw his sword against the offspring of the woman he had loved so well seemed to him the last degradation of the memory of that beautiful companionship, not realizing after the manner of so many parents that chastisement in the long run may be the greater kindness. In this unwise tenderness he stood by in despair while the four brothers fell upon one another, and his own army, seeing in his inaction only weakness with which they feared to be entangled, melted away among the conflicting forces. Each ambitious leader, hoping to ally himself with the eventual conqueror, chose the side which seemed most promising. Courage and the wisdom to support Dara, to proclaim him the legitimate heir, might have enabled Shah

Jahan to escape from the difficulties in which he found himself, but while he hesitated, in the fear of what might be the fate of his other sons if he definitely became allied to one of them, the whole situation escaped from his grasp.

Aurengzebe, still persuading Murad of his own loyalty to the latter's ambitions, succeeded in driving Shah Riyar a fugitive to Persia, then turned upon Dara and, having defeated him, seized Delhi and Agra, imprisoned his father, assassinated the foolish Murad, and sent Dara's bloody head wrapped in a magnificent cloth as a gift to the Emperor. Having thus secured his own path he took over the reins of power.

Even in the East a parricide was likely to expose him to more horror than he quite cared to face; therefore Aurengzebe endeavoured to justify himself by putting about infamous libels upon his prisoner. Many of these libels have been duly repeated by historians who have not taken the pains to examine their origin and purpose. Aurengzebe's method is illustrated in a letter which he sent to his father replying to Shah Jahan's protest against his imprisonment. Written at the moment when Dara was making his last advance upon the capital, into which Aurengzebe had thrown himself, this letter he carefully read aloud to his followers with the evident intention, for the moment, of persuading them that his aims were less infamous than they appeared.

"I can not better explain my conduct than by stating that while you professed extraordinary partiality for me, and expressed your displeasure at Dara's proceedings, I was informed, on indisputable authority that you had sent him two elephants laden with golden rupees. Thus is he furnished with means to collect new armies and to prolong this disastrous war; I therefore put it to you plainly whether I am not driven by his pertinacity to resort to measures which appear harsh and unnatural? Is he not, properly speaking, the cause of your imprisonment, and is it not owing to him that I have so long been deprived of the pleasure of throwing myself at your feet, and discharging the duties and paying the attentions you have a right to demand from an affectionate son? It only remains for me to beg that you will pardon what now seems strange in my conduct, and to recommend the exercise of patience under the temporary loss of liberty; for be assured that as soon as Dara shall be rendered incapable of disturbing our repose, I shall fly to the citadel and with my own hands open the doors of your prison."

Whatever may have been the cruel impression made by this letter upon the recipient, Shah Jahan abandoned all effort to punish the usurper or to regain power.

Never had a downfall been more complete and tremendous; for at once he was robbed of untrammelled rule, of unimaginable riches; the love of his life was in her grave; one son was in exile; two had met a bloody and treacherous end; and he himself was a hardfast prisoner, daily in danger of poisoning or secret assassination.

No word of his remains to tell his thoughts; no Lear-like ravings. Plainly he scorned the indignity of the bitter scufflings necessary to regain the pomp and power ravished by his unnatural son. What were these, now that his immortal work was accomplished, India left crowned with beauty? Pomp and power were bubbles to break and vanish, but his great gifts would remain for the joy of the generations. He could endure in silence till the end.

Twice he asked that his son should present himself at the palace where he was confined. Aurengzebe, who held the great fortress of Akbar, of which the palace was a part, pretended to have had secret warning that his father was planning his murder at the hands of certain Tartar women who had taken the place of the usual eunuchs as guards of the harem. He declined all invitations and never again beheld his father's face till he looked upon it in death.

Constant endeavours, however, were made by the usurper to possess himself of the hoard of jewels which Shah Jahan still retained, Aurengzebe's plea being that he was in great need of money, and further that he wished to make certain additions to the Peacock Throne. The captive monarch's only reply was that if Aurengzebe needed money he should be careful to govern the kingdom with more wisdom, since he himself had always found the revenues sufficient for all needs, including his building. As for the Peacock Throne he demanded that it be not meddled with, and finally announced that if further troubled about the jewels, hammers had been provided to beat them into powder the next time he should be importuned upon the subject.

How the days passed during those seven long years in which he never left his palace we are not told. Aurengzebe, uneasy as long as his father lived, did not fail to declare that the Emperor was plunged into sottish indulgences and degrading vices, but information from such a source may be wholly ignored. The wrong doer never fails to malign those whom he has wronged.

Again must imagination be trusted to reconstruct those empty days as they lapsed like a weary recurrent dream, or those star- and moonlit nights in which, from his prison tower, loomed the vision of that ghostly dome beneath which lay the lovely broken spring of his existence; that rounded grace of white marble rising from the dark foliage and mirroring its noble purity in Jumna's stream.

We know only that Jahanara remained his devoted attendant and companion, that in her arms died this erstwhile Prince of Faery, broken of heart and body; old, sad, and abandoned by all others, looking from the Jasmine Tower toward the tomb built for the beloved mother of this faithful daughter. So passed, on the twenty-second of January, 1666, this inscrutable monarch into final peace and inviolability, leaving behind him, in the place of words or violent deeds, unmatched poems in stone; the most lovely speech of spaces, of forms, of colours ever uttered by one man. A great strange character: little understood by his contemporaries, and even less valued and renowned by succeeding generations, though all authentic historical documents record of him nothing that was not admirable. Nevertheless, after two hundred and fifty years, still "his works do praise him" and reveal that noble and lonely soul which could utter itself only in marble.

Aurengzebe expressed much loud grief at the death of his injured parent. At Delhi at the time, he set out in frantic haste to Agra lest the coveted jewels might escape him. Being what he was, he naturally suspected his sister of any possible greed and treachery and appeared at the palace surrounded by armed attendants, ready to seize her. Jahanara received him with distinguished honours

THE GREAT LOVER

at the entrance to the Pearl Mosque, where his father's body lay waiting for burial spread with magnificent tapestries and covered with the roses and the jasmines which he had so much loved. In her hands she bore a large golden basin full of her own jewels, and attendants carried in the same manner Shah Jahan's great treasure of precious stones.

The naïvely delightful comment of Aurengzebe's chroniclers upon this episode is: "Moved by this affectionate reception, Aurengzebe forgave his sister her former behaviour and thereafter treated her with kindness and liberality."

Records of the time declare that this loving brother really conveyed her to Delhi as a prisoner and finally poisoned her. We see and hear no more of Jahanara. It is only known she begged that she might not find her last resting place in one of the mighty tombs built for the monarchs of her race. She desired to lie under the grass and beneath the blue canopy of heaven.

The long plain of Delhi, between the crumbled capitals which mark each step in its tumultuous history, is strewn with tombs—tombs of kings and saints, of prophets, of poets, and martyrs. Not the most majestic but perhaps the most interesting of these dwellings of the dead is the garden, shadowed by tall trees and surrounded by walls, where lies Khusru, the poet, author of the famous "Garden of Beauty" so beloved of all the scholars of India. Lichens stain the marble under which he lies; the hand of time has softened and mellowed its outline; but for three hundred years not one day has passed that his tomb has failed of being covered with flowers. The poets and musicians of India come long journeys to recite beside him their compositions of words or of music and to sing the songs they have created.

Very near this altar-tomb, at which beauty has so long been worshipped, is a little space of grass closed in on its four sides by delicate pierced-marble screens, open above to the sky. Under it lies that loving daughter, an Indian Cordelia, and on the screen is inscribed in bold and flowing Persian lettering the epitaph chosen by herself:

"Let no canopy over-arch my grave; this grass is the best covering for the humble, and transitory Jahanara, daughter of the Emperor Shah Jahan."

Her one form of pride was to have been the child of the great Poet and Lover whom she and her mother, alone, had cherished and understood.

II

CHIEN LUNG

THE MAGNIFICENT EMPEROR

CHIEN LUNG

In 1911 there crumbled into ruin the oldest political structure in the world. The Chinese Empire had had a continuous existence of more than four thousand years. Giles, in *Historic China*, speaking of one dynasty alone, says:

"The nine centuries covered by the history of the Chows were full of stirring incidents in other parts of the world. The Trojan War had just been brought to an end, and Aeneas had taken refuge in Italy from the sack of Troy. Early in the dynasty, Zoroaster was founding in Persia the religion of the Magi, the worship of fire, which survives in the Parseeism of Bombay. Saul was made king of Israel, and Solomon built the temple of Jerusalem. Later on Lycurgus gave laws to the Spartans, and Romulus laid the first stone of the Eternal City. Then came the Babylonian captivity, the appearance of Buddha, the conquest of Asia Minor by Cyrus, the rise of the Roman Republic, the defeats of Darius at Marathon and of Xerxes at Salamis, the Peloponnesian War, and the retreat of the Ten Thousand, and Roman conquests down to the end of the first Punic War. From a literary point of view the Chow dynasty was the age of the Vedas in India, of Homer, Aeschylus, Herodotus, Aristophanes, Thucydides, Aristotle, and Demosthenes, in Greece, of the Jewish prophets from Samuel to Daniel, and of the Talmud as originally undertaken by the Scribes, subsequent to the return from captivity in Babylon."

Such a catalogue visualizes China's immense story sweeping past the landmarks on the shores of Time. Not smoothly always has that tremendous tide flowed. Many whirlpools of disaster and disorder there have been—conquest by other races, long periods of confusion. Yet this great race had heretofore known no real break in the continuity of its political edifice. All the intruders had been gradually absorbed and modified until they were one with the Chinese themselves. Dynasty after dynasty had come and gone. Emperors had mounted the throne with swords still wet with the blood of predecessors, but always the great structure in its original intention had remained intact, founded deep upon the cornerstone of the family, passing upward stage by stage, a mighty pyramid, to that capstone at its very peak, the man who stood between the people and the invisible powers of Heaven and Earth.

An Emperor of China held a position unique in the history of mankind, because the Chinese mind, a mind dowered with the capacity for passionate

THE MAGNIFICENT EMPEROR

reverence combined with a hard streak of criticism and practicality, held a conception of Empiry unlike that of other races. It has been said that a Chinaman may knock his head nine times before the throne in humble obeisance and raise it to voice the most stinging criticisms of the sovereign to whom he is willing to demonstrate bodily humility. Chinese archives show petitions from subjects mingling humble pleas with bitter imputations upon the conduct of the monarch to whom these pleas are presented—petitions which would have roused a murderous fury in any more Western despot. On the other hand, proclamations of the emperors frequently admit the most serious faults on the part of the writers, containing frank declarations of their own responsibility for disasters and misgovernments.

All of which is the simple expression of the Chinese conception of their ruler. He is the head of their religion and the only one qualified to adore Heaven: the source of law and the dispenser of mercy; no right can be held in opposition to his pleasure; no claim maintained against him; no privilege protect from his wrath. All the forces and revenues of the realm are his. The whole empire is his property. At the same time it is implied that this enormous power must be wisely used. If the Emperor fails in discretion and efficiency his subjects have the well understood right to get rid of him and to find some more satisfactory representative. If floods come or droughts waste the land, it is obvious that he is an unsatisfactory mediator between Earth and Heaven. He must either set himself right with the Invisible Powers or make way for someone who can—a conception perfectly in accord with the Chinese mentality.

Among the numerous titles given the monarch may be mentioned *hwang shang*, the august lofty one; *tien hwang*, celestial lofty one; *shing hwang*, the wise and august, i.e., infinite in knowledge and complete in virtue; *tien ti*, celestial sovereign; and *shing ti*, sacred sovereign, because he is able to act on heavenly principles. He is also called *tien tsz*, Son of Heaven, because heaven is his father and earth his mother, and *shing tien tsz*, wise son of heaven, as being born of heaven and having infinite knowledge; terms which are given him as the ruler of the world by the gift of heaven.

All this is very flattering and agreeable, but nevertheless it carries implications, and the bearer of these towering titles must see to it that he really is the thing implied. All is given him but much is exacted, considering the infirmities of human mind and morals. That very few of those raised to this prodigious eminence succeeded in keeping their bargain might naturally be inferred. Chien Lung, fourth emperor of the Manchu Dynasty, came as near to the ideal as any, and very much nearer than most.

The Chinese Empire under his rule reached its apogee. He was perhaps the greatest Emperor the world has ever seen. Rome ruled over less territory and fewer people; the British Empire has been the suzerain of more human beings: but no one man has ever ruled a compact territory of a homogeneous race at all comparable to that under the sceptre of Chien Lung, for China comprises one-fifth of the world's inhabitants, one-tenth of its solid land. Its area is larger than the whole of the United States including Alaska, the Philippines, and all other dependencies; what is left from these is still larger than Germany, Belgium, France, and Spain.

Like Shah Jahan, Chien Lung came of a Northern race, but the house of Gioro, from which he sprang, had constantly accepted wives sent them from China by the native dynasty of the Mings. This infiltration of blood must always be taken into account when considering the characteristics of these monarchs of alien conquering origin. Chien Lung undoubtedly had a strong strain of Chinese blood, for none of even her native rulers was so completely an example of the Chinaman at his best. All the finest qualities of "the Sons of Han" he embodied, which may account for his eminent success in ruling them. That interesting commingling, which marks the typical Chinaman, of charming sensibility to all that is noble, subtle, and exquisite with a shrewd, cynical realism, was his in its highest development. Despite his Manchu origin never had the Chinese a ruler more sympathetic to their racial genius.

Though the Chinaman can fight furiously when he must, in all his long history he has been almost entirely free from the lust of conquest, and Chien Lung used his armies only when some interest or integrity of the empire was directly attacked. He loved literature, learning, and beauty with complete passion. He had the Chinese fondness for accumulating wealth, and did not disdain the smallest thrift, though he could be, on occasion, imperially profuse and generous. Filial love and reverence he possessed in a degree marked even in a land where these were the highest virtues. Perhaps the only quality in which he was not wholly like his subjects was in his honesty and love of justice—usually a beloved ideal to the Chinaman but too precious to be soiled and vulgarized by frequent use.

But the Manchu conquerors from which Chien Lung sprang were not the first of the Northern raiders to make themselves masters of China. Always southern Asia had suffered from the forages of the wild races of the uplands. Two centuries before Christ, in the days of the Emperor Chi'n Shih Huang, that bold adventurer, son of a dancing girl and a Tartar merchant, who had made himself emperor and was famous for his attempt to destroy all Chinese learning—this menace from the North had hung over the Southern people. It was to meet this danger that Chi'n Shih Huang had built the Great Wall, which still stretches two thousand miles along the mountain border like a guarding dragon, one of the most astonishing of human achievements.

But even this gigantic effort was unavailing to protect them always from the Tartar hordes. Kublai Khan, a descendant from the terrible Genghis, finally burst through the barrier, consolidated his conquest, and reigned in Peking, being Marco Polo's renowned host and leaving a dynasty which endured until 1368. Kublai's descendants gradually lost their dominance through the process of absorption and disintegration which Southern luxury has so often used effectively against these wild warriors of the North. By the middle of the fourteenth century the Chinese, always restive of foreign intrusion, succeeded in freeing themselves under the leadership of Hung Wu, the Beggar Emperor, founder of the native dynasty of the Mings.

Under Chu Yuan-Chang, Buddhist priest, administrator, and fighter, who finally crushed the power of the Mongols, and under his nephew and successor, Yung Lo, this dynasty fully earned the title of *Ming* signifying either "Bright" or "Illustrious," according to the taste of the translator. During

THE MAGNIFICENT EMPEROR 101

the next two hundred and seventy-five years China knew one of those supreme intellectual blossomings which come at certain intervals in the history of all civilizations. Such a flowering of the human spirit is attributed to various causes in various lands, but the vernal wind of the spirit bloweth where and when it listeth. No irrefragable reason can be given for either its coming or its going. The one thing certain is that during this time the word *Ming* took on a magic significance of glorious achievement in architecture, decoration, poetry, and literature, sculpture and painting, pottery, and textile creation. In every museum in the world what the Chinese hand and mind wrought in that period are among the most valued treasures, while still in China, despite all the drums and tramplings of conquest, buildings and gardens and a thousand lovely objects remain to show how exquisitely life was adorned in that golden period.

Unluckily the same cause which had eaten away the manhood of the Mongol debauched the native rulers. Whether this cause was a large polygamy in the palace, the insidious intrigues of eunuchs—that band of lamentable abnormalities clad in scarlet and supple and poisonous as snakes—or merely the destruction of character inevitable to those entrusted with unlimited power, is uncertain. At all events, early in the seventeenth century the barbarians of the North were again hammering at the gates, and there was no one strong enough to resist them.

Nur-hachi, the head of the house of Gioro, which had made itself master of a large part of Manchuria, was the first of his line to conduct any really serious raids into China behind the Wall, making no attempts himself upon Peking, which he likened to a great tree to be best attacked by cutting the outlying roots. His son and successor completed the work. In 1643 his armies returned to Moukden, the Manchu capital, having taken possession of sixty-seven cities and routed the Chinese in thirty-seven engagements. It gives some idea of the enormous wealth of the Middle Empire that though not actually entering the capital, the invaders had, according to their carefully computed list, secured booty to the amount of twelve thousand two hundred and fifty ounces of gold, over twelve million two hundred and fifty thousand ounces of silver, four thousand four hundred and forty ounces of pearls, fifty-two thousand two hundred and thirty-four rolls of satin and silk, thirty-three thousand seven hundred and twenty suits of raiment, one hundred and eleven fur coats, five hundred sable skins, and sixteen hundred deer horns. They had taken three hundred and sixty-nine thousand captives, and over five hundred and fifty-one thousand beasts of burden, camels, and oxen. One-third of this booty was divided among the officers and men; immense quantities of private loot were also secreted by the army of camp followers.

Not until the next spring did the Manchus finally enter Peking under the command of a regent, and the end of the Mings—the Bright, the Illustrious—came in horror and tragedy. It is told by the chronicler with all the stark simplicity of an Old Testament narrative:

"The last of the Mings, summoning his Empress Consort and the concubines, said to them:—

" 'All is over. It is time for you to die.'

"The Senior Concubine, Lady Yuan, on hearing these words, rose in terror from her knees and tried to escape, but his Majesty pursued her with a sword. Shouting: 'You too must die,' he wounded her in the shoulder. She continued to run, but the Emperor thrust at her a second time, whereat she fell, weltering in blood. The Empress Consort fled to her Palace of Feminine Tranquillity, and there hanged herself. Next the Emperor summoned the Princess Imperial from the Palace of Peaceful Old Age. She was only fifteen years of age. Wildly he glared at her, saying: 'By what evil fortune were you born into our ill-starred house?' Seizing his sword and hacking off her arm she sank, dying to the floor. He then went to the Pavilion of Charity Made Manifest and there killed his second daughter, the Princess of Feminine Propriety. Finally he sent eunuchs to greet in his name the Empress Consort, and to the senior concubines of his late brother, Hsi Tsung, strongly advising them all to commit suicide. Entering the Palace of Feminine Tranquillity, he saw his Consort hanging dead from the rafters, whereat he cried aloud: 'Death is best; the only way for us all.'

"It was now nearly 5 A.M. and the dawn was breaking. The Emperor changed his apparel and removed his long Imperial robe. The bell rang in the palace for the morning audience, but none attended. The Emperor donned a short, dragon-embroidered tunic and a robe of purple and yellow, and his left foot was bare. Accompanied by the faithful eunuch, Wang Ch'eng-en, he left the Palace by the Gate of Divine Military Prowess, and entered the Coal Hill enclosure. Gazing sorrowfully upon the city, he wrote, on the lapel of his robe, a valedictory decree:

" 'I, feeble and of small virtue, have offended against Heaven; the rebels have seized my capital because my Ministers deceived me. Ashamed to face my ancestors, I die. Removing my Imperial cap and with my hair disheveled about my face, I leave to the rebels the dismemberment of my body. Let them not harm my people!' Then he strangled himself in the pavilion known as the Imperial Hat and Girdle Department, and the faithful eunuch did likewise."

In 1651 the young prince of the house of Gioro formally ascended the throne under the title of Schunchih, living but ten years thereafter and being succeeded by his second son, K'ang Hsi. By this time the Manchus had routed such poor remnants of the house of Ming as had contested their power in Nanking, had subdued all rebellions, and had thoroughly organized their rule.

K'ang Hsi, the grandfather of Chien Lung, had been born in Peking and had thoroughly assimilated the Chinese civilization. His early years, passed in the beautiful palaces that the Mings had created and adorned with every treasure of refined and exquisite art, had modified greatly his Northern inheritance and had taught him the value of the culture—far greater than gold and gems—acquired in the conquests made by his forebears. Strangely those wild horsemen of the Northern plains, hunting and devouring like wolf packs the people of the South, seem always to have been ardent lovers of literature. K'ang Hsi became a magnificent patron of letters.

Already there was in existence an admirable foundation laid by the Mings. The third emperor of the Ming dynasty, Yung Lo, had issued a commission for the production of a work on a scale which was colossal even for China. His plan was to collect all that had ever been written in the four departments of the Confucian canon, and in history, philosophy, and general literature, including also astronomy, geography, cosmogony, medicine, divination, Buddhism, Taoism, arts and handicrafts. In 1408 the encyclopedia was laid before the throne, received the imperial approval, and was named *Yung Lo Ta Tien*, the *Great Standard of Yung Lo*. To produce it three commissioners, with five directors, twenty sub-directors, and a staff of two thousand one hundred and forty-one assistants, had labored for the space of five years. Three copies of this work were transcribed, one of which the Manchus found when they seized Peking. It was bound up in eleven thousand one hundred volumes covered with yellow silk, each volume being one foot eight inches in length by one foot in breadth and averaging a little more than an inch in thickness.

Inspired by this great work, K'ang Hsi caused to be published under his personal supervision an encyclopedia of a hundred and sixty volumes; a huge thesaurus of extracts in a hundred and ten volumes; an herbarium of a hundred books containing coloured drawings of most of the plants of China; and a complete collection in sixty-six volumes of the most important philosophic writings of the time of the Sungs. In addition to these, he created the first great modern dictionary of the Chinese language, which contained over forty thousand characters under separate entries, accompanied in each case by appropriate citations from the works of authors of every age and of every style.

K'ang Hsi was an equally ardent patron of pottery, and the creations of his reign are among the greatest treasures in that long story of the almost incredible loveliness that a Chinaman can achieve, given clay, water, and fire.

Not less did he concern himself with the administration of his great inheritance. Native Chinese laws were taken over and somewhat modified to include Manchu customs. The revenues were organized, the population numbered, the statistics of the land-tax brought into order. K'ang Hsi even attempted to persuade the Chinese women to abandon the practice of footbinding, but even a Chinese Emperor is less strong than feminine fashion, and after a short experience of the irresistible force pitted against an immovable body he wisely abandoned the attempt.

As is so often the case, the great father had an inferior son, and Yung Chang, the son of K'ang Hsi, seems to have done nothing of much importance except to marry a woman of notable character, who became the mother of Chien Lung.

This wise ruler first saw the light in 1711. His was a happy inheritance. From his grandfather and from his mother he had drawn elements of wisdom, strength, and good temper. His kingdom was well consolidated, for the dozen years of his father's incumbency had been too short to undo K'ang Hsi's great work. He found himself monarch of the most magnificent empire in existence, and during the cycle of his control he governed his realm with such intelligence that in all Chinese history there is no period in which the people experienced greater happiness and prosperity.

Not only was his dominion the most extensive, but his capital was one of the wonders of the world. Within its walls with a circuit of twenty-five miles, lived a population of some three million. The city itself was very old, known in ancient history as the capital of the Yen Kwoh, "Land of Swallows," but first made a central place of rule by Kublai in

1264. It was Kublai who had enclosed it with those mighty ramparts sixty feet at the base, fifty feet high, and forty feet broad at the top, entered by sixteen gates, each surmounted by a tower a hundred feet high. Dividing the city were main thoroughfares more than a hundred feet in width, the side streets being forty feet wide.

In Chien Lung's time this vast area was crowded with the palaces of the Mandarins and the Bannermen. Each of these palaces consisted of a great number of separate houses and pavilions, and each was enclosed within a wall; for the Chinese and Manchus are equally "wall-mad," and, put down anywhere on earth, set about making a wall as instinctively as a bee, with wax, must perforce create a cell. Within these enclosures were always many trees and flowers, even the humblest dwelling boasting at least one tree, so that looking out over his capital the Emperor saw it more as a great grove than as a city.

Shops were everywhere—shops by the thousands, all adorned by façades of the most elaborate and intricate carvings which were gilded, scarlet, blue, green, black, with waving vertical signs of vivid colors, the cloth painted in bold decorative Chinese characters.

Everywhere life pullulated. The veiled scarlet chair of the bride passed by, carried on the shoulders of sweating coolies, attended by banners, music, and dower gifts borne on open palanquins, and followed by a swarm of servants in costumes of sharp bright hues. Great brayings of brass and the moaning of horns accompanied the dead on their last journey as they fared outward through the city gates in ponderous coffins—coffins so huge that fifty men bent under the poles from which the mortuary chests swung. Gaunt lines of camels, grey with the dust of Mongolian plains, lurched along the streets bringing tallow, wax, sables, ermine, priceless furs of many sorts, and the emerald-green royal jade from the river beds of Turkestan. Panting bearers passed, swinging between poles the sacks of tribute rice pouring in like streams from most of the eighteen million householders paying thus their land taxes. Endless packages in bamboo matting contained fragrant teas of delicious flavours. From many poles hung great bales of tribute silks with special weavings of exquisite tintings and textures. Other poles bore large bamboo baskets in which were packed in rice-straw porcelains from the Imperial Kilns—porcelains thin as eggshells, of marvelous glazes, of unmatched colourings. Ten thousand pieces of such porcelain were sent annually to the palace as gifts from the officials.

Along these great arteries of traffic and tribute the whole life of the city had its noisy, confused being. Artisans sat in their doorways creating those thousand ingenuities of which only the Chinese hand and the Chinese patience are capable. Food was everywhere displayed. Little charcoal braziers sent up from stewpans myriad mingled odours of cooking rice, duck, pork, and chicken—savory messes of complicated flavours. The crab-apple man strolled along with a broom over his shoulder, every straw strung with little bright-tinted apples preserved in honey—a Mongolian innovation this, for the Mongols brought with them the fashion of preserving their tart fruits in honey. Others had trays about their necks, heaped with candies made of peanuts and sesame seed. Both Mongols and Manchus had a passion for sweets, and it is said that one may trace the path of the conquering Tartars all over Asia by the sugared and honeyed confections they brought with them. Most delightful of all of these were the walnuts rolled in honey and fried in sesame oil. There were stands heaped with salted peanuts—a Chinese invention—and dried melon-seeds which everyone cracked and ate as he walked. Chestnuts were roasted in black sand set in shallow pans over the mud-oven fireplaces. Other stands and swinging baskets were piled with the fine pears for which Peking was famous, and with bunches of grapes preserved by the ancient cold-storage system of pottery jars buried in the ground. There were gorgeous orange-red persimmons and the dried fruit of the jujube, from which a tinted paste was made and cast into a thousand curious and amusing forms. Hanks and skeins of millet-and-buckwheat macaroni swung drying in the sun. Cabbages were being skillfully carved into fine threads for the favourite cold slaw.

All this wealth pouring up from the provinces flowed through the gates in the mighty Wall toward the centre of the Nation's power. The Imperial enclosure was walled about and might be approached through magnificent avenues and imposing portals. Behind the walls clustered innumerable palaces with poetic names, such as the Hall of Perfect Peace, the Hall of Intense Mental Exercise, the Palace of Earth's Repose—the Empress's Residence—and the Coal Palace, where those were sent who were in disgrace. The Tranquil Palace of Heaven was the Emperor's own dwelling. In the Pavilion of Purple Light envoys were received. All these Imperial palaces, and these only, were roofed with shining yellow tiles, the pleasure pavilions using green or rose. Magaillans enthusiastically says of these royal roofs:

"You would think them all covered with pure gold or enamelled in azure or green, so that the spectacle is at once majestic and charming. Everywhere within that four miles of rose-coloured wall was the same richness of verdure, and looking down upon them, these splendid roofs appear from amidst the billowing of leaves."

It was here that Chien Lung, who was later to add much beauty to the Imperial enclosure, had found his residence awaiting him, set among delicious gardens, wide lakes, smooth canals, noble trees, and offering every sumptuous refinement of loveliness. From the Emperor's throne-room the hundred-foot-wide avenues stretched away to the great gates of the city. Along them the Emperor was supposed to look out to the four points of the compass over his mighty empire. He was the hub in which centred every spoke of the vast wheel upon which the entire life of China revolved.

The young monarch set by fate in this prodigious station was by position and nature a personage. A sanguine full-blooded man, it appears, enormously industrious, of wide-ranging interests, and withal having a profound sense of humour. Nothing was too big for him and nothing too small.

The likeness of Chien Lung painted by Alexander, an artist who accompanied Lord Macartney's Embassy, shows him a tall, broad-shouldered Manchu, slender but muscular. The face is one of great firmness, wisdom, and character, with long straight nose, small curving moustaches, heavy arched brows, a fine dome-shaped head, and eyes longer and more lateral than is usual in his race. Alexander paints him dressed in a richly embroidered long Manchu coat with the "hoofed" sleeves marking the costume of ceremony of all that race of horsemen, and in high velvet boots with inch-thick cork soles. The upturned velvet Manchu hat carries the button of supreme rank in the shape of an enormous pearl. A chain of great pearls falls to his knees. On his hand is the square jade thumb-ring of the archer—special adornment of Manchu warriors. Hardly the type, one might guess, to lead contentedly the sacrosanct existence expected of a Chinese monarch, supposedly too elevated above the human level to be gazed at by the subject eye. Like the bees, whom they so much resemble in many of their social manifestations, the Chinese hive was rather inclined to imitate bee-policy—once having selected their Queen, to wall her up carefully in a royal cell against any rude event or inclination to wander.

It is impossible to imagine the lusty, powerful Chien Lung submitting patiently to being helplessly embedded in the wax of those endless formalities and ceremonials which the Chinese so loved. Nor did he. The hawk vision and the whip-cord muscles of waist and loins, inherited from uncounted generations of wild Tartar horsemen, were little adapted to silken confinement. From his earliest childhood to his eightieth year he loved to feel a horse between his thighs. Once out of sight of Peking, he was wont to abandon for the saddle the ponderous Imperial palanquin rocking on the shoulders of sweating bearers, and to distress plump attendants by the speed with which he covered the long miles of his many journeys. Several times a year he escaped to his Hunting Park at Jehol to indulge his passion for movement, but at all times he went and came at his own pleasure, without consideration of the entangling web of Imperial etiquette.

This was, however, by way of relaxation and refreshment from much labour. The task of ruling an Empire was the real occupation of his days, and at home in the palace he led a life of enormous industry. Every morning, after the Chinese rulers' manner, rising at four o'clock, he took a scant meal of tea and rice-wafers and shortly thereafter received his cabinet and high officials.

A cabinet member in China enjoyed no sinecure. All were expected, along with every great official, to be present to lay the affairs of the Empire before the Ruler long ere the dawn. To expedite the business of administration the custom was for the Ministers to have previously read and formed an opinion upon each document and to write this opinion upon a slip of paper fastened at its foot—or on more than one, if the opinions differed. These were presented to His Majesty, who, after considering them and asking questions, proceeded to make his own decision and write this across the document with the Vermilion Pencil—in reality a brush dipped in red ink with which he wrote the character *Chien Ngon*, meaning "Ourself." In this way an astonishing amount of business was quickly transacted. Every appointment throughout the entire Empire was submitted to him, as well as removals and degradations, all the orders respecting the apportionment or remittal of revenues and taxes, and the disposition of the army. In short, every concern of his great dominion was brought to the attention of the Emperor.

No *roi fainéant* this. Five hours or more of hard incessant labour began each day. The modern business magnate is not more industrious.

Retiring to his private apartment he was served with a meal and slept for a while. Waking, he made a visit every day to his mother, who lived in the

THE MAGNIFICENT EMPEROR 113

Palace of Benevolent Old Age, to rehearse his filial reverences, inquire after her health, and discuss domestic matters. The afternoon was given to amusement or to study.

Chien Lung had an insatiable thirst for knowledge and was an ardent collector of the literary treasures of the past. Under his direction were published eight large volumes of specimens of the poetry of the Yuan Dynasty. New editions of important historical works and of encyclopedias were issued by Imperial order, superintended by the Emperor himself. In 1772 a general search was made for all literary works worthy of preservation, and ten years later a voluminous collection of these was published, embracing many rare books taken from the great encyclopedia of the Emperor Yung Lo.

A descriptive catalogue of the Imperial Library, containing three thousand, six hundred and forty works was arranged under the four heads of Classics, History, Philosophy, and General Literature, with historical and critical notes for each work. The vastness of this catalogue led to the publication of an abridgment, which omits all works not actually preserved in the Library. Its contents ran to no fewer than twenty-two thousand, eight hundred and seventy-seven separate sections, to which must be added an index filling sixty sections. Each section contained about twenty leaves, making a total of nine hundred and seventeen thousand, four hundred and eighty pages for the whole work. Each page consisted of sixteen columns of characters, averaging twenty-five to each column, or a total of three hundred and sixty-six million, nine hundred and ninety-two thousand characters.

This extraordinary work was never printed, as the expense would have been too great, although it was actually transcribed for that purpose. Later two more copies were made, one of which was finally stored in Peking and the other, with the original, in Nanking. Both these Nanking copies perished at the time of the Taiping rebellion. A similar fate overtook the Peking copy, with the exception of a few odd volumes, at the Siege of the Legations in 1900.

Another great literary monument remains to mark Chien Lung's sixty years of power, a magnificent bibliographical work in two hundred parts consisting of a catalogue of the books in the Imperial Library with valuable historical and critical notices attached to the entries of each, and a huge topography of the whole Empire, in five hundred books—beyond doubt one of the most comprehensive and exhaustive works of the kind ever published. Such a prodigious compilation as this was necessarily not personal labour. Rather it was the imposing Imperial gesture of a lover of letters who could command at will the services of many industrious scholars for many years. Yet gestures were not his only efforts. His personal compositions were voluminous. He wrote prefaces to a number of these volumes, as well as a great variety of notes and papers on current and ancient topics.

Like all highly educated Chinese he was a persistent writer of verse. When his collected poems were published, they reached the almost incredible total of thirty-three thousand, nine hundred and fifty separate pieces, which gives an idea of the enormous vitality of the man. It is to be remembered, however, that most Chinese poems are very brief. Though conforming to the most rigid rules of versification, his compositions are not rated among the classics, because usually they were wanting in that prized feature, the "stop-short," signifying that "although the words end the meaning still goes on."

An example of this is "On Hearing the Cicada":

> The season is a month behind
>   in this land of northern breeze,
> When first I hear the harsh cicada
>   shrieking through the trees.
> I look, but cannot mark its form
>   amid the foliage fair—
> Naught but a flash of shadow
>   which goes flitting here and there.

Here, as Giles points out, instead of being carried away into some suggested train of thought, the reader is fairly entitled to ask "What then?" More popular is a song called "Picking up Gold," which he wrote to be inserted in a play, but his "Praise of Tea" was his most successful composition. Thousands of teapots and teacups are still inscribed with these famous verses, which he published as part of his well known description of Manchuria written after a visit made to Moukden to worship at the tombs of his ancestors. Though he was born and brought up in China his heart was filled with emotion at the sight of the country of his origin.

"Arriving in this place I found my heart overflowing with filial piety. I went to visit everything I could find which pertained to my ancestors. I looked with inexpressible joy at those mountains covered with verdure, those rivers which rolled in crystal floods, those fertile fields, and enchanting landscapes which seemed yet to hold the spirit of their ancient master. I admired above all those good sincere people who live happily because they are content with their lot, existing without inquietude because they live in honest abundance. Behold! I said then to myself with delight, behold truly a kingdom which Heaven favours. I was penetrated with that which makes the true happiness of a sovereign. At last I have become familiar with those august places which were the cradle of my house and the root from which sprang great kings."

The rest of the book is filled with a careful record of agriculture and industries, and praises of the people and their manner of life. It is a true pastoral, an eclogue, combining a poetic passion for the simple beauties of the land with a shrewd insight into its practical condition. It was at the end of this description of Moukden that he appended his "Praise of Tea," but tradition says that it was composed in the house of his brother in Peking, a place he loved to visit for the joy of casting off all ceremony and being for a few hours a man and not merely a monarch.

To see Chien Lung as the man and not the Emperor, relaxing happily in this family environment and indulging all his natural tastes, it is here necessary to look back a minute into historical records. In the days of his grandfather, K'ang Hsi, the Catholic Church sent out many missionaries to China, choosing for the difficult task the most learned and gifted members of the Society of Jesus. K'ang Hsi was intelligent enough to discern their possibility of usefulness. They founded his great Observatory, and under their inspiration were made those noble bronze instruments for the study of astronomy which combined so much beauty with their scientific value. The Chinese savants learned from the Jesuits many of the secrets of Western science.

Yung Chang, K'ang Hsi's son, who was a devout Buddhist, frowned upon their efforts to insinuate religious teaching alongside of these more worldly

THE MAGNIFICENT EMPEROR 117

matters. But when Chien Lung came to the throne he lightened the pressure his father had put upon the missionaries, skillfully using the knowledge they brought, while checking their too ardent religious propaganda. He interested himself in European art and architecture, literature and science. While the Western world was developing Chippendale furniture, learning the delights of Chinese tea sipped from Oriental porcelain, collecting hawthorne jars, importing Palace sleeve-dogs for the pets of fine ladies, and decorating interiors with very Occidentalized Chinoiseries, the Court of Peking was also amusing itself with a craze for European toys in the shape of enamelled French watches and bibelots.

The missionaries—who appear to have practised all the arts—built pavilions in the French manner at the Summer Palace, surrounding them with gardens like a miniature Versailles, and at Chien Lung's desire made for him numerous translations of French books. Father Amiot was allowed to paint the Emperor's portrait, and while doing so spoke to him of Voltaire, giving so agreeable a description of the sage of Ferney (it may be guessed this Amiot was no bigot), that the Emperor conceived a great admiration for the Frenchman. He even entered into a correspondence with Voltaire, Amiot serving as the translator. If these letters still exist—no mousing scholar or antiquarian has yet come upon them—it would be extremely interesting to see what these two unusual men had to say to each other.

Two beings more remote from each other in race and environment it would be difficult to imagine. Did their translators do them justice? Did the Chinaman catch the fine savour of the Frenchman's mordant wit? Did Voltaire relish the ornate and mellifluous style with which the Emperor loved to wreathe his forthright, practical ideas? The historian reviving the psychological reaction of this queer correspondence could evoke from it more precious revelations than are contained in the many dead and futile military adventures with which chroniclers are prone to load their pages.

Receiving a Voltaire letter, Chien Lung, one learns, was wont to carry it with him on visiting the "Fu" of his brother and to read it aloud. What a priceless opportunity anyone eavesdropping upon their comments might have had of really knowing the Chinese mind—an opportunity none could have appreciated more than the old Frenchman with his ironic interest in all manifestations of the human spirit.

One can imagine the Emperor lounging in the great carved chair reserved for his use, pausing over a phrase to exchange with his brother one of those glances of bland, veiled humour never more possible than to the Chinese eye. If the visit were in winter he would occupy the "kang," that stone shelf against the wall common to all well-to-do Chinese houses, heated by fires built underneath it from outside and softly padded with rich furs. The two brothers would smoke and sip tea together and gossip at their ease, served by the brother's daughters, tall, free-striding Manchu women, standing high on their "flower-pot shoes" with three-inch soles, clad in long Manchu gowns of brocade or embroidered satin, over which were slipped the short sleeveless jackets. Colourful girls they were, rustling in azure and green, with jackets of gold thread or plum colour and purple, or sometimes of turquoise with lavender, mulberry with orange, or maize contrasted with rose, all splendidly decorated with needlework of flowers, butterflies, birds, or the curling waves of the sea. Each blue-black head must have shone like lacquer, the hair wound over a broad golden hairpin, from the two ends of which balanced great clusters of jewelled flowers.

It was in this easy, home-like environment that Chien Lung set down, in the exquisite characters he commanded—one of his many talents—that famous "Praise of Tea":

"Graceful are the leaves of Mei-hoa, sweetly scented and clear the leaves of Fo-cheou, but place upon a gentle fire the tripod, whose colour and form show its antiquity, fill it with water of molten snow. Let it seethe till it be hot enough to redden a crab. Then pour it in a cup made from the earth of Yui upon the tender leaves of selected tea. Let is rest till the mists have formed themselves into thicker clouds and then gradually cease to weigh upon its surface until the last vapours float away, then slowly sip the clear deliciousness. It will drive away the five causes of disquietude. You may taste and you may feel, but never can you tell in verse or song the sweet tranquillity drawn from the leaves' essence."

No long-winded and cumbrous English translation can give more than a rough suggestion of the intricate rhymes and oblique suggestions of the succinct Chinese ideographs of the original verse.

Not often, however, could Chien Lung indulge in these gentle family delights in the midst of the strenuous existence demanded of an efficient ruler, though rumours are not wanting that he played Haroun al Raschid at times, going forth in the night in disguise to see for himself matters he suspected of having been misrepresented by his courtiers, and occasionally indulging in adventures of gallantry. Only a rich, powerful, and vigourous nature could have dealt with his multitudinous duties.

One of the first works undertaken was a reorganization of the land taxes and the regulation of the revenue, by which reform the revenue was raised from about fifteen million taels to forty million, the tael at that time being worth about the same as the pound sterling of today. This although Chien Lung left it on record that he was well aware of enormous fortunes being made in the provinces by his administrators, those "rats under the altar" as the Chinese proverb dubs them, peculation being the irremediable curse of every administration in China. The Chinese attest to this in such proverbs as "Underlings see money as a fly sees blood," or "Cash drops into an underling's paw as sheep falls into a tiger's jaw." Nevertheless, Chien Lung, despite leaks, kept so strong a hand upon the balance of expenditures and receipts that throughout his reign there was always a reserve on hand of somewhere between sixty and seventy million taels, even during intervals of warfare.

On one occasion he was obliged to send seventy thousand men into Nepaul to subjugate the Gurkhas who had invaded Thibet, over which China claimed suzerainty. On another he was forced to deal with outbreaks among the Miaotsze, hill tribes living in the remote highlands in the provinces of Kwei-chow and Kwang-si: wild survivals these of what were probably the autochthons of China, who, secure in their mountain lairs, had never been subdued or amalgamated during the four-thousand-year history of the Empire.

Ordinarily, peace was very adequately kept throughout Chien Lung's vast realm. Expenditures were usually for construction rather than destruction. He never made the mistake, however, of neglecting his army or of allowing its pay to be in arrears. Two hundred thousand men were kept with the colours at all times, the army being organized under Bannermen, the original formation of the Manchu army. During his reign twenty-four Banners, eight of them being Manchus and the others Mongols and Chinese, were always maintained on a war footing. The élite of the Banner forces served as guards for the Emperor, but at certain vital provincial centres, such as Canton, Foochow, and Hangchow, the Banner garrisons with their families formed a sort of hereditary privileged caste within the inner wall, always under a Tartar general and holding the keys of the city gate.

Though having the wisdom properly to maintain his military establishment, Chien Lung had many matters much nearer his heart. One of these was the regulation and improvement of trade and commerce. A mistaken assertion, constantly reiterated, is that China fell into a formalism because of reluctance to accept contact with the outside world and to receive fresh impulses from the minds and civilizations of other races. As far back as the fifth and sixth centuries two Chinese monks had wandered widely afield and written records of their observations. I-tsing, in his long account of his travels, which extended from 643 to 713, gives a list of sixty priests who had made the grand tour either by land or sea, mostly for the study of Buddhism but also keen-eyed to observe the culture of other peoples. Parker says, "The fact is that hundreds of Nestorian, Hindu, and Chinese priests were able to move freely by land and sea all over Asia, and the trade routes were frequented along exactly the same lines as they are now." There was a large commerce with Persia both by land and sea, and the Roman Emperors procured all their silks from China. As early as 1087 Chinese junks were carrying cargo to Java, Sumatra, Borneo, and Ceylon, and as far west as Zanzibar and the Persian Gulf.

Not till the Manchu Empire was established did Europeans begin to send their traders to Chinese ports, as usual, with an advance guard of missionaries. The instinct of the rulers—very rightly as the event proved—warned them that this new element contained a menace not inherent in free intercourse with the rest of Asia. Westerners were received at first with a courtesy which they later proved to have ill deserved. Trade flourished, and for a while it seemed that there might eventually be a close rapprochement between the East and the West, but both missionaries and traders gradually became violent and aggressive, and K'ang Hsi warned Europe of the mistake that was being made. It was because of this constant aggression against their religion and their traditions that the reaction took place. Two or three times revolt broke out, which had to be bloodily repressed. It was then that the Chinese conceived their hatred of the Western world, which has never been appeased and which today makes itself potently felt.

European traders were permitted to enter only Canton, and even there many restrictions and regulations were imposed, against which the Westerners constantly protested. Embassies were sent by both the English and the Dutch, but, though they were splendidly entertained, Chien Lung would never agree to their requests. Considering how scornfully and ruthlessly the Western world has treated China for the last century, amusing reading is Chien Lung's letter to the King of England, a reply to his Ambassador's demand for permission to establish an embassy in the capital and to found trading places at other points and ports. At that date China still looked down on the outer world with a pride as remote and indifferent as the stars. The text of this delightful document follows:

"You, O King, live beyond the confines of many seas, nevertheless impelled by your humble desire to partake of the benefits of our civilization, you have dispatched a mission respectfully bearing your memorial. Your Envoy has crossed the seas and paid his respects at my court on the anniversary of my birthday. To show your devotion you have also sent offerings of your country's produce.

"I have perused your memorial: the earnest terms in which it is couched reveal a respectful humility on your part, which is highly praiseworthy. In consideration of the fact that your Ambassador and his deputy have come a long way with your memorial and tribute I have showed them high favour and have allowed them to be introduced into my presence. To manifest my indulgence I have entertained them at a banquet, and made them many gifts. I have also caused presents to be forwarded to the Naval Commander and six hundred of his officers and men, although they did not come to Peking, so that they too may share in my all-embracing kindness.

"As to your entreaty to send one of your nationals to be accredited to my Celestial Court and to be in control of your country's trade with China, this request is contrary to all usage in my dynasty and cannot possibly be entertained. It is true that Europeans, in the service of the dynasty, have been permitted to live at Peking, but they are compelled to adopt Chinese dress, they are strictly confined to their own precincts and are never permitted to return home. You are presumably familiar with our dynastic regulations. Your proposed Envoy to my Court could not be placed in a position similar to that of European officials in Peking who are forbidden to leave China, nor could he, on the other hand, be allowed liberty of movement and the privilege of corresponding with his own country; so that you would gain nothing by his residence in our midst.

"Moreover our Celestial dynasty possesses vast territories, and tribute missions from the dependencies are provided for by the Department for Tributary States, which ministers to their wants and exercises strict control over their movements. It would be quite impossible to leave them to their own devices. Supposing that your Envoy should come to our Court, his language and national dress differ from that of our people, and there would be no place in which to bestow him. It may be suggested that he might imitate the Europeans permanently resident in Peking and adopt the dress and customs of China, but, it has never been our dynasty's wish to force people to do things unseemly and inconvenient. Besides, suppose I sent an Ambassador to reside in your Country, how could you possibly make for him the requisite arrangements? Europe consists of many other nations besides your own: if each and all demanded to be represented at our Court, how could we possibly consent? The thing is utterly impracticable. How can our dynasty alter its whole procedure and system of etiquette, established for more than a century, in order to meet your individual views? . . .

"If you assert that your reverence for our Celestial dynasty fills you with a desire to acquire our civiliza-

THE MAGNIFICENT EMPEROR 125

tion, our ceremonies and code of laws differ so completely from your own that, even if your Envoy were able to acquire the rudiments of our civilization, you could not possibly transplant our manners and customs to your alien soil. Therefore, however adept the Envoy might become, nothing would be gained thereby.

"Swaying the wide world, I have but one aim in view, namely to maintain a perfect governance and to fulfil the duties of the State: strange and costly objects do not interest me. If I have commanded that the tribute offerings sent by you, O King, are to be accepted, this was solely in consideration for the spirit which prompted you to dispatch them from afar. Our dynasty's majestic virtue has penetrated into every country under Heaven, and Kings of all nations have offered their costly tribute by land and sea. As your Ambassador can see for himself we possess all things. I set no value on objects strange and ingenious, and have no use for your country's manufactures. This then is my answer to your request to appoint a representative at my Court, a request contrary to our dynastic usage, which could only result in inconvenience to yourself. I have expounded my wishes in detail and have commanded your tribute Envoys to leave in peace on their homeward journeys. It behooves you, O King, to respect my sentiments and to display even greater devotion and loyalty in future, so that, by perpetual submission to our throne, you may secure peace and prosperity for your country hereafter. Besides making gifts (of which I enclose an inventory) to each member of your Mission, I confer upon you, O King, valuable presents in excess of the number bestowed on such occasions, including silks and curios—a list of which is likewise enclosed. Do you reverently receive them and take note of my tender goodwill toward you! A special mandate."

So spoke China to Europe in the eighteenth century. Behind these calmly contemptuous phrases lay a deeper meaning: the fundamental objection to granting further privileges to the British was based upon their importation of opium from India. The first mention of the poppy in Chinese literature is found in a book written in the eighth century, and its medical qualities were already understood, but there is no evidence to show that the Chinese ever took opium other than for illness until this foreign importation began. Already in the time of K'ang Hsi the Emperor was protesting against its introduction, saying: "There is cause in this trade for apprehension lest, in the centuries to come, China may be endangered by collision with the nations of the West come hither from beyond the sea."

Chien Lung issued edicts against the menace to his people, aware that the insidious drug was making inroads upon their morals. As early as 1796 the importation was declared illegal.

How justly the Emperors had foreseen the risk of dealing with Western nations became evident when the great endeavour of 1860 to shut out opium brought the Opium War, for at that time the English reached the walls of Peking, and, as the culmination of the many sorrows inflicted upon China, destroyed that triumph of Chien Lung's creativeness, the Yuan Ming Wang, or Round Bright Garden.

Chien Lung, so firm in discouraging Western commerce, let nothing pertaining to the development of trade within his own dominions escape attention. Efforts were made to control the great

THE MAGNIFICENT EMPEROR 127

rivers, arteries of internal exchange, from whose mouths an active traffic along the coast was conducted from port to port by skilled Chinese sailors. During a very disastrous flood of the Hoangho one of the Emperor's best engineers was sent to undertake measures to prevent a recurrence. His letter of instruction says:

"My intention is that this work should be successfully carried on, in order to secure for the people a solid advantage both for the present and in the time to come. Share my views, and in order to accomplish them forget nothing in the carrying out of your project, which I regard as my own, since I entirely approve of it and the idea which originated it was mine. For the rest it is at my own charge and not at the cost of the province that I wish all this to be done. Let expenses not be stinted; I take upon myself the consequences, whatever they may be."

And so successfully was the work accomplished that during his life the turbulent Hoangho gave no further trouble.

At Hangchow, at the cost of ten million taels, was built the embankment of the Tsien-tang, where junks shelter from two million tons of water which thunder past each minute as the famous tide, or bore, comes into that port on the three full-moon nights in April and October. So well built was this defense that much of it still remains, despite the hundreds of vast tides which have since flung themselves upon it. Canton was given great ports and godowns. Chien Lung's statue in one of the Cantonese temples bears an inscription commemorating his splendid benefactions to that city.

The peace which he so forcefully ensured and his skill in the promotion of the Empire's prosperity naturally resulted in an enormous increase of population. There came a year of unfavourable crops, and proliferating humanity suffered a famine so serious that even the Emperor's free spending of the revenues proved inadequate to meet it. The people, seeking a scapegoat, riotously attacked the Western missionaries and the numerous followers of the new faith, which they blamed for the disaster. Skillfully taking advantage of it, the Emperor gathered up the native converts, planting them in colonies in certain uninhabited precincts in order to lighten the pressure of population in the cities—a characteristic example of Chien Lung's practice of killing two birds with one stone and achieving his ends without brute violence. To relieve the people he readjusted the land taxes, reducing them to a sum equalling about sixty cents an acre.

Very firm he was meanwhile with his well-to-do subjects, whom he thought less ready to aid him in famine relief than they should be, intimating, after a fashion which, coming from an Emperor, was difficult to resist, that a very small amount from each one of them would accumulate a sum which he found desirable for support of the orphans of those who had died during the time of scarcity. This suggestion, which they deemed it wise to act upon, was couched, of course, in his usual magniloquent style. He dearly loved a rotund phrase:

"If for the extension of kindness to our fellow creatures and to those poor and destitute who have no father and mother, all the good and benevolent would daily give one cash [1100ths of a dollar] it would be sufficient for the maintenance of the foundlings for one day. Let no one consider a small good unmeritorious, nor small subscriptions as of no

THE MAGNIFICENT EMPEROR 129

avail. Either you may induce others to subscribe by the vernal breeze from your mouth, or you may nourish the blade of benevolence in the field of happiness, or cherish the already sprouting bud. Thus by taking advantage of opportunities as they present themselves and using your endeavours to accomplish your object, you may immeasurably benefit and extend the institution."

Human nature being what it is, not even so absolute a ruler nor one so wise and shrewd was able to accomplish all his desire for the good of his people. The laws of China have always been in many respects admirable, and immediately upon Chien Lung's accession to the throne he improved the code and took active measures to see it enforced. He added to it his famous Sixteen Moral Maxims, known as the Sacred Edict: a complete code of rules for the guidance of everyday life, presented in such terse yet intelligible terms that they at once took firm hold of the public mind and have retained their position ever since.

Like Shah Jahan, Chien Lung was not primarily a reformer or an innovator. The philosophy of government held by both seems to have been that the ideals and needs of their people were already embodied in the nation's laws. The idealism and aspiration of humanity nearly always outruns its practice. Men see the good and the desirable, though reluctant to accept the limitations of good rules upon their personal wishes and desires. So that in large part a nation's wise and reasonable laws are more honoured in the breach than in the observance.

The Chinese ruler realized, as did the Indian Emperor, that were the laws and customs already sanctioned adequately administered, there would be small need for their readjustment, and both men proved the wisdom of their theory. But few changes in the codes they inherited were attempted by either the one or the other. With wisdom and firmness they executed the laws which their people had decided were for their best good, and by putting into practice the already existing codes of the land they succeeded in achieving that desired good. The same laws in the hands of their successors resulted in confusion and corruption. Historians have endlessly disputed whether conditions or the will and personality of great men control a nation's fate. The Chinese and the Hindus have been in many respects gifted and noble races, but without great leaders their history demonstrates that they fail to achieve what they *wish* but do not really and potently *will*. No laws, however wise, wholly alter the instincts of the people. A lover of the Chinese, who understood their many admirable qualities, yet says of them:

"The Chinese Officials put all their happiness in pleasures in dignities and wealth, and to get those they break without any scruple divine and human laws, trampling under foot, reason, religion, justice, honesty, and the rights of blood and friendship. The inferior officers do not think of anything else than fooling the superior Mandarins, the Mandarins the supreme Tribunals, and all together their King. They know how to do that with so much artifice and skill, using in their memorials words so soft, so honest, so humble, so respectful, and so flattering, and their arguments are so well coloured, and look so disinterested, that the poor Prince takes very often a lie for a truth. And so the people, seeing themselves badly treated and overpowered without

THE MAGNIFICENT EMPEROR 131

any reason, grumble and rouse riots and revolts which have caused many ruins and changes in this Empire. Yet the wickedness of the magistrates must not do any wrong to the goodness and excellence of the Laws of China."

Chien Lung strove all his life to stop the peculations of his officials and their tendency to allow portions of the revenue to stick to their fingers. Although he was not invariably successful, perhaps at no time in Chinese history was official dishonesty so firmly curbed as during his reign, and one of the missionaries of the day, commenting upon this fact, writes to his European superiors: "He is a truly great prince doing and seeing everything for himself." One of the French Jesuits received often at his courts inscribed beneath the portrait of Chien Lung, which he included in his Memoirs of his experiences in China, an enthusiastic quatrain:

"Occupé sans relache à touts les soins divers,
  D'un gouvernement qu'on admire,
Le plus grand potentat qui soit dans l'universe
  Et le meilleur lettré qui soit dans son Empire."

Chien Lung, hating extravagance and waste, watched the expenditures of his household with the same care he devoted to the business of the Empire. This was a constant struggle because of the ingrained habit of the Chinese servant of expecting to exact his "squeeze" from everything passing through his hands. Two amusing stories are related in this connection. While journeying through the Yangtsze provinces, his Majesty desired to try a famous Yangchou receipt for bean curd. Finding it to his taste, he asked the cost, and being told that it was only thirty cash (about a penny) directed that this cheap and excellent fare be added to the menus of the Palace at Peking. After returning to the capital, he discovered, however, that the eunuchs entered the dish in the household kitchen accounts at twelve taels. His protest was countered with the smooth reply that "Southern delicacies are not easily prepared in the north."

One cold winter's day, receiving an official named Wang Yu-tun in audience, Chien Lung inquired politely whether he had had anything to eat before attending the court at dawn.

"We are very poor," said Wang. "All the breakfast that I can afford consists of two or three eggs."

The Emperor exclaimed: "You dare tell me that you are poor; yet you confess to eating three eggs at a time! Eggs cost me seventy-five cents apiece—I would never dream of ordering three."

Wang, not venturing to tell the true price of eggs, said: "I was speaking of an inferior type of egg, not the sort which would be suitable for your Majesty's table. My sort can be bought for about a cash apiece." The Emperor twinklingly understood, and gave orders that the Palace eggs were henceforward to be charged at a more reasonable figure.

While he sometimes succeeded in reducing the constant peculations of his attendants, he seems never to have been able wholly to rid his capital of its famous guild of beggars which was said to number, later, in the days of Abbé Huc, eighty thousand members, possessing their own king and officers and having strange regulations. The Abbé gives a droll account of the famous Feather-bed Lodging House of the Peking mendicants of his day:

"As the beggars stole the coverings at their lodging house, some keen one devised a single great coverlet the size of the floor, with holes for the sleepers' heads. It was raised and lowered by tackle, a tom-tom sounding each morning to warn the lodgers to get their heads in under the coverlet. Beneath the great communal bedspread the area was covered thickly with loose feathers."

While the Emperor carried on this unceasing effort against "squeeze" for the sixty years of his reign, with, on the whole, a fair success, it is to be remembered that in these things he was warring against men. When, however, he turned his attention towards women, though he was the most powerful ruler in the world he encountered a humiliating defeat, as have all his sex when they attempted to meddle with what women consider their special prerogatives. Doubtless Adam criticised the exiguity of Eve's fig-leaf petticoats—and was promptly snubbed as a result. The whole history of man shows prophets, priests, and kings violently fulminating against women's methods of dealing with their own clothes and persons, and not one single male triumph lightens the melancholy tale of universal defeat. The Manchu conquerors successfully imposed upon the Chinaman as a mark of submission the shaving of the forehead and the wearing of a queue, but when Chien Lung, like his grandfather, undertook to stop the binding of the Chinese women's feet, he met with such an outbreak of furious disobedience that even he quailed before the hornet's nest he had stirred up. He then hastily and apologetically rescinded his edicts, though remaining convinced of the superiority of the Manchu women's free-striding and graceful gait with a natural foot in a high-soled silk or velvet shoe.

This humourous and reasonable despot accepted defeat at the hands of the other sex promptly and handsomely because of having a soft heart and an innate reverence for women. In a country where filial devotion to the mother was so universal, few were more completely the ideal son than the Emperor. His mother, Lady Niuhulu, entered the palace of Yung Chang as a very young girl but already gifted with many talents. She recited poems beautifully, was reputed to be very learned, and was also a musician and an artist. She so pleased Yung Chang, especially when she became the mother of a handsome boy, that he raised her to the rank of queen. Surviving him forty-two years, she died at the age of eighty-six. Chien Lung adored her, never missing a day, when in residence in Peking, in making her a visit. After the conquest of the turbulent Tartars he held a special feast for his mother, going to her palace with all his generals to attribute to her virtues his whole success, and presenting her with a golden tablet on which was engraved all her titles. In her name he dispensed all the honours of the occasion to the generals and the men of letters, revoking punishments for the smaller faults which he had decreed for the officers. Three years were allowed for the repayment of money lent from the royal treasury. He made grants to the wounded and to those who had contracted diseases in service, and gave a month's leave to all who had served in the last campaign. Exiles were recalled and orders given that throughout the entire Empire grants should be given to the old and poor and to those unable to work because of illness. All of which was done in the name of his mother that she might be blessed by the whole nation.

Of his amatory relations with women Bland says:

"Where women were concerned Chien Lung was, naturally, polygamous and patriarchal, after the

Oriental manner, but ever mindful of the proprieties and jealous of his Consort's dignity, and for the rest of his harem was courteous, gentle and generous. His domestic life was free from bickerings and scandals and his children were well brought up, for he knew how to combine the *suaviter in modo*, with the *fortiter in re*. According to the annalists, His Majesty was wont, in the *moments perdus* of his manifold official and domestic duties, to indulge occasionally in emotional adventures and even escapades. There were entr'acts in the dignified drama of his public life."

Eleven sons were born to him, but in their usual fashion historians make no report of his female offspring, supposed also to be numerous, showing that he was not unpopular among the ladies who were chosen for the companions of his softer moments.

All this was quite in the patriarchal manner; yet the one romantic love of his life was tragically unsuccessful. The beautiful red Mohammedan Mosque which used to stand just outside the South Wall of the Lake Palace of the Forbidden City (known to the Chinese as the "Home-looking Palace"), was a monument to this unhappy love, built to please a princess from Turkestan, in order that when saying her prayers she could turn her face at once towards Mecca and Turkestan.

During the first campaign in Sungaria, Chien Lung heard rumours of the remarkable beauty of the wife of one of the tribal chiefs, Ali Arslan, then in arms against him. She was known all over the Western frontierland as the "Model Beauty," and was celebrated for the softness of her skin, upon which she never used cosmetics. At a farewell audience given to his Commander-in-chief, Chao Hui,

Chien Lung casually told him of the reports he had heard of this lady and bade him to do his best to secure her for the court. After the successful end of the war, when her husband, the Prince, had committed suicide, Chao Hui brought her prisoner to Peking, sending couriers ahead to inform the Emperor of his success.

Greatly pleased, Chien Lung decreed that special honours should be shown her en route, and every care taken lest the hardships of the journey should impair her beauty, also ordering Chao Hui to see to it that she did not commit suicide. Arriving at Peking she was quartered in the Western Palace by the Southern Lake. The Emperor decreed that her title should be the Hsiang (Fragrant) Concubine. At first she appeared quite contented and indifferent to her former husband's death and the ruin of her tribe. But when Chien Lung, delighted with his exotic prize, approached her, she proved hostile and silent.

The baffled lover bade some of his concubines, in whose powers of persuasion he had confidence, to inform her of the high destinies awaiting her if she would be amiable. The only reply of the savage beauty was to draw a dagger from her sleeve. When asked what this meant, she answered with cold ferocity:

"My tribe is destroyed and my husband is dead. Long since I have resolved on death, but when I die I shall not be alone like any meek peasant girl perishing by the roadside. I mean to avenge my lord's memory by slaying his enemy. If the Emperor forces me to become his concubine, I shall kill him and myself too."

The Palace women, horrified, bade her attendants take the dagger. With a bitter smile she declared:

"Whatever you may do, I shall find a way. As for you, if you do not cease from troubling me, I shall kill one of you first."

Abandoning their efforts the superseded favourites —no doubt with a certain cheerful malice—reported themselves helpless in the face of such ungrateful and improper wilfulness, intimating that hanging such a wild woman would be a natural gesture from a wise and benevolent Sovereign. Chien Lung had never developed a taste for diversions of that nature, more especially where women were involved. Moreover, for the first time in his life he had fallen genuinely and humbly in love.

Realizing that for the moment it was hopeless to try to win her, he ceased his wooing, only visiting her apartment and sitting for a while in her company, trusting that time would heal her wound and that ultimately she might regard him with favour. Meanwhile he ordered that she be carefully guarded to prevent her from making any attempt on his life or her own.

Finding that she was continually watched, she seemed to abandon the idea of suicide, but one day, after she had been in the Palace about two years, her attendants reported that on the occasion of the Moslem New Year she had been found weeping bitterly. It was then that Chien Lung gave orders for the Mosque to be built, hoping this proof of his consideration might soften her rancour and awaken some gratitude and indulgence in the heart of the beautiful widow. After the usual masculine manner her unattainableness made her ever more passionately desirable in his sight.

In the whole roster of royal love tales none is more curious ... this autocrat over many hundreds of millions, standing meek and abashed before the passionate determination of one small defenseless female.

The Empress Dowager, then in her eightieth year, roused herself to end this situation, which she considered unworthy of her son's dignity. Sorely distressed at Chien Lung's infatuation and fearing his assassination at the hands of his captive tigress she said to him:

"As the woman is obstinately resolved not to yield to your advances, and as she is sick of life, why not put her to death? Or at least send her back to her own home, and trouble yourself no more about her."

The infatuated Emperor could not bear the idea of losing her, and hoping against hope he continued to wait. On the day of the winter solstice, when he was due to be absent from the Palace and to spend the night in the Hall of Fasting at the Temple of Heaven, the Empress Dowager was swift to act. The stark simplicity of the chronicle in the original—without adjective or comment—sets forth with abundant clarity how wholly these women, seemingly of such silken submissiveness, were of the same iron fibre as the men of their race and time:

"Waiting until the Emperor had quitted the Palace the Dowager bade the 'Model Beauty' attend her at the Palace of Motherly Tranquillity. When she had come into the presence the outer gates were made fast.

THE MAGNIFICENT EMPEROR

"'I hear that you will not submit to His Majesty,' said the Empress sternly. 'What is it that you propose to do?'

"The implacable widow replied, 'I mean to die.'

"'So be it! I am ready to grant you the privilege of committing suicide here and now.'

"The unhappy woman expressed her gratitude by kotowing several times. 'Your Majesty the Empress is showing me undeserved kindness in thus meeting my wishes. I submitted to the ignominy of being compelled to make this long journey under escort in the hopes that I should not die alone, that I might be able to avenge my husband's memory by a deed which should stagger the Empire. But this cannot be, for I am too closely guarded. What then is the use of my continuing this useless and aimless existence? Is it not far better that I should rejoin my late lord in the other world and close my eyes, satisfied, in death? I thank Your Majesty for your grace in acceding to my wishes, and in the realms of Hades shall not forget your benevolence.'

"At the end of speaking tears welled from her eyes. The Empress, greatly touched, bade a eunuch convey her immediately to a room in one of the wings of the Palace, where she hanged herself to a beam.

"The Emperor was at the Hall of Fasting, but a confidential eunuch sped breathlessly to inform him that his beloved concubine had been summoned to the presence of the Empress Dowager. Fearing the worst, in great distress of mind, he set out in all haste for the Palace, although in so doing he violated the rule which required him to remain in the Hall of Fasting till the morrow. On his arrival finding the doors of the Empress Dowager's palace barred, he stood there weeping, till the gates were opened and a eunuch said:

"'Her Majesty desires that you will repair to her presence.'

"He entered, and the Empress took him to the side room where the concubine was hanging from the rafter quite dead. There was no sign of pain or struggle on the beautiful and placid face. Chien Lung, greatly grieved at her death, had her buried with the honours of a concubine of the first rank."

It demonstrates the influence of that ruthless old lady upon her son, that in spite of his grief for one who was the only passion of his life, he showed no resentment toward his mother nor any failure in his lifelong tenderness and respect.

Love affairs, however, absorbed but little of the time of the tremendous Emperor. His activities were so multifarious the wonder is that twenty-four hours a day were sufficient for his labours. Like all great men and rulers who do not waste their time in butchering their fellow men, he was a passionate builder. There is scarcely one great monument of the capital but owes part of its splendour to his creative energies. The lofty Drum Tower, which contains that mighty tambour whose huge voice called the city to arms in time of danger, was rebuilt and repaired. Its companion, the Bell Tower, in which was seated the bell of Yung Lo, said to weigh a hundred and twenty thousand pounds, was also restored.

The resonant murmurs of that huge bowl of metal, which could be heard throughout the whole great city, seemed to the Chinese to say with wistful yearning: "*Ko-ngai, Ko-ngai,*" giving rise to the legend that Yung Lo commanded his master Bell-Founder to cast for him the largest and sweetest-

THE MAGNIFICENT EMPEROR 141

voiced bell in the world. Half a dozen times was the casting made, but always its tone was harsh and flat, and Yung Lo intimated that another failure would be paid for by the Founder's head.

The little daughter of the maker of bells, alarmed for her father's life, secretly consulting a soothsayer, learned that into the casting must be thrown the thing he loved best. Dressing herself in her most beautiful costume the girl, Ko-ngai, at the crucial moment of the casting took her stand beside the cauldron in which bubbled the metal just about to be poured into its mould, and with a last salutation to her father, who stood beside her, threw herself into the molten mass. The agonized parent, catching at the lovely figure in its shining silks as it slipped past him, succeeded in saving only her little shoe which came off in his grasp. Not realizing what had happened the workmen poured the metal.

When cooled and the form broken away, the great bell proved to have a voice silvery and sweet, which sang with argent reverberations the name of the devoted daughter. When the people of Peking heard the rich echoes rolling across the city, they lifted their heads for a moment to say to one another: "It is little Ko-ngai calling for her shoe. It is little Ko-ngai crying for her shoe...."

The reroofing of the famous Temple of Heaven, fallen badly into disrepair, was another addition made by the Emperor to the glories of Peking. Beautifully restoring it from top to bottom, he crowned it with tiles the very tint of the heavens above, having set his tile-makers the task of achieving the exact turquoise of a Chinese midsummer sky.

The task was a long and difficult one, for tile of that shade had not heretofore been used, and labourious experiments were required ere the roof matched the heavens bending over it. With fine reserve and feeling, the Emperor declined to use this colour, so hardly arrived at, on other buildings, convinced that only on that great shrine where the Celestial Powers were worshipped was the use of the celestial tint justified. Occasionally, small groups of tiles were mingled with other colours, but no other building was allowed to serve as a perfect mirror to reflect the azure face of Heaven with its own exact hues.

Chien Lung had grown up under those golden roofs of the Imperial city, which curve into lines airy and piquant—those roofs of which a French traveller has said:

"Les amples toits aux lignes courbées surgissent comme les tentes à jamais fixées; le soleil lustre et glorifie les tiares de tuiles des pavillons angulaires,"

and from the early impressions of his childhood he had imbibed a passion for the use of tile. He reroofed in numerous beautiful colours the many detached pavilions of the park of the Winter Palace. These he loved to look down upon from the white marble pagoda set by the Mings on an eminence in the midst of that most luxurious of imperial pleasances: pavilions which still rise like magnificent jewels along the borders of the great lakes among the ancient emblossoming trees.

Across the wide avenue leading inward from the entrance of the Winter Park he set the renowned Dragon Screen, a long and lofty wall against whose background of white porcelain writhe huge five-clawed dragons of many-tinted tiles, crimson, violet, green, and gold—a riot of shining splendour which takes the breath with its gorgeousness.

THE MAGNIFICENT EMPEROR

Every Chinese house possesses one of these spirit-screens somewhere within its walled enclosures. With their curious mingling of logic and childishness the Chinese trust these screens to prevent the entrance of maleficent influences, the theory being that evil spirits can travel only straight forward and never possess the intelligence to go around an obstacle lying across their path. Plainly even the most malignant demon would be arrested in his course by Chien Lung's screen. He would naturally sit down in front of it to gloat upon its glory.

A screen guarded by dragons was held peculiarly efficacious, for the dragon, mythical monster typifying profound and occult forces, has in all ages dominated the Chinese imagination. Its symbolism is infinite, its significations subtle and far-reaching. It is figurative of the clouds, of thunder and rain, of the encircling seas and the heavens above, of majesty and power, of fate, and of all the blind tremendous forces of the universe amid which man moves trembling and mystified. Until the recent revolution the dragon always adorned the Chinese flag. From the earliest period it was used in every form of decoration: woven into silks, painted upon porcelain, cast in bronze, wrought in gold, carved in jade and marble. Even walls of gardens were topped with wavy undulations of blazing tiles to give the outline of the sinuous chimera. Especially was it sacred to the Emperor. Dying, he was said to have "Mounted the Dragon":

"Deeply sunk in his consciousness it must be, for on every hand the image of the 'Lung' in some form is present to his gaze. It is on the robes he wears, 'the dragon robes,' the chairs he sits in, the kang upon which he reposes, the gold and silver and porcelain dishes from which he eats. His hands are the 'dragon claws'; the Imperial glance is known as 'Dragon's eyes.' The Dragon Hour is the twelfth, or climax hour, as is the twelfth day, month, and year. Shen Lung, the Spirit Dragon, is the most popular of the eight species. It is in this form that it is depicted on all the 'spirit ways' laid down for the Imperial foot. It is used in all the acts of the Emperor's official life. His throne is the 'dragon's seat,' the pen he uses is the dragon's brush. The character which means an Emperor's love is a dragon under a roof. Intertwined with the silver-crested love pheasant, usually called the phoenix, it permeates all his love life, and as such, the two emblems joined have come to signify marriage and are used upon all betrothal certificates throughout the eighteen provinces."

A legend, given by Bying, from Tan Chin, tells that the Emperor Yuen Tsung of the Tang dynasty had an Imperial ink with the delightful name of Dragon Fragrance. Once he saw in the ink little Taoist priests like flies walking about. They called out to him:

"Oh King! Live forever! Your servants are the spiritual essence of the ink, the ambassadors of the black pine. Whoever in this world has literary powers must have twelve of us dragon guests in his ink."

The Manchus had found the Winter Palace, which is really a park enclosing many palaces, already adorned and beautified by the Ming Emperors. K'ang Hsi and Chien Lung added greatly to its beauty, making of it a sumptuous resort for royalty in its hours of diversion. Across the spacious lakes, where acres of lotus lifted up their cupped jade-green leaves and perfumed rosy blossoms, they flung graceful arched bridges of marble, carved always with the Imperial five-clawed dragon in low relief. They built wharves of the same stone, from which they embarked upon their pleasure barges, which were decorated with all the fantastic incredible exquisiteness which only a Chinese mind can conceive. They built theatres and banquet halls of teak carved like lace; these, walled with glass that was gaily painted with flowers and glorious plumaged birds, admitted the light in soft delicate hues.

Chien Lung built the splendid Arch of Confucius at Peking. Indeed, throughout China, arrested by the presence of beauty and asking its origin, one is told the name of the great Emperor either as its creator, rebuilder, or decorator. In the Hall of the Classics still remain the Nine Books of the ancient classics cut in permanent text upon stone by Chien Lung, that these treasures might run no risk of fire or time.

The two places upon which he spent his most loving care were the Summer Palace, known as the Yuan Ming Wang—the Round Bright Garden—and his Hunting Palace at Jehol. Of the Summer Palace Father Attiret, one of the Jesuit missionaries stationed at Peking, wrote in 1743:

"All the mountains and hillocks are covered with trees, especially those of blossoming varieties which are very common here; it is a real terrestial Paradise. The canals are not as with us, bordered with dressed stone, but are quite rustic and edged with great rocks, some pushed forward others drawn back, which are placed with such art that one feels it must be the work of Nature. At times the canals are wide, at others narrow, here they are serpentine, and there bend sharply as though really pushed by the hills and boulders. The banks are sown with flowers which seem to have grown naturally; each season has its own. All the façade of the palace is in columns and windows; the woodwork is guilded, painted, and varnished, the walls are of grey bricks, well made and polished; the roofs are covered with glazed tiles, red, yellow, blue and violet, which by their harmonious arrangement, form an agreeable variety of compartments and designs. Nearly all the buildings have but one floor. Each valley has its pleasure house, small in comparison to the whole enclosure, but in itself large enough to accommodate the highest of our European seigneurs with his whole suite. Several of the houses are built of cedar wood brought at great expense from a distance of five hundred leagues. But how many palaces do you suppose there are in the different vales of this vast enclosure? There are more than two hundred, without counting the houses provided for the eunuchs. The Palace where the Emperor generally lives is a prodigious assembly of buildings, courts and gardens; in a word it is a city, at least the size of our little town of Dole. It is in the compartments of which it is composed that one sees all that can be imagined of the most beautiful in the way of furniture, ornaments, paintings (I speak of these in the Chinese taste), precious woods, lacquer, both Japanese and Chinese, antique porcelain vases, silks and brocades of gold and silver. Here has been assembled all that art and good taste can add to the riches of nature. I admit that the manner of building in this country pleases me greatly, my eye and my taste, since I have been in China, have become a little Chinese. Here there is only one man: the Emperor. Everything is made for him alone; this superb treasure house is only seen by him and his people; it is but rarely that he introduces princes or nobles beyond the audience hall. Of all the Europeans who are here only painters and clock-makers, by necessity of their employment, have access everywhere."

The Emperor amused himself by adding to all this Chinese charm one portion to be planned in the European style, with which he had become familiar through many engravings presented as gifts from the French government: a palace and a garden in the style of Versailles, with pompous outer staircases, waterfalls, and fountains—curious contrast to the fantasies of the Chinese taste.

This great summer resort some miles from the city remained fairly intact and a constant pleasure to the Chinese court until 1860, when at the end of the Opium War Lord Elgin, the commander of the British forces, destroyed it with the most ruthless thoroughness; today it is but a melancholy mass of ruins, weed-grown and desolate. When the Western world finds cause to regret the inimical attitude of the Chinese, it is well for them to ponder a little upon some of the seed, sowed by themselves, from which this hate has sprung. The attitude of mind in which the sowing was accomplished is naïvely set forth in the report of the chaplain named M'Ghee, who accompanied the British forces and witnessed the horrible work:

"Yes a good work, I repeat it, though I write it with regret, with sorrow; stern and dire was the need that a blow should be struck which should be felt at the very heart's core of the Government of China, and it was done. It was a sacrifice of all that was most ancient and most beautiful, but it was offered to the names of the true, the honest, and the valiant, and it was not too costly; oh no! one of such lives was worth it all. It is gone, but I do not know how to tear myself from it. I love to linger over the recollection and to picture it to myself, but I cannot make you see it. A man must be a poet, a painter, an historian, a virtuoso, a Chinese scholar, and I do not know how many other things besides, to give you even an idea of it, and I am not an approach to any one of them. But whenever I think of beauty and taste, of skill and antiquity, while I live, I shall see before my mind's eye some scene from those grounds, those palaces, and ever regret the stern but just necessity which laid them in ashes."

A modern lover of China writes of this episode: "The piteous ruins of what was once a place of beauty are today a strange monument to the memory of Lord Elgin, who describes himself as 'guardian of the good name and interests of a great Christian Nation.'" As Borel says: "It is as if the Prussians had burned and looted the Louvre."

The Hunting Park of Jehol, lying a hundred miles north of Peking, was the work originally of Kublai Khan. This walled park, some eighteen miles in circumference, lay five thousand feet above sea level and for the most part was thickly wooded with oak, pine, and chestnut covering the sides of the mountains where a great number of deer were kept for the chase. Purchas, in his *Pilgrimages* has told how:

"In Zanadu did Cublia Can build a stately palace, encompassing sixteen miles of plaine ground with a wall, wherein are fertile Meddowes, pleasant springs, delightful Streams, and all sorts of beasts of chase and game, and in the middle thereof a sumptuous house of pleasure," the "stately pleasure dome" of Coleridge's magic verse.

THE MAGNIFICENT EMPEROR

The Mings were not lovers of the chase and the park was little used and fell into neglect, but the prodigious Chien Lung could not find sufficient outlet for his inexhaustible energies in the mere ruling of China and in composing poems. He was also a mighty hunter before the Lord, and spent a portion of every summer there occupying those spare moments, of which he found so many, in adornments of his favourite resort.

An ardent Buddhist, he built near his Palace on the side of a steep hill the magnificent temple of Poo-ta-la, largest and richest in the whole Empire, covering twenty acres of ground. It was an immense square, eleven stories in height, each story having galleries running around the four sides of the building, opening from the apartments of the eight hundred priests. In the centre was a golden chapel with three altars richly adorned, each supporting a colossal gold-plated statue of Gautama.

When Lord Macartney's Embassy arrived in China in the month of August, 1793, Chien Lung was at Jehol, and they were obliged to follow him there. The English had landed in Tien Tsien and had gone up by water toward Peking until the narrowing of the river obliged them to land. At that time the road to the capital was well paved and kept in beautiful condition, with travelling palaces along the route, a day's march apart, in which the visitors were entertained each night.

Deeply impressed with the great hunting park, they mention that they counted in the ornamental grounds fifty handsome pavilions magnificently furnished, each containing a state room with a throne, and some having in addition a large banqueting hall where entertainments were given on special occasions. Sir George Staunton, writing the account of the journey of the Embassy, mentions with special admiration the beauty of the buildings and the many crystal-clear lakes filled with gold and silver fish, and a broad canal in which were several islands adorned with pagodas and summerhouses sheltered by groves of trees and fragrant shrubs. This was the first time that an English nobleman was presented at the Court of the most ancient monarchy in the world, and, as he himself expresses it, they beheld "King Solomon in all his glory."

After the Eastern fashion the reception of the Embassy took place at dawn in the magnificent Hall of Audience, filled with the principal officers of state, a great number of mandarins, and several Mongol chiefs. The Englishman mentions many great painted lanterns hung from the roof, which he thought unequalled in beauty. In his account he gives a vivid picture of the occasion.

The Emperor's approach was announced by the sound of gongs and trumpets—the never-failing accompaniments of all state processions in China, whether of the monarch or the mandarins. He was carried in a palanquin by 16 bearers, a number that is not permitted to any other individual in the Empire, and was surrounded by the usual appendages of Chinese dignity—flags, standards, fans and parasols. He was plainly dressed as suited his venerable years, in a robe of brown silk, with no ornaments about his person except a large pearl in the front of his black velvet cap. Some compliments were exchanged with several presents also; for the etiquette of the Court of China requires that every envoy who approaches the throne shall be provided with a suitable offering for which he usually receives a gift in return, but it should be observed that the former is accepted as a humble tribute due from an inferior, while the latter is conferred as a mark of extreme condescension. When the ceremonies were ended a sumptuous breakfast was served in the tent, in the Chinese fashion, and while all present partook of the repast, a band of music played on the lawn, where tumblers and rope dancers exhibited various feats of agility, and a play was performed on a raised stage. They had no scenery but very fine dresses and as no women were allowed on the stage, the female parts were always performed by boys. At Jehol the ladies of the court had a theatre for their own special amusement, where plays were acted every day and were sometimes attended by the Emperor and his ministers, but more frequently by the ladies only, who having but little occupation, naturally turned to any frivolous pursuit that might help to pass the time. One of their greatest enjoyments was to form parties of pleasure on the canal, for which purpose there were yachts always in readiness, fitted up in the most elegant manner, but so contrived that the fair occupants were entirely screened from observation.

The English visitors remained for a week at Jehol, and were present at the anniversary of Chien Lung's birthday.

The ceremonies of the Court consisted principally of the grand Birthday Ode sung in chorus by voices innumerable, accompanied by deep-toned bells and solemn music. The Emperor was present but not visible, being seated behind a screen in a large hall where all the courtiers were assembled in their state dresses to pay the customary homage, which was done by falling prostrate at the conclusion of every stanza of the Ode, which has been thus translated: "Bow down your heads, all ye dwellers on the earth; bow down your heads before the great Chien Lung!" an exhortation that was literally obeyed.

The two or three days succeeding the birthday were entirely devoted to shows, sports, and festivities, in which all classes participated. As soon as the gaieties were over, it was intimated to the British Ambassador that it would be proper to take his leave of Jehol, and return without delay to Peking, where the Emperor's answer on the subject of the embassy would be given to him. This was done, and there was no longer any excuse for the Embassy's remaining in China.

Instead of returning to Canton by sea as they had come, the strangers travelled by means of canals and rivers, the journey occupying considerably more than two months; thus they saw the interior of the Empire and reported themselves greatly impressed with the highly cultivated state of the country, the number, wealth, and greatness of its cities, its abundant resources, and myriads of inhabitants.

Two years later a Dutch embassy under the direction of A. E. Van Braam Houckgeest was received, but, arriving in winter, had audience at Peking. The Hollander wrote a very elaborate account of his impressions, and his dry and formal style, bare of all emotion or ornament, is yet packed full of suggestiveness. He speaks of being received with much honour in several towns, where the Emperor was represented by a little altar covered with yellow cloth, a vase with burning incense, and a tablet with the names and titles of the Ruler in golden letters. Behind this was placed a yellow wind-screen. Cushions were laid on the floor, and under command of a Mandarin the foreigners had to salute the Emperor, "which consists of kneeling down three times; with each kneeling the head

THE MAGNIFICENT EMPEROR 153

touches the floor and the third time one rises in order to kneel again." When they had finished the reverences meat-juice and birds' nest were served.

Houckgeest mentions that on the road from Canton to Peking they saw many stone arches built in honour of several Chinese who had lived a hundred years, as Chinese think that one cannot become so old unless one has lived a sober and virtuous life; they also saw arches built in memory of children who had given proof of their love for their parents, and in memory of women who were celebrated for their chastity. One was made in remembrance of three sisters, who lost their fiancés by death before their marriage and who then refused to marry any other men. Arches were found in memory of well-behaved Mandarins or other people who did great deeds for the people. Also to their great astonishment they met a "fleet" of wheelbarrows. Each wheelbarrow had a sail of cloth five to six feet high, attached to a mast, which stood in communication with the handles of the wheelbarrow in order that the men could govern the sail.

The season may account for the very frigid and unadmiring attitude of Van Braam Houckgeest, who was bored by almost everything that he saw in the Chinese capital. One thing, however, which roused his interest was the skating on the frozen lakes of the Winter Palace. The Dutch envoys were taken to see the skating, the Emperor occupying an armchair placed on a sledge covered with yellow cloth and decorated with precious stones and images of golden dragons. This was pushed by attendants while the other skaters circled about him, he being buried in magnificent furs.

The Dutchman also sets down with interest the fact that the streets of Peking were daily swept and kept in order by four thousand men, which appealed to this tidy Dutch soul far more than the splendours of the Palaces.

Apparently the festivities with which they were greeted and the many displays of fireworks still left Van Braam very indifferent, and most of the things he mentioned, whether buildings or gardens, he thought in very bad taste—the characteristic attitude of the Western mind of that day toward Eastern art. In 1816 Ellis, in his account of Amherst's Embassy, "interspersed with observations upon the Chinese nation," seems apologetic about his pleasure in Chinese painting when he says:

"I have often endeavoured to express the impression made by beautiful scenery, and have never been able to satisfy myself; indeed, I should be disposed to doubt the possibility of doing so, where there are no moral feelings connected with the scene. We have this day been passing through a beautiful country, the lesser features as yesterday, but the general effect heightened by a nearer approach to the more distant mountains, of an elevation and form imposing and varied. It strikes me that the landscape paintings of different nations would form a good criterion of their notions of picturesque scenery, as the artist will probably select those subjects most generally agreeable; thus Chinese paintings represent precipitous hills, with boats sailing near them, trees of the most vivid autumnal tints, under combinations that might seem unnatural to European eyes, but which are perfectly correspondent to the banks of the Yang-tse-keang."

Mrs. Ayscough, commenting on this quotation from Ellis, says:

"A curious passage! He must have been a person of sensibility this Third Commissioner of His Majesty's Embassy. A person of sensibility, struggling with unwanted and unintelligible emotions. Remember he wrote before Constable the 'father of landscape painting' had shown his pictures in England; before Turner was known to the world; while Wordsworth was still Distributer of Stamps for Westmorland, and while Keats and Shelley were mere boys. The possibility of expression unconnected with 'moral feelings' evidently shocked his sense of fitness.

"To us a century later, his attitude of mind is necessarily difficult to grasp, but making all allowance for inevitable ignorance, it is almost impossible to pardon the complacent superiority with which Occidentals set out to establish relations with countries which had no desire whatever for their presence.

"Ellis was a highly educated English gentleman worthy to hold a responsible post in an important Embassy and, as we have seen, he was a person of sensibility, yet he could calmly pronounce, after a few short weeks in China, the following dictum:

" 'I felt most forcibly the deficiency of interest in everything relating to China, from the whole being unconnected with classical or chivalrous recollections. Here are no temples, once decorated, and still bearing the marks of the genius of Phidias and Praxiteles; no sites of forums once filled with the eloquence of Cicero or Demosthenes; no plains once stained with the sacred blood of patriots and heroes; no,—it is antiquity without dignity or veneration, and continuous civilization without generosity or refinement.' "

Being what he was, wide ranging in interests, wholly at one with all manifestations of the Chinese soul, Chien Lung's strong hand is seen upon every one of his people's activities. Everywhere moulding, shaping, developing, he was an ardent patron of the art of painting, and a great collector of the works of the older masters.

Even the sun of an Emperor's patronage, however, cannot cause the finest flower of an art to bloom. Outbursts of inspiration spring from some unknown seed of which the sowing is obscure. Much admirable work of the Chinese brush was produced in this period, but no fostering could teach it to rival the gay and gracious flowering it knew under the Mings, or produce equals of the great Sung period, when the ink sketch reached perfection and was the most typical expression of the Chinese genius. The Japanese, always quick to see the best in art and to adapt it to their purposes, made the masters of the Sung and Tang epochs their models, where the utmost vigour of stroke was combined with the utmost delicacy of modulation.

Though Chien Lung was not able to create a great school of painting, yet in another direction his fostering care resulted in admirable achievements. China has always been famous for its porcelains and pottery, so much so as to give the name of "china" as a generic term to the whole product. In every age "the Sons of Han" have fabricated treasures which the world has preserved in museums for their unrivalled loveliness.

Century after century the great kilns at King-te-chen had kept their fires alight. The famous potters had produced incredible triumphs, handing down from generation to generation exquisite methods of grinding and triturating their clays, secrets of col-

THE MAGNIFICENT EMPEROR 157

ours and glazes unknown to other nations, tricks of firing which produced luminosities unbelievable. Out of those glowing furnaces came bowls, pots, and vases of apple-green, the tint of willow leaves in Spring; peach-blow, the very shade of fruit blossom petals; coral red, blues the colour of the sky, or deep in tone as tropic seas; yellows that glowed like gold; pots massive as stone; bowls and cups almost as delicate and translucent as soap bubbles. For a time after the downfall of the Mings a noble period of Chinese porcelain came to an end. The factories of King-te-chen were more than once destroyed, but the art remained inherent in the artists, for under K'ang-Hsi, Chang, and Chien Lung, there was, for a century and a half, a second culminating period in which the high-water mark of artistic production was reached and passed. Protected and encouraged, the potters were full of eager experiment and developed new glazes, new forms, and new decorations.

Within this time the famous green and blood-red Lang-yao were discovered, the latter known to the Western world as "sang de boeuf." A revival of the traditional blue and white of the Ming period was successfully accomplished, and the K'ang Hsi blue and white are difficult to distinguish from their Ming predecessors. The so-called "hawthorne ginger jars" were more highly developed than ever before. In the same way the decoration in underglaze was revived, and the finest pieces of this ware date from the reign of Chien Lung. Eggshell ware and pierced or reticulated pieces of that period have a special perfection, and the coloured glazes in light green, turquoise, purple, and black reached their height. The vessels were first fired to the biscuit state, and then soft alkaline glazes covered with copper, or manganese, were fired over them at a much lower temperature, so as to give the peacock blue, kingfisher green, and aubergine purple glazes.

One of Chien Lung's officials under the Emperor's orders made a careful collection of ancient porcelain and potteries, and sent them to King-te-chen to be reproduced, the court making it worth the potter's while to study the older methods as well as to develop new effects. It was during the reign of Chien Lung that the iron-rust and tea-dust glazes were first used. A vast number of the finest wares in the collection at Moukden were part of the purchases of Chien Lung, as were also those splendid treasures of the potter's art which crowded the storerooms of the Imperial City before the Western world broke in upon that sanctuary of beauty and destroyed and looted in so ruthless a manner.

Still another glory of his reign was the unrivalled carving of jade, crystal, lapis lazuli, rose and purple amethysts, and agates, an art of which the Emperor was passionately fond and of which he was an ardent collector. The examples remaining of his favourite pieces are unexcelled in beauty and value.

In his crowded and strenuous life, every hour of which seemed full of interest and occupation, one would hardly suppose that the Emperor had much time left for spiritual emotion, but Chien Lung was a poet as well as a man of affairs, and religion was one of his deepest emotions. Like the typical Chinaman that he was, there was no bigotry in his composition, and, as with most of his countrymen, his ardent Buddhism lived side by side with the noble philosophy of Confucius, which concerned itself with daily behaviour rather than with mystic emotion. These were linked to that third influence which emanated from Lao tze: that "Way" so intangible, so indefinable, so difficult for anyone not of Chinese blood to understand, and yet woven like a thread of gold and colour through all Chinese thinking. Even the Jesuits he regarded with indulgence and a certain interest, though he firmly repressed any attempt on their part to force their fixed way of thinking upon his people.

His Buddhism caused him one difficult episode. The Dalai Lama of Thibet (who held a position among the Northern followers of Gautama very similar to that of the Pope among the Catholics), fled from Lhasa to Peking at the time when the Gurkhas attacked the city. His great sanctity made it necessary for the Emperor to receive him with extreme respect and consideration. Housed in the Yellow Temple, the Lama found his quarters so much to his liking that when the Chinese troops had restored the freedom of his own city he was reluctant to return to it. The Emperor, under the necessity of making almost daily visits to the Lama, found himself greatly bored. He, before whom all China prostrated itself, was expected to perform the same act of humility before the haughty prelate, an act he relished not at all, apart from the fact that these visits and protestations interrupted his own busy days. No hints served to induce the Pontiff to consider removing himself, and the Court whispered that Chien Lung shed no tears when smallpox attacked the sanctified person of the head of his church and succeeded at last in putting an end to the over-long visit.

The body of the "Gem of Learning" was sent to Lhasa in a golden coffin, and his infected garments were incased in another precious casket and buried in the temple grounds, over which the cheerfully resigned monarch built that famous Dagoba which remains perhaps the most perfect example of the Imperial builder's taste and splendour.

"The pinnacled monument of white marble, with its four attendant pagodas and fretted white pillow, are raised on a stone and marble terrace, and from its wave-patterned base to the gilded tee thirty feet in the air, it is as fair and as perfect as when finished, chiseled all over with reliefs as fine and white as frost traceries. There are bands of symbols, diaper work, and inscriptions, eight panel scenes from the life of the great Lama, beside the Buddhist trinity. In the high medallions Kwanyin and the company of bodhisattvas in the cloud-land of Nirvana are seated on its successive stories. Each tiny figure is as exquisitely finished as an ivory carving, and the lines of the floral symbols, the bands of svastikas and phenixes, medallions and geometrical designs make it a very text-book and grammar of Chinese and Buddhist ornament. Its perfect whole shows what we know of the latter by the fragments rescued from Amrawati and Gandhara; and the fine carvings, the snowy relief of white on white, recall Mogul tombs and palaces at Agra and Delhi."

Yet, underlying all the philosophies and religions and the foreign faiths which through the centuries have been grafted upon them, the Chinese have always retained their original worship of the three invisible forces to which they felt they owed their profoundest reverence: one, the spirits of their ancestors; the other two, the overarching heavens, from which all blessings came, and the earth which received and developed these blessings in tangible form. The reverence paid these three forces was the state religion of China, apparently existing from the remotest antiquity, though the Chinese had no generic term for religion in its usual sense. The word "kiao" which means "to teach" or "doctrines taught" is applied to all sects and associations having a creed or ritual.

The prime idea in this worship is that the Emperor is *Tien-tsz*, or the Son of Heaven, the coördinate with Heaven and Earth, from which he directly derives his right and power to rule on earth among mankind. He is the One Man who is their vice-regent, the third of the trinity (san tsai) of Heaven, Earth, and Man. With these ideas of his exalted position, he claims the homage of all his fellow men. He cannot properly devolve on any other mortal his functions as their high priest—to offer their oblations on the altars of Heaven and Earth at Peking at the two solstices. He is not, therefore, a despot by mere power, as other rulers are, but is so in the ordinance of nature. The basis of his authority is divine. He is accountable personally to his two superordinate powers for the fate of his nation. If the people suffer from pestilence or famine, he is at fault and must atone by prayer.

Williams, a missionary to China, speaking of their religion says, in substance:

Two features of Chinese religion deserve to be noticed, which distinguish it from the faith of most other heathen nations. These are the absence of human sacrifices and the non-deification of vice. The prevalence of human offerings in almost all ages of the world, and among nations of different degrees of civilization, not only widely separated in respect of situation and power, but flourishing in ages remote from each other, and having little or no mutual influence, has often been noticed. But no clear record of the sacrificial immolation of man by his fellow, "offering the fruit of his body for the sin of his soul," has been found in Chinese annals in such shape as to carry the conviction that it formed part of the belief or practice of the people. This feature, negative though it may be, stands in strong contrast with the appalling destruction of human life for religious reasons, sanctioned among Aztecs and Egyptians, Hindus and Carthaginians, and other ancient nations, not excepting Syrians and Jews, Greeks and Romans. The other, and still more remarkable, trait of Chinese religion, is that there is no deification of sensuality, which, in the name of religion, could shield and countenance those licentious rites and orgies that enervated the minds of worshippers and polluted their hearts in so many other pagan countries. No Aphrodite or Lakshmi occurs in the list of Chinese goddesses; no weeping for Thammuz, no exposure in the temple of Mylitta or obscene rites of the Durga-puja, have ever been required or sanctioned by the Chinese; no nautch girls as in Indian temples, or courtesans as at Corinth are kept in their sacred buildings. Their speculation upon the dual powers of the Yin and Yang have never degenerated into the vile worship of the Linga and Yoni of the Hindus, or of Amunkem, as pictured on the ruins of Thebes. Although they are a licentious people in word and deed, the Chinese have not endeavoured to lead the votaries of pleasure, falsely so called, further down the road of ruin, by making its path lie through a temple and trying to sanctify its acts by putting them under the protection of a goddess. Nor does their mythology teem with disgusting relations of the amours of their deities; on the contrary they exalt and deify chastity and seclusion as a means of bringing the soul and body nearer the highest excellence. Vice is, in a great degree, kept out of sight, as well as out of reli-

THE MAGNIFICENT EMPEROR 163

gion, and it may be safely said that no such significant sign as has been uncovered at Pompeii, with the inscription *Hic habitat felicitas*, was ever exhibited in a Chinese city.

At the time of the winter solstice the Emperor performed the first of his great duties, embodying in himself the worship of Heaven by his whole race and bearing upon his spirit the sins of all his people to be atoned for. On the first day of February, the day before the Chinese New Year, the Emperor went at midnight to the great enclosure several miles beyond the city where stood the Altar of Heaven. All houses were closed along the route; no spectators permitted to see the great torchlight procession. Curtains were held up along the way by soldiers, so that no outsider might gape at this sacred progress. The procession was led by tribute elephants from Cochin China magnificently housed in crimson silks, followed by a crowd of attendants dressed in long satin gowns of imperial yellow, embroidered at the borders with the wave pattern. Sixteen chair-bearers in scarlet carried the Emperor in his jewelled and gilded palanquin. The cortege passed out by the Southern road escorted by some two thousand mandarins, princes, and musicians, as well as banner bearers, along the two-mile course to the Tien Tan, the great walled enclosure about the park containing the Temple and the Altar of Heaven, a park rich with ancient trees. The Emperor spent the night in the Chai Kung or Palace of Fasting, where he prepared himself for the great ceremony by silence and meditation for his duty; "for the idea is that if there be not pious thought in his mind the spirits of the unseen will not come to the sacrifice." This fast continued until midnight of the New

Year's Day, when the ceremony of the sacrifice began.

For twenty-four hours, silent and solitary in that shadowy chamber, Chien Lung communed with his own soul. All the sins and sorrows of hundreds of millions of his fellow beings were laid in his hands to be atoned for and assuaged. He was to be the reconciler. He alone was to stand face to face with the mysterious forces of the universe and find some link to bind suffering, toiling, sinning humanity to a potent will which moved through the cosmos towards ends and purposes which none could discern, but which all dimly felt made somehow for right. These dark, fasting hours stripped him of the facile temptations of the world, and yearly cleansed his spirit to meet adequately his tremendous task of ruling wisely and well.

This worship of the Supreme Ruler with burnt offerings and upon an open altar, is the most ancient cult observed anywhere in the world, far antedating Confucian and Taoist and Buddhist doctrines. It is a survival of those primitive beliefs which had force in Asia before the gods were personified, their images enshrined in temples, or creeds and ceremonies elaborated.

The fast ended, the Emperor went on foot, dressed in his finest garments, surrounded by the highest officials of the Empire, to what is perhaps the most noble and beautiful place of worship man has ever made. The great altar lay open to the stars—a beautiful triple circular terrace of white marble more than two hundred feet in width, each terrace surrounded by a richly carved balustrade of the same stone. The uppermost terrace, at a height above the ground of about twenty feet, was paved with white marble slabs, forming nine concentric circles—the inner of nine stones enclosing a central piece, and around this each receding layer consisting of a successive multiple of nine until the square of nine (a favourite number of Chinese philosophy), is reached in the outermost row. It was upon the single round stone in the centre of the upper plateau that the Emperor prostrated himself. Four flights of nine steps led to the altar.

Here beneath a vast star-spangled canopy, the kneeling Emperor bowed his head, confessed all the sins of his nation, which he took upon his own head, and prayed for blessings on his people to the mighty intangible forces which rule the universe. Meanwhile in a huge furnace south of the altar was offered up through fire a whole ox without blemish. The smoke of the burned sacrifice rose into the air mingled with the clouds of sweet-smelling gums from the great bronze incense burners at the foot of the stairs, while strange instruments clashed and vibrated, and ancient hymns of the ruler of Heaven rose in the darkness.

As dawn lightened the skies and whitened the great altar the Emperor, after nine reverences, passed down and made his way to the blue-roofed Temple of Heaven, where the early light shone through windows barred with delicate rods of blue glass, making a magic radiance inside. There he offered homage to the moon and stars and the spirits of all the Chinese ancestors.

Another great ceremony was celebrated later in a park opposite the Tien Tan where stood the Altar of Earth. The worship here was performed at the vernal equinox, the Emperor first ploughing a furrow to symbolize the turning of the earth for sowing of grain. Still another ceremony took place once a year within the Imperial City at the Tai

Maio, or Great Temple of the Imperial Ancestors, a large collection of buildings enclosed by a wall three thousand feet in circuit. It was the most honoured of religious structures next to the Temple of Heaven, containing tablets to princes and meritorious officers. Here offerings were presented before the tablets of deceased emperors and empresses by the Imperial family and clan to their departed forefathers.

It would seem as if the vital and mental forces of this great Chinaman were inexhaustible, but time was stronger in the end than even the most highly dowered of human beings. As the Emperor passed into his seventh decade he began to show that softening of will and tendency to lean upon others which inevitably overtakes even the most powerful as their forces begin to fail. Thus, in his late sixties, his attention was attracted by a sergeant of the Palace guard, a strong and handsome man who was especially selected to escort the Imperial sedan. It happened one day as Chien Lung was leaving the Eastern gate of the Forbidden City in his chair he was reading a memorial of an outbreak of disorder in one of the provinces.

"The Everlasting Lord's face was clouded as he read, and his bearers overheard him saying: 'If the tiger or the rhinoceros escapes from his cage, if the gem be injured in the casket, who is to blame?' This well known quotation from the Discourses of Confucius means that the party responsible for a misfortune must expect to bear the blame. None of the bearers understood the allusion, but Ho Shen, the sergeant, who was riding alongside said to them: 'yeh (the Master) means that officials holding responsible posts must be made accountable for every dereliction of duty.'"

Chien Lung was so pleased with the quick intelligence of this reply he commanded Ho Shen to become his special personal attendant and never ceased to delight in his ready wit, his knowledge of the classics, and his pointed epigrams. This first and only favourite rose rapidly to power, and his patron more and more made him his delegate in all the affairs of the Empire. His influence became enormous, and since influence in China has its price and a high one, his wealth ever growing and his influence ever for sale aroused the enmity of all the envious. As long as the Emperor lived no one could shake Ho Shen, but one false step, one outburst of temper, brought about his ruin.

In the early years of his power the Emperor had appointed him as tutor and governor of Prince Chia, who eventually succeeded his father to the throne. Ho Shen disliked the young prince, whose character was surly, and did his best to dissuade Chien Lung from selecting him as his heir. So thoroughly had this beggar on horseback become intoxicated with his own power that on one occasion he lost his temper with his pupil and dared to kick him. The insult was never forgotten or forgiven by Prince Chia, and when the Emperor died the new Monarch laid a heavy hand on the late favourite. He stripped him of all his offices, seized his entire property, and ordered him to commit suicide.

As the Emperor grew older he appeared to suffer no abatement of his bodily vigour. Up to his eightieth year he still hunted at Jehol and kept a vigilant eye upon the affairs of the Empire. But the great Chinese Imperial sun was sloping to the west and nearing its setting. The clouds that close in round the end of any long life had dimmed the radiance of even this shining being. His beloved and revered mother, who lived to a very great age, had been taken from him. Probably this was the greatest grief of his life, greater even than the tragedy of the lovely princess whom he had wooed in vain. The ceremonies attendant upon the burial of this parent were of incredible gorgeousness and occupied many months. Chien Lung had also outlived two sons who were his favourites, whom he had chosen, one after the other, to be his successor. Even the son of his son had predeceased him. He had no great respect for, or confidence in, his son, Chia Ching, to whose hands he found it necessary to transfer his powers though filled with doubt as to whether the admirable order he had instituted in the affairs of the country would be safe during his son's reign. To so ardent a patriot this was a matter of distress, and though he began to contemplate an abdication in the sixtieth year of his rule, he took pains even after vacating the throne to keep the direction of the government largely in his own hands.

It was more or less an unwritten law among the Chinese dynasts that a man should not reign more than sixty years. Partly this was founded on certain esoteric beliefs in the magic quality of the number five multiplied by twelve which formed the famous "Cycle of Cathay," the cycle which was supposed to close an era, and from which all things must date again, beginning with the number one. Beside this superstition the Emperor harboured the sensible notion that a man who had reached such ripeness of years was no longer fitted for the strenuous tasks of ruling so vast an empire, and Chien Lung, with his usual fondness for making himself clear on all subjects, and doing it in rolling phrases, announced his intention in 1795 in a delightful mingling of respect for omens and cynical contempt for them. His statement reads:

"I have now reigned for fifty-nine years. By the favour of high Heaven and the protection of my ancestors, peace prevails through my dominions, and new territories have come to share the blessings of China's civilization. During all these years, I have striven to alleviate my people's lot, and to show myself worthy of Heaven's blessings. Again and again have I granted exemptions of land tax in times of flood and famine and bestowed upon the sufferers over ten million taels from my privy purse.
"Next year will witness the sixtieth anniversary of my succession to this goodly heritage of the Throne: few, indeed, of my predecessors in this and other dynasties, have completed a sixty-year cycle. Those among them who have reigned over sixty years came to the throne in early childhood whereas I was twenty-five years of age at my accession. Today I am eighty-four, and my natural strength is not abated. I rejoice in the possession of perfect health, and my descendants to the fourth generation surround me. Immeasurably thankful as I am to the Almighty for his protection I feel encouraged to yet further endeavour. On New Year's Day of the sixtieth year of my reign an eclipse of the sun is due, and on the Festival of Lanterns [1st moon, 15th day] there will be a lunar eclipse. Heaven sends these portents as warnings, but a Sovereign's duty

is to be guided by his conscience and to be aware of his shortcomings at all times, so that an eclipse is not needed to awaken him to a sense of duty. To find favour in the sight of Heaven he must regulate his conduct. There is no need for empty catchwords and platitudes on the occasion of such natural events.

"During the course of the next year, I shall prepare for my impending abdication, and the new Emperor will mount the Throne on New Year's Day of the year following. In recognition of the warning conveyed by these eclipses, I purpose to hold no New Year's Court next year, and the customary banquet to the Princes will be omitted. During the period of the eclipse I shall array myself in everyday raiment and doff my Imperial robes of ceremony. These phenomena can be foretold, as Mencius says, a thousand years before they occur, but in the present case, the coincidence of two eclipses is a fresh indication of the favour of Heaven towards me, for had this phenomenon taken place in the following year, it would have signified an inauspicious opening for my son's reign. I feel profoundly grateful to Heaven for its favour, and in return I hereby cancel all birthday celebrations in the capital for next year, and shall content myself with receiving the congratulations of my Court at Jehol."

His jubilee year, 1796, the Emperor celebrated by a great feast given to more than two thousand guests over sixty years of age. This took place in the Chien Ching Kung, or the Palace of Heavenly Purity, considered the most important of all the Imperial edifices, the loftiest and most magnificent of them all, into which no one could enter without special license. The guests, who came from every part of the empire, were served with food and wine by the Emperor's own sons and grandsons, and those who had reached ninety years of age were invited to the table at which the Emperor himself sat, where, standing, they shared with him his special dishes.

Although he had passed his three score years and ten, after which existence, according to the Hebrews, is but vanity and vexation of the spirit, this lusty and vivid old Manchu found it difficult to occupy his still vigourous mind so accustomed to enormous labours. While he continued to keep a hand upon the affairs of the Empire, he was freed from the daily councils and the endless ceremonies required of an Emperor, and he found it difficult to fill the long days of the years still left to him.

No doubt to this old man waiting calmly for death his best solace was the reflection that under his rule for more than half a century four hundred millions of his fellow creatures had lain down and risen up in peace and security; that, as far as government may achieve it, his people had known happiness through his industry and wisdom; that China had been beautified from end to end by his efforts; that, as far as a mere human being might, he had reigned wisely and well.

He spent many months of every summer at Jehol hunting as much as his powers permitted, writing poems, presiding over tea ceremonies and flower-arrangement parties of the Ladies of his Court, listening to music, indulging in that endless delight of the Chinese, the flight and songs of pet larks, or lending an ear to the fairy melody made by the whistling pigeons, those aërial cadences which Chinese ingenuity has added to the lovely movements and subtle iridescences of the dove's wings.

Miss Scidmore, speaking of these pigeon whistles says:

"They are made of the thinnest bamboo and of little gourds scraped to paper thinness and when fastened beneath the tail feathers of a pigeon, the tiny organ-pipes emit a weird, elfin, Aeolian melody as the bird flies. Every morning and afternoon the vault of the Peking sky is swept with the sweet sad notes of scores of pigeon whistles as the carrier-birds wing their ways across the walls with bankers' messages and quotations of silver sales—a stock report and ticker service older than the telegraph and automatic tape.... These swirls and sweeps of melody were strangely sad and thrilling, and the whistling flight of these musical pigeons, the 'mid-sky houris' of the hoary East, was something that I waited for and listened for each day."

Chien Lung is said to have always carried with him to Jehol many of these musical messengers.

Another diversion of his day was to amuse himself with theatrical performances, or to watch his courtiers play the game of Wei Chi, which he himself never mastered. The educated Chinese hold that this deliberate and intricate amusement is beyond the power of any foreigner to learn, not only because they have insufficient intelligence, but because it is impossible for one not thoroughly familiar with the Chinese classics to understand its meaning. A war game of the utmost intricacy, it is played on a board containing three hundred and twenty-four squares; and three hundred and sixty black and white pips are used in making the moves. The player who makes the first move, holding

THE MAGNIFICENT EMPEROR 173

either the black or white pips, establishes his point of strength, the object of his opponent being so to surround him that his pips cannot break through. Many of China's greatest heroes have been famous for their skill at Wei Chi. The greatest general, Meng Chang Chun, played it daily to keep his hand in practice for war.

So unusual is it in China for a man of high literary tastes and abilities to be ignorant of Wei Chi, that history has deigned to record the fact of the ignorance of Chien Lung. It chanced one day that a Japanese envoy petitioned his Imperial Majesty for the honour of a game. Ashamed to say that he could not play, the Emperor caused a board and pips to be brought and gravely sat down as if he knew all about it. Royalty of course took the first move, but his Majesty, not knowing where to begin, thought the middle of the board would be as good a place as any and, accordingly, put his pip down on the very centre cross of all, to the no small astonishment of his opponent. The Japanese then made such a move as he deemed advantageous, which the Emperor immediately imitated by placing a second pip in exactly relative position on the opposite side of the middle pip, and this he continued to do all through the game, at the end of which he was necessarily the winner by the pip he put down first.

There was no want of the feminine element in the old Emperor's court. No Empress existed at this period, for the princess who had enjoyed the dignity was dead, and Chien Lung had not thought proper to raise another to the throne. The laws of China admit only one lawful wife; but the Tartar sovereigns did not restrict themselves to this rule, although they generally gave to one a rank above the rest and she alone was called Empress, while the others bore the title of queen. There were eight queens at that time, two of the first and six of the second rank; and these had each a certain number of ladies in her train, making altogether upwards of one hundred females belonging to the court. Chien Lung seems, however, to have escaped the tendency of the aged and unoccupied male to fall a victim to the wiles of a youthful enchantress. No record reaches posterity of any amorous adventures on the part of the Emperor in his last years.

His health remained vigourous up to his eighty-eighth year. A stroke of paralysis closed his life.

Fortune had loved him to the last. Given the widest opportunity, he had used it wisely and well. Wholesome of nature, violence and grossness were repugnant to his genial humour, and his rich appetite for life found satisfaction in immense activities, covering not only the administration of a huge realm but also every interest of the human intellect. Never intoxicated by unlimited power, he refrained his hand from cruelties while rewarding with generous magnificence good service to himself and the nation. His brain was as vigourous as his body, and the exercise of both gave him unflagging pleasure; a well dowered, buoyant personality was his, uniting all the noblest qualities of his race. He happily escaped those faults which have often overweighted the admirable character of the Chinaman—faults which, despite his virtues, have yet so often plunged the nation into disorder and misery.

Chia Ching decreed for his Father the most sumptuous of obsequies, though it is to be supposed that he was not overcome with grief when that strong hand was lifted and he felt himself free to follow his meaner purposes and instincts, long held

THE MAGNIFICENT EMPEROR 175

in abeyance by fear of his great predecessor.

The deliberation of Chinese interment is so great as to amaze more impetuous races. At long last, however, there wound across the grey plains to the Eastern Tombs a huge procession of motley mourners, the blaring and wailing instruments clashing and shrieking, the multitudinous banners waving, and the pompous military and civil escort accompanying the ponderous coffin of the Chinese ruler carried upon the shoulders of a regiment of bearers.

All Chinese royal tombs bear a close resemblance. Soothsayers, sorcerers, and astrologers select the spot where the Imperial clay is to be laid. A mighty mound is built, lined with stone to form a great chamber within. The way to the door of the tomb is a broad paved road overarched at several points by magnificently carved, gilded, and lacquered pavilions, housing huge bronze incense burners, the tablets of the deceased, and tables for funerary offerings.

Between these pavilions, on either side of the road, tower stone figures more than life size, of elephants, lions, camels, and full-armed warriors. Enclosing the whole, a great wall protects the wide park of ancient trees surrounding the Imperial mausoleum.

In earlier epochs the custom was to provide the tomb of the dead Emperor with many tall jars of oil lest his spirit might lack for light, and vats of wine lest he might thirst. Gorgeous garments were stored there against his need of the pomp and beauty to which he had been used while living. Along with jewels and insignia of rank were his favourite jade toys and priceless paintings and sculptures to divert his mind in the long weary night of death. That he might not lack attendants to serve him sixteen of the most beautiful boys of the palace were strangled and laid near one side of the coffin. Sixteen young and lovely girls, with silken knots drawn tight around their throats, were laid at his left hand lest that tenuous adumbration which lingered in his clay might feel the need of some tender intercourse.

There is no record that these human sacrifices were made to the manes of Chien Lung. Milder ages contented themselves with paper reproductions of these terrific offerings, symbols which were burnt at the time of the entombment. Supposedly the spirit of the dead required only spirit pleasures which were inherent in the light smoke which curled up from the images of the objects treasured during his mortal years. It is probable that only these fragile simulacra flamed in the still air before the entrance of that long tunnel which passed underneath the mound to the chamber into which the Emperor entered alone.

Chien Lung, who had bulked so large in the living world, vanished at last into darkness and silence, letting fall behind him a heavy curtain of earth which none might ever raise. All that was left to lament a great era and a great Emperor was the voice of the wind which sighed through the leaves of the tall dark evergreens clustered about the place of his repose.

A noble period, a magnificent monarch had come to an end. Truly, a Wise Man of the East....

III
HIDEYOSHI
THE DELIGHTFUL PARVENU

HIDEYOSHI

A large room in a convent in Kyoto. . . . The shoji have been pushed back to open half a dozen chambers into one. Some fifteen guests stand about in groups waiting for the hostess, a lady of the Imperial family, abbess of the convent. Deep reverences are exchanged as a white linen-clad figure enters—a woman of middle age, but of slender form and pale golden complexion. Her fine features are markedly those of the Japanese aristocracy. A Buddhist nun, she wears a coarse linen kimono without ornament of any kind. The head, entirely shaven, lends an air of great purity and benevolence to the smooth countenance.

The gathering is a reception and a concert, for there is no sternness or seclusion in Japanese convents. Art, music, the tea ceremony, and the pleasures of gardening render suave and gracious the conventual life. When all are seated upon silken cushions five *kotos* (long Japanese harps) are brought. The most gifted players of Kyoto are to entertain the company.

Strange and exotic is their music to Western ears, strange as the pictorial art of the East, so puzzling to the Occidental on first acquaintance—one would say a mere outline of music, achieving its purposes with austere economy of means and poignant with suggestion of harmonies refined to the last essentials. It is the result of profound subtilizing of notes; as seemingly simple as that reserved and yet suggestive line, the *notan*, of Japanese drawing and flowing with the same grace and surety. A music but little known and little understood in the Western world.

A long repertoire is given, sometimes accompanied by songs in recitative. One of these causes a perceptible stir of interest and attention among the guests. Even a stranger can hear in the song echoes of something tragic and moving, rumours of "old unhappy far-off things and battles long ago," ghosts of pain and despair, of things lost and destroyed and forever past. The faces of the listeners grow tense, and tears flow quietly down many cheeks. It is the story of the battle of Dan-no-ura seven centuries ago, the final decisive struggle of the Taira and the Minamoto in the Bay of Shimonoseki, where the powerful clan of the Taira was utterly destroyed.

That great sea-and-land battle was so bloody, so ruthless, so tremendous that the heart of the race has never ceased to vibrate to its tragedy. Ghostly tales were whispered of strangely marked crabs that crawled on the shore from out the waters where so many brave spirits sent up their last despairing cry—crabs marked with the Taira insignia and of a grisly aspect; plainly some goblin emanation of the defeated dead, whose bones still lay heaped far down in the dark sea with the broken ships. Eerie legends grew of a blind singer led nightly by a gauntleted, clanking figure to a magnificent palace and made to sing before what his visionless senses told him was a crowd of murmuring and rustling guests who hung breathless upon his famous song of the battle of Dan-no-ura, breaking into passionate weeping as he chanted the heart-breaking words. When the blind singer was tracked at last by curious neighbours, who wondered at his frequent absences, nothing was seen of mail-clad guide or crowded palace. Only, in the night and the dreary rain, the lonely figure of the blind man crouched at the foot of the tall stone marking the woeful memory of the defeated clan and chanted to his biwa the story of Dan-no-ura.

So close-knit and continuous is the history and the life of Japan that every auditor is completely familiar with the story of that great agonism which for centuries rang through the land with the sound of swords and the clanging of armour; a struggle sown with a thousand tales of heroism and courage, of chivalrous adventure and of a haughty pride which hesitated at no sacrifice; a period in which the Japanese gentleman and warrior, knowing that his head would be taken by his conqueror, always before battle beautifully dressed and perfumed his hair ere putting on his helmet, in order that even in death he should still be exquisite and proudly fine before the gloating eyes of those who had overcome him.

It was into this sixteenth-century world of desperate confusion, ringing with the sound of steel on steel, that Hideyoshi was born. His patron was the ferocious and tremendous Oda Nobunaga, a survivor of the Taira Clan; his associate and successor, Ieyasu Tokugawa, came of the victorious Minamoto line.

At what date the Japanese race entered the islands of Japan or from whence they came no one is quite sure. Nor is their racial origin known. When they appeared, the land was scantly populated by a big, powerful race of white-skinned people, hairy and savage, resembling the Russians of the mainland to the north—a primitive people with the bear as a totem. They lived in rude tribal formation, with families clustered in enormous huts where all those immediately consanguineous huddled together.

The new comers entered the islands in two lines, from the south and from the north, bearing with them all the qualities which have marked the race through the whole of its history, and apparently already capable of delicate handicrafts. A small, powerful, sturdy people was the lower class; the rulers a finely featured, haughty aristocracy, taller, much paler of tint, of a different cast of countenance, unlike in facial angle.

Slowly the invaders pushed back the autochthons, with whom they never interbred, hunting and crushing them as the white race did the American Indian, forcing them to find refuge in the remote fastnesses of the Northern Islands, where they linger on—slowly dying—to this day.

Even yet, when a new Emperor is crowned, the feast of his coronation is eaten from reproductions of simple unglazed pottery and served on fragile trays of unpainted wood, as a memorial of the original furnishings of those first comers. The exquisite lacquers and porcelains which they were

THE DELIGHTFUL PARVENU 183

later to develop were then unknown, but all was clean, delicate, and beautiful in form. Even in those early days, the people evidently loved simplicity and daintiness. This unique taste in art deepens the mystery of their origin, for no other race is characterized by the same qualities. Their language, too, is unrelated to any other.

The Japanese, through all their history, have been possessed of three essential ideals: beauty, cleanliness, and fine manners. They have loved, too, all things subtle, light, and airy. Solidity and permanence have for them no charm. Their most sacred shrines are constructed of unpainted wood, and at Isé every twenty years these central altars of the race are demolished and constructed afresh so that they may be always immaculate and sweetly smelling of the natural perfume of new wood. Not only for the gods but for themselves they have preferred dwellings easily replaced, easily kept clean, easily renewable in every part: dwellings not cluttered with accumulations; beautiful with the beauty of natural things, with the essential loveliness which breathes from the thing itself rather than from that imposed upon it by human labour. Yet labour was not spared in the exquisite adjustment of form and placing, in order that intrinsic beauty might have opportunity for its complete revelation.

This love of airy, graceful impermanence and liberty of the spirit was strangely allied with qualities wholly opposite: an iron courage, a granitic firmness. Lafcadio Hearn comments upon this silken covering of the Japanese nature over a core strong, close-knit, and fierce.

Descent they claimed from the Sun Goddess Amaterasu and from her brother Susano-o, known by the delightful title of "The Impetuous Male."

Of her their legends tell a charming story. Offended by the Impetuous Male's impetuous ways, she retired to a cave thereby leaving the world in darkness. Prayers nor persuasions could induce her to shine again. Eventually the gods hit upon the device of causing a famous dancer to perform in front of the closed cavern. Hearing the applause and laughter of the divine spectators, the goddess yielded to curiosity and ventured forth to discover the cause of such enthusiasm. Quickly the gods rolled the stone back to the mouth of the cave, leaving her outside, and, having presumably recovered a more amiable frame of mind, she accepted the situation and returned to the society of Heaven. Fifth in descent from this bright divinity was Jimmu-Tenno, leader of the Japanese invaders and founder of the Japanese Imperial line.

That the race brought with it a nascent civilization is proven by the fact that when Buddhism was introduced in the sixth century, the Japanese began shortly to create admirable sculptures in bronze and in wood to embody their conception of the founder of the Buddhist faith. Nothing in their original beliefs had required this ocular embodiment. Shinto, The Way of the Gods, their ancient cult, which has maintained itself in amity with all imported belief, except the jealous exclusiveness of Christianity, was a nature-worship and tie with the dead, requiring neither priests nor elaborate ceremonies nor ponderous temples. Only shrines without images or altars were needed; shrines before which the worshipper clapped his hands to intimate the driving forth of all personal and material instincts, and bowed in silent reverence and spiritual communion before the intangible powers of the uni-

THE DELIGHTFUL PARVENU

verse; this in order that through him might flow their beneficent impulses.

In those dimly visioned early days, when the barbarians had still to be pushed farther and farther back, the rule of the Emperors was strong and wise, demanding and receiving unlimited reverence from a compact and well-knit people.

As early as the twelfth century that famous first Japanese novel, *The Tale of Genji*, reveals how highly developed were the graces and the order of their civilization. It pictures a court life refined and cheerfully vivacious, occupied with such charming festivities and amatory diversions as distinguished Provence in the reign of King René.

The astonishing Lady Murasaki, who introduced the art of novel-writing into Japan and whose sophisticated, suave style modern critics find the last word in our own modernism, shows her hero, the gay Genji, participating in poetical contests where oblique suggestiveness and subtle phraseology were a test of merit. She represents him, too, as a connoisseur of ancient Chinese art and that of his own time; as a critic and creator of music; very squeamish as to the handwriting of his lady-loves; censorious of any lack of perfect taste in their costumes, of their skill in versification, of the melody of their voices.

Meantime, on the borders of the Empire, the captains who had commanded in the barbarian wars were consolidating their conquests, occupying and settling regions remote from the capital. Transportation being difficult, the rulers of these distant provinces were slowly assuming power and developing a spirit independent of the central government, ruling according to their immediate necessities and erecting semi-independent centres of administration. The daimyos, or dukes, were jealous of the encroachment of other daimyos and inclined to enlarge the borders of their own territories where possible. While the court amused itself with exquisite developments of art and the graces of conduct, these strong men-of-their-hands clashed with one another, without asking permission of the Emperor, in order to enforce their private rights or greeds.

The first great capital had been established at Nara, and not until 784 A.D. was it transferred to Kyoto, which was to remain the seat of authority until the nineteenth century, when the Emperor moved to Tokio.

By the middle of the eighth century the Fujiwara family had established themselves as mayors of the palace, and the Emperors had begun to sink more and more into the position of spiritual rather than political rulers. The Fujiwaras succeeded in retaining the actual power in their own hands until the beginning of the eleventh century, when the seventy-first Mikado, Go San Jo Tenno, made a strenuous effort to reform the abuses which had crept into the Fujiwara administration. The struggle of several succeeding emperors to control their aggressive vassals lasted for three quarters of a century, but the feudal development of society had advanced too far for any peaceful return to centralized administration.

The Fujiwara fell, but between the two great clans of the Taira and the Minamoto began that terrific struggle which, as already told, wrecked the land for generations. The first decisive victory in the long struggle fell to the Taira, but for twenty-two years the Minamoto contested their dominance, until Yoritomo finally crushed the Taira and assumed for himself the title of Shogun, equivalent to

THE DELIGHTFUL PARVENU 187

Captain General. Distrusting the intrigues and conspiracies of the court nobles, he took up his residence at Kamakura, where from a new military capital he ruled the whole kingdom, though leaving to the Mikado the title of Emperor and affecting to be but the administrator of the shadowy crown in Kyoto.

Wealth and ambition naturally centred about the real source of power, and in Kamakura a stirring and martial world arose, rich with thrilling tales of knighthood and chivalry, The jongleurs and tale-tellers elaborated the epic of the amazing and amusing adventures of Yoshitsune and his giant squire, Benkei, whose rebellions and wanderings are still the inexhaustible delight of Japanese youth. At Kamakura was cast that bronze Buddha—the famous Dai Butsu—which remains the noblest of man's efforts to embody his spiritual ideals in human form. It was housed in a splendid temple fifty yards square, a temple destroyed by the earthquake and tidal wave which swept away the capital and the whole Kamakura period. The majestic figure of Gautama the Buddha, still sitting upon his pedestal among the pine and cherry trees that now cover the site of the vanished capital, still an object of wonder to pilgrims from the uttermost parts of the earth, is the only survival of that magnificent capital and its complete desolation.

It was at the height of Kamakura's glory that Marco Polo told to a wondering Europe his Oriental travels and the stories he had heard at the Court of Kublai Khan concerning Zipangu (Japan) and its fabulous wealth. Gold had never been abundant in Japan, and it is difficult to guess whence arose these persistent rumours of its profusion in the Mikado's empire. Kublai Khan, after conquering China, sent a great expedition to annex the Islands—an expedition which met with total disaster. It has been suggested that escaped prisoners returning to China might have supposed the many gold lacquer utensils to be fashioned of the precious metal and had thus started the story of Japan's rich stores of gold. However this may have been, the rumours grew in Europe as they passed from mouth to mouth, and Columbus included in his plan of finding a westward passage to India a hope of touching somewhere at the ports of the reputedly auriferous Zipangu.

After the fall of the Minamoto régime, there arose another great family of aristocrats, the Hojo, who were content to exercise their power at Kamakura. They were succeeded in turn by the Ashikaga, under whose rule Kyoto regained all its original splendour, and there the arts and beauties of life reached perhaps the most exquisite development ever known.

Hideyoshi may not be understood without some knowledge of this epoch of the Ashikaga, when the essential spirit of the Japanese mind found its preëminent expression—an epoch which permanently stamped the tastes and standards of all classes. It left an impress which neither time nor turmoil could eradicate, so that even Hideyoshi, that plebeian wanderer of the roads, was able to find his relaxation and delight in diversions inconceivable to the fighters and workers of other lands.

The Japanese passion for the garden, with all its lovely suggestiveness, was in this period brought to perfection. Though the Chinese garden art had been an inspiration to the Japanese, yet in their own creations they broke away from the intricate and rigid rules which governed the Chinese. Massive walls, with many buildings and bridges, did

THE DELIGHTFUL PARVENU 189

not appeal to them; they sought quite other effects. The extreme artificiality and heavy grotesqueries of the former were unsympathetic to the lighter and airier spirit of the Island race. The beauty and use of stones they understood, but chose them for their natural charm and colour rather than for fantastic suggestiveness. Plants were moulded and guided into strange outlines and mirrored in placid waters, and all flowering things were used with that fine discretion and delicate austerity which governed Japanese preferences in the search for beauty. The strange and the fantastic, so often the dominating notes in the Chinese pleasances, were in Japan replaced by a soft tenderness and grace, by an arch and half-humourous sweetness of aspect. Great garden artists arose, as renowned and valued as painters and sculptors, the nobles vying with one another for their services. Yoshimitsu Ashikaga laid out the famous Kinkakuji garden about his golden pavilion, still beautiful after centuries, with its Moon-gazing Platform of silvery sand, its lotus-adorned lakes, its strangely wrought trees, its soft vistas, its esoteric symbolism, its gentle charm.

In these gardens was developed the great art of Ceremonial Tea. Indeed the garden was created largely as a frame for the tiny pavilions in which the ceremony was held. The Garden Master was the Tea Master as well, spending infinite pains upon these simple-seeming little centres of the Rite. An elaborate code of rules was developed governing every detail. A stream must cross the path to the tea-house portal, the "dew-drop path" of stepping stones making a way through the clear shining water. The portal must be low that there might be ensured a reverence of the head upon entering. Special woods were chosen for the building, all fitted together with the perfection of a jewel casket, the soft-flowing grain of the unpainted wood and the spirit of perfume emanating from its fibres being the only adornments. All was of an extreme and exquisite simplicity. Here, under the rule of the Tea Master, was celebrated the making of the Ceremonial Tea, according to an ancient and elaborate formula. Every article used was required to be simple, almost primitive in character, but beautiful in form and in quality.

The Tea Ceremony was held to be of esoteric and symbolic significance, a training of the spirit to silence, to perfect accuracy of method, to beautiful and deliberate movement, to concentration and purity of thought. By drawing the attention of the celebrant away from all worldly matters, it cleansed and elevated his soul and refined all its instincts. Luxury, ostentation, haste, and noise were rigidly excluded from any part in the rite. The participant was supposed to pass, by its means, into a finer air of clear thought and pure sweetness. Those who had done wrong sought its aid to purge their souls of darkness, and those who had not attained full development of spirit climbed higher and higher, through its aid, into a rarer element.

It was in the Ashikaga period, also, that the most famous schools of flower arrangement found their perfect growth. It was characteristic of the Japanese that all the nation—generals home from the stricken field and the simplest workmen—gave hours to this sublimated diversion of combining leaves and blossoms in such a way as to create an inexplicable delight through the mere manner of their juxtaposition. Prizes were offered and contests held in this cultivated diversion. Beautiful tools were perfected to aid the fine hand and tastes of the contestants. Not only was flower arrangement a part of the education of every gentlewoman, but also in its practice warriors laid aside their intricate armour—woven of silk, bronze, and steel adorned with gold, so that the wearer resembled some brilliant sharded coleopter—to pore over the enchanting possibilities of combining dark pine boughs, drooping withes of the willow, the dawn colours of the lotus set amid its jade-tinted leaves, or the curved petals of the mauve and purple iris.

All the diversions of the period had this ethereal quality. Incense parties tested the discriminating olfactories of the participants. Hands of warriors and great ladies, almost equally supple and beautiful, sketched upon sheets of black lacquer with poured silver sand, picturing landscapes with the shifting medium. Everyone wrote poetry; half the correspondence of lovers, friends, and courtiers was conducted by means of verse—verse compact, suggestive, oblique, in which, in a few syllables, little was said but a thousand emotions were implied.

The music of that day resembled the verse, bearing in its brief strains endless implications of sublimated half-told harmony. Calligraphy was a high art, and all the qualities of the writer were guessed not only from these brief poems but from the grace and boldness of the brushwork which expressed them. Great artists adorned the sliding walls of lacquer and paper by which at will an apartment could be enlarged or diminished. They painted transparent silk to be suspended as kakemonos in the one shallow alcove where a single work of art was allowed to hang, accompanied by some rare bibelot and a carefully thought-out flower arrangement.

Many notable artists made difficult and labourious journeys to China to study the methods of the older masters, as the artists of Northern Europe pilgrimaged to Italy to drink at the fount of inspiration, collecting originals where possible, or copying masterpieces not to be purchased. With sure taste these Japanese painters dipped themselves deep into the treasures of the Sung and Tang periods, when the Chinese art was at its purest before it declined into intricacy and elaboration.

The sliding wall spaces, the folding screens, the rolled kakemono were adorned with landscapes, with great court pageants and processions, with reproductions of the fair gardens, with the thousand beauties of the world the artists saw about them. For the Eastern spirit, unlike the Western never found a special satisfaction in depicting the human body. It did not turn its eye upon itself or set up as its one central model of beauty the naked human frame, as did the Indian fakir who discovered all heaven in the contemplation of his own navel. Perhaps, to the Oriental mind, man was unfortunate in being the one animal whose carcass was not covered by any natural clothing of silken and dappled fur or shining feathers. Eastern artists delighted rather in the fluent outlines and glowing colours of the garments man had wrought to hide his nakedness. But most of all they turned to the world of nature, with which their faith knitted them so closely in the belief that they too had passed and would pass again through avatars of all these forms.

The Japanese artist, trained to the utmost finesse, austerely ignored all unnecessary and intrusive detail. He sought rather by implication to suggest things tender and lovely, things moving and wistful, by an ineffable line: the half seen curve of a fish through the water, the gracile shape of a bird in the air, the moon glimpsed through bending

THE DELIGHTFUL PARVENU 193

grasses of the marsh, the dewy glowing of the sun rising through mists beyond the many tall stems of a bamboo brake. With a flower or two, or with a single pallid branch of the blossoming plum, the artist could wake emotions deeper than tears, or with a few magic shadows evoke a whole mountain landscape feathered with snow—a landscape breathing a thousand rhythms of yearning and lonely melancholy.

The same qualities of fine reserve characterized all the life of the time. Beauty and grace distinguished all the furniture and accoutrements of daily living. The art of behaviour was governed by codes exquisite and severe, and a super-perfection of manners fitted men to move about perfectly in the gossamer world with which they had surrounded themselves. Perhaps never before had anything so superfine in the conduct of life been realized. But the structure could not bear the weight of human passion, and with the death of Yoshimitsu Ashikaga in 1408 the whole Empire fell once more into disorder.

In the years that followed, the material ruin of the country was appalling. Disputes as to the succession to the throne, as well as the struggle for power among the great vassals, rent the land. To the horrors of the never ending civil wars were added frequent violent earthquakes, failures of crops, terrible famines, and devastating plagues. While the nobles warred among themselves, the people fell into the utmost misery and distress.

As always when material living becomes agonized and uncertain, the less violent spirits turned to the shrines of religious faith, clinging in despair to its altars as a possible refuge. The Buddhist temples swarmed with refugees bringing their treasures with them, and the great Buddhist monasteries became so populous and so rich that they felt obliged to arm themselves to insure their protection from the greedy and turbulent factions of the warring nobles. With this growth in numbers and in wealth, the old simple purity of monastic life was disintegrated by pride and violence. Armed retainers of the monasteries even descended at times upon the capital, endeavouring to enforce their rights by battle, and the nobles began to realize that a new and dangerous contestant had entered the field where they clashed with one another.

From the monastery of Hiei-san, high among the mountains overlooking Kyoto, came the founder of Hideyoshi's house, a monk by the name of Shosei. His grandson Yaemon took service with the father of Oda Nobunaga, in whose wars he received an arrow wound in the knee disqualifying him for further service and forcing him to take up farming for a living. As is usual in the case of great men, rumours of a royal or noble bar-sinister endeavoured to account for the genius displayed by Shosei's great-grandson, for men find it hard to believe that genius can spring from a lowly root. There seems no reason to believe, however, that Shosei's grandson was not the father of Hideyoshi, whose mother, Naka, a farmer's daughter, proved to be a woman of uncommon intelligence and character.

Marvels were reputed to have attended Hideyoshi's birth. After his rise to power legends grew of a new star that had appeared in the sky on the date of his appearance, January 1, 1536. It was also said that he had been a twelve months' child. What is more certain is that the newcomer bore a remarkable resemblance to a monkey. Though his

THE DELIGHTFUL PARVENU 195

mother called him Hiyoshi-maru, he was known to the neighbours as Sarunosuke, "the monkey-faced," and the poor little "pithecanthropoid baby" for a long time supposed it to be his real name.

His character justified the title. He was as agile as his namesake, as wild and active, climbing all the trees, swift of foot, always in high spirits, astonishingly cunning, and perfectly indifferent to any will but his own. The neighbours gossiped that Naka had given birth to a creature hardly human, and in despair at his very un-Japanese-like resentment of all discipline and rules of manners, his parents finally determined that he should be apprenticed as a servitor in the temple of Komyoji. Through the efforts of a cousin, Genzaemon, he was especially recommended to the Abbot. The kind priest, at first very much impressed with the child's intelligence, soon discovered that he had no love for learning but was always escaping studies and duties to arm the other children in the temple's care with lances fashioned of bamboo and to set them fighting with one another under his direction. All questions of religion bored him inexpressibly, but to tales of war he would listen by the hour, his little bright eyes under their overhanging brows shining with interest. To the reproofs of his teachers he answered impudently, "Priests are always beggars. I mean to learn something more important than how to beg."

Unteachable and unmanageable as he proved to be, yet out of regard for his family the priest bore with him until he had reached the age of twelve years; then one of his most outrageous escapades brought his expulsion. His daily duty being to make offerings of food upon the altar before the image of Amida, the boy always hungrily regarded the vessels which contained delicacies he dared not touch. In the mornings the bowls were invariably empty, and the curious child determined to see at what time during the night Amida made his feast. Growing weary through the hours of darkness and observing no movement on the part of the revered image to avail itself of the offering, he fell into a fury. Seizing one of the candlesticks from the altar he began to beat the calm golden figure which showed so little appreciation of the food he himself longed to take. The priest, wakened by the noise, found him engaged in this blasphemous outrage and immediately summoning his cousin Genzaemon, ordered him to remove the obstreperous iconoclast from the temple precincts.

The boy's own father had died, his mother had remarried, and the stepfather, who had now two children of his own, declined to be bothered with Hideyoshi. The worried cousin, who had also his own responsibilities, apprenticed the lad to half a dozen different trades, but found him returned again and again, without thanks, by angry masters. It is recorded that he was dismissed from thirty-eight places in succession, and finally Genzaemon breathed a sigh of relief when his charge quietly vanished, determined, evidently, to go and see the world for himself.

In after years little Monkey-Face related with great amusement the adventures of this wandering career. When hungry he asked for food and would accept nothing else; at night, curled up by the roadside under the open sky, he slept as cheerfully as if he had been the animal he so much resembled. On one occasion, roused out of his slumber by the sound of many feet, the clang of armour, and the light of torches, he sat up, and rubbing his eyes he saw a boy considerably younger than himself borne past in a lacquered palanquin surrounded by armed retainers. It was the young Ieyasu Tokugawa, heir of one of the Minamoto families. An attendant, finding the little waif in his way, kicked him out of the road, and the disgusted boy grumbled threats at the petted aristocrat; not guessing that they two were destined to fight side by side on many a field, and to rebuild the broken fabric of the nation's life.

That same night, hours later, the boy was once more awakened by someone stepping upon him as he slept. Springing up, very much angered by this second interruption of his slumber, he struck at the man who had disturbed him. This time there were no torches, and he could but dimly see an armed group stealthily making its way across the bridge. The man he had tried to strike caught the lad by the arm and held him tightly, threatening him with a drawn sword.

"If you sleep by the roadside, you may expect to be trodden upon," he said, "and it would be a small matter if your neck were broken. I have half a mind to cut off your head as it is."

The angry little monkey, undaunted, countered haughtily: "The highway is as much mine as yours and I sleep where I like. It is the duty of everyone passing along the road to treat those he meets with courtesy."

The impudence and courage of the child so amused the man that he burst out laughing, began to ask questions of the young cockerel, and finding he came of his own province of Owari, took the boy along with him into the forest and fed him at the camping place of the band. Hideyoshi thus found himself affiliated with a group of highwaymen under the leadership of Koroku, sometimes known as Hidoye-mon, a man of good birth fallen upon evil days, who, like many in those troublous times, had taken to the road with a group of followers as a means of making a living. The whole land was troubled by these Ronins, masterless men, the broken fragments of the armies of defeated nobles.

For a while the waif followed the fortunes of this band of Ronins, and in the many books written to record the life of the great consolidator of Japan are endless gay tales of their adventures. Koroku apparently delighted in his young follower's impertinence and quick-wittedness and employed him in scaling walls and opening gates from the inside so that the band might enter at their ease for plunder; and many times the boy's lightning-like tricks saved his master from capture when hard pressed. This indulgence more and more developing the ambition and pride of the lad, he finally flatly refused to go on any further expeditions unless armed with a sword, the insigne of manhood. Koroku, amused at his presumption, tossed him an old and shabby weapon which the boy refused to accept, declaring it no fit arm for a person of his ability; he must have one made by some noted man. Koroku smilingly questioned: "What sort do you want; what make pleases you? If you would have the indulgence to inform me of your exact wishes I might be able to accommodate you."

Twinkling with delight the boy announced pompously, "The one you wear yourself would satisfy me perfectly."

"I should think so indeed! But I am hardly likely to dispose of it. It is my family sword, and one does not give away the family sword without disrespect to one's ancestors," adding with a laugh: "If you are able to steal it from me then my ancestors could not blame me, and if you can do that you are welcome to it, but that is impossible."

Knowing the obstinacy and enterprise of his little follower, Koroku took pains for several nights to lie awake to watch for an attempt upon his weapon. But the boy having humbly admitted that his master was too much for him, Koroku grew careless, and, sleepy from his vigil threw himself down for a nap, awaking to find himself swordless. Immediately Hideyoshi walked into the room and pointing to the sword thrust into his own girdle said politely:

"This no doubt is what you are looking for. According to your own promise it is now mine. How foolish you were to suppose that I should not be biding my time to throw you off guard, and be waiting for just such a piece of unpardonable carelessness, sleeping in the daylight without taking any precaution."

Whether these tales are, or are not, the amiable inventions of admiring chroniclers, apparently Koroku never quarreled with the bold child, for many years later when Hideyoshi ruled the Empire, the latter sought out his whilom master and gave him power and place.

The life of a highwayman did not long satisfy the aspiring boy. In the course of the year he drifted back to his home and was for a while employed among the workmen who were repairing the castle of Oda Nobunaga. It is possible that even then there was forming in his head some plan to attach himself to the fortunes of this young noble, already becoming known for his forays and his growing power. There was small chance at his age, however, for such aspiration to be gratified, and he returned to his old habits of drifting about from one master to another, always amusing them with his tall talk and impudent boldness, his quick-witted capacity for getting his own way, his gaiety and good humour, but invariably in the end exhausting their patience.

Finally, he succeeded in insinuating himself into the household of the Samurai Yukitsuna whose occupation it was to instruct the young retainers of his master, Yoshimoto, in the knightly arts. This, at last, was an employer the boy respected and admired, and under this tutelage he became highly proficient in the use of the sword, lance, and bow. Here he learned to be a good horseman and gave invariable attention to the older man's lectures upon military matters. Apparently he was quite willing in return for this instruction to perform any menial duty and make himself useful as a servant, but in the fencing yard he soon became so skilled that none of the other pupils could hold their own with him.

In his sixteenth year the daimyo Yoshimoto, Yukitsuna's master, was attacked by the Lord Ujiyasu. Hideyoshi begged to be allowed to march with the defending forces but was refused as being too small and too young: a useless refusal, it would seem, since once he had determined upon anything it was always simpler to let him have his own way.

No sooner had Ujiyasu's troops disappeared than Hideyoshi managed to possess himself of an abandoned suit of armour much too big for him, following hotfoot in clanking and ill-matched mail; and Yukitsuna, arrived at camp, suddenly became aware of a queer figure clothed in fantastic odds and ends saluting at the side of his horse. As usual Hideyoshi's impudence and willfulness seemed to strike some vein of amusement in his master, who, looking down into the queer little simian face shining up at him from a much too big helmet slidden over one ear, laughed and forgave the disobedience. Much to the boy's disgust, however, Yukitsuna sent him to serve in the sutler's camp.

Again he might have known that it was useless to give Hideyoshi orders which did not march with his intention, for, soon slipping away from the commissariat, the lad plunged into the thick of the fight, which was going badly for his overlord. Squirming through the mounted combatants, he managed to sink his sword into the hindquarters of the mount of the opposing general. As the horse plunged and fell, Hideyoshi sprang on the entangled rider with the speed and fierceness of a tiger, and before his foe could recover he succeeded in shearing the prostrate general's head clean from his shoulders, throwing thereby the attacking forces into a confusion that resulted in their rout.

After the battle, Yukitsuna, pleased with this feat, offered to adopt Hideyoshi as his own son and give him his name, but the boy refused, declaring in the pride of his achievement that he intended to make his own name eventually far more famous than that of any fencing master. He willingly remained, nevertheless, in Yukitsuna's service and rose to the position of his most trusted attendant.

Four years went by. Hideyoshi was now a man, still small and ugly, but powerful, agile, and of inexhaustible vitality; and still the pride of the fencing yard and the archery butts. Yukitsuna began to think the boy ready to be wived. Kiku, a pretty girl (whose name signified Chrysanthemum), was selected. Naturally, at that date, even pretty girls were not consulted as to their taste in mates. Her very respectable Samurai family arranged the affair with Yukitsuna. The landless waif strutted at the idea of so dignified an alliance, but to his deep abashment found Kiku sullen and scornful. She hated his low birth and queer countenance. Endless pouts and furies countered his humble blandishments. His promises of some day giving her reason for pride were treated as mere vulgar boasting.

Hideyoshi, constitutionally incapable of being tied, was already growing restive at his want of advancement, and this, added to Chrysanthemum's repugnance and contempt, decided the moving on to new adventures.

The armourers of Owari, Hideyoshi's native province, were unrivalled for their mail, and Yukitsuna longed to possess a complete suit. Monkey-Face, who in his various apprenticeships had badly served many of these smiths, yet knew which were most skilled and so was chosen for the commission. As this implied a rather lengthy absence, Kiku—knowing something of his thoughts—renewed her entreaties.

"I doubt whether you will ever return," she cried, "and before you go it is only fair so to arrange matters that I should be at liberty to become another man's wife without bringing reproach on myself and my family."

Thus she obtained from the reluctant boy her bill of divorcement, though Hideyoshi warned her she would eventually regret not sharing his future grandeurs.

Kiku's intuition proved correct. Hideyoshi lightheartedly set out for Owari, composedly appropriating the money with which Yukitsuna had entrusted him for the purchase of the armour. Settling down pleasantly in his parent's house for a while, he spent with cheerful liberality the funds he had brought, offering as excuse that neither his master nor his overlord had ever adequately rewarded him for saving the day and turning their defeat into victory. He always maintained that he was simply availing himself of an opportunity to collect a just debt. Throughout his life he had a more or less shadowy conception of the line between *Meum* and *Tuum*, and, while lavishly open-handed with all who served him, he never hesitated to help himself freely to the goods of those he considered his debtors.

Looking about for a new master whose career would be likely to afford his best opportunity, he finally settled on the near-by Oda Nobunaga, the Daimyo of Nagoya. Employing the last of what remained of Yukitsuna's funds, he fitted himself out with the proper equipment of a baron's retainer. His cousin Genzaemon, who had so often found him positions and who seems to have been an incurable optimist in spite of the many times the boy had failed to profit by his labours, offered to persuade Nobunaga to take the wanderer into his employ. Hideyoshi's reply was characteristic:

"What you say might suit ordinary people well enough, but in the case of a man like myself, who chooses a master on account of his capacity, such a course would be undignified in the extreme. If Nobunaga has not the sense to see that I am a man worth employing, he is not the baron I take him for, and in that case I am not anxious to serve him. We will have no middle man: I will manage the affair myself."

Bidding his family a jaunty adieu and telling them not to expect to hear from him, he set out on his new road. Nobunaga, who was resting after the chase, hearing outcries and scuffles outside his tent, sent to inquire the cause; there was brought before him a young man who, his attendants explained, had attempted to force a way into his presence. Angrily questioned as to the reason of this impertinence, Hideyoshi, with his usual self-contained insolence, explained he had chosen Nobunaga as his master, and had come to present himself, knowing that he would be a valuable retainer for so ambitious a captain. Undoubtedly Monkey-Face had a "way with him" and a personality which impressed and disarmed everyone he met. Nobunaga, like so many predecessors, was diverted instead of angry and took the young man into his service, saying gaily to his attendants: "We have had good sport today. We bagged a young monkey; we can afford to go home."

Learning that Hideyoshi was a son of Yaemon, who had served under Nobunaga's father, and that he had already distinguished himself in battle, the baron offered his new retainer the land which his great-grandfather had possessed, but Hideyoshi haughtily refused, saying: "What I receive I wish to receive for my own merits. I care not for things inherited."

This, like everything his new retainer did, amused Nobunaga greatly. It was he whom the baron constantly summoned to accompany him on his wild rides in the early winter dawns, liking them the better the greater the inclemency of the weather. Before the day broke Lord Oda might be seen galloping madly in the face of the gale, stung by snow, lashed by sleet, finding some furious joy in the fury of the weather, some cooling for the black torments of his diseased spirit. At his stirrup rode, in patient sympathy, the young retainer, who understood and condoned the madness of his liege. Oda had also a habit of sending for him in the evenings to amuse himself with Hideyoshi's inextinguishable wit, bland impertinence, and gay tales of varied experiences.

"Young Monkey" was his affectionate name for his youthful favourite, the court all using the same term. Pride of personal dignity has always been markedly characteristic of the Japanese, and that Hideyoshi should allow his associates to use such a term in addressing him aroused the remonstrance of one of his friends.

"But I do look like a monkey," said the young man cheerfully, "and the name causes me no annoyance. I know how to exact respect when I require it, but a name is a matter of no importance."

That he knew how to protect his dignity he proved when one of the Samurai, having taken a little more saké than was wise, said insolently to the young favourite: "I mean to lie down and you can come and give me a massage."

In Japan massage was a form of restorative treatment after fatigue, practised from the earliest periods, long before it was known in the Western world; but the masseurs were usually of the lowest classes. "Sworded men" never condescended to practise it. Hideyoshi, however, replied calmly that he was not a professional, but would be glad to do what he could. He managed the business so well that the recipient expressing his astonishment added contemptuously: "Of course if you do this sort of thing you can never hope to be a soldier. What do you expect to become? I suppose every man has some sort of ambition."

Hideyoshi sitting back upon his heels, his eyes shining wickedly, answered composedly: "One never can tell what the changes and chances of these disorderly times may bring about, but I hope some day to make you little barons glad to hold my sandals."

The rest of the group, watching the episode with great interest as likely to end in bloodshed, broke into wild laughter, so typical was this reply of the favourite's cool pride and insolence.

Dark and violent was the Lord Oda whom Hideyoshi had chosen for a master, resembling those sombre, sinister figures who passed across the scene of the States of Italy in the Cinque Cento—ruthless, bold, and supple, grasping at domination, reckless of the means by which they might achieve it; magnificent while in power, but always playing a dangerous game, and likely at any moment to be hurled from their dazzling positions by the victory of a rival, the intrigue of conspirators, or the hand of the assassin. Nobunaga was a far-Eastern replica of a Sforza, a d'Este, or a Gian Galeazzo. Born in 1534 of the clan of the Taira, a descendant of the great Kiyomori who had brought the clan to the apex of its power, and who had been overwhelmed at the battle of Dan-no-ura, he inherited many of the traits of his ferocious ancestor.

The Jesuit missionaries, whom he afterwards played with as a cat might with a mouse and whom he used for his own ends, have left a portrait of Oda in which lives again a fine face, haughty and delicate, with features inexorably cruel. Slender of figure, and not of a robust aspect, according to their report, his passionate spirit and iron constitution enabled him to continue undebilitated by a wild life of war and voluptuousness, a life of frenzied luxury and of ferocious activity. They represent him as taciturn, distrustful, and cunning. He struck with the swiftness of a thunderbolt and inspired in his opponents an almost superstitious terror.

For some unexplained reason the Buddhists had incurred Oda's insane hatred. Priests and monks, he said, were vile impostors who abused the credulity and simplicity of the people and dissimulated their debaucheries under the veil of religion. There seems to have existed in this sombre and turbulent soul, however, some conception of patriotism, some desire to save his country from the agonized disorders which rent her in fragments, though his methods of cure were but little less terrible than the disease he aspired to heal. His desire was to destroy not only the great feudal families struggling amongst themselves, but also the military power of the enormous and wealthy monasteries.

Nobunaga began his work by attacking, one after another, his immediate neighbours. His military genius was indubitable and his tactics were so sudden, so unexpected, and so violent that none was long able to maintain effective resistance. He counted upon the exacerbated jealousies between the nobles to prevent the coöperation that would have enabled them to meet him successfully. An opponent once down he savagely destroyed the ruling family of the clan and annexed the province to his own originally small fief of Owari. By the beginning of 1560 he controlled thirty-three of these baronies, more than half the Empire. A few months later, in the great battle of Okehazama, he annihilated the armies of Imagawa Yoshimoto and became the greatest feudal power of the land.

In the course of these wild years he not only had availed himself of Hideyoshi's prowess in the field, but constantly found him employment in a manner still more fitted to his genius. Here, there, everywhere, the ugly little man penetrated, a whole Intelligence Staff in himself. Before a thunderbolt was launched, Hideyoshi explored the province of any prey which his master had marked down. He discovered its every point of weakness; he suggested the vital spot to be attacked, and carried in his head an amazingly detailed map of the country he had been quietly examining. He learned who were the enemies of the predestined victim. If the doomed man had a friend Hideyoshi was soon whispering in his ear that it would be wise to hold his hand until he could guess the likely outcome of the struggle with the redoubtable Lord of Nagoya, lest he be pulled down by the other's disaster. So utterly had the national spirit disintegrated that his argument usually proved effective, and, the bundle of sticks being untied, Nobunaga had small difficulty in breaking them one by one.

In diplomatic work Hideyoshi delighted. He had small love for fighting, convinced that violence was the last resource of able men, the first instinct of the stupid. Throughout his whole career he put his trust in the superior efficiency of persuasion and appeals to reason. Only when all these failed was he ready to have recourse to arms. A beaten foe, he said, was always dangerously resentful and ready to take advantage of misfortune or indiscretion on the part of his adversary, while the man persuaded that his own interests lay on the side of one who had offered convincing arguments was unlikely to be guilty of those cynical treacheries which so often brought about the ruin of the most powerful. Nobunaga loved war for its own sake, and while willing enough to avail himself of Hideyoshi's methods when necessary, he found some solace for his tene-

THE DELIGHTFUL PARVENU 209

brous spirit in the shedding of blood and in the clangour of mortal combat, indifferent to the fact that he stored up for himself a creeping fire of resentment which must one day burst into flame.

More and more he leaned upon the services of his young Monkey-Face, assigning to him a regular revenue, and entrusting him more and more with the government of his household. The Lord Oda had learned that his favourite was a skillful economist and manager, who set straight his master's disordered affairs and cut off the waste and negligence so common in a great military establishment. The favourite had eyes for everything, carefully budgeting the expenses of each department and managing with skill the servitors who carried out his orders. He displayed none of the hard ruthlessness to those under him so common at that time, for here again his principles persuaded him that resentment was always dangerous, and that ends could be accomplished more effectively through cheerful coöperation and hope of reward than by the tyranny of fear. On one occasion a terrible typhoon seriously damaged the walls of Nobunaga's castle, and Hideyoshi, becoming alarmed when he saw how languidly the repairs proceeded, called Nobunaga's attention to the danger he ran by exposure to a sudden attack while their defenses were thus enfeebled.

"You are fond of criticizing the work of others," said the Daimyo sneeringly, "but I doubt if you could do better yourself."

"If my Lord will entrust the task to me," said the young retainer, "I will undertake to see that we are in a position to defend ourselves within three days."

Calling the workmen together he explained that they themselves were exposed by the damaged wall and had no protection for their own wives and children. Speed, he said, was as necessary for them as for their superiors, and because of Nobunaga's love for his people and his wish to ensure their safety, he had engaged to pay them two days' wages for one and give them a bonus as well.

The first morning no great progress was made, the workmen being too accustomed to leisurely methods to alter their progress suddenly, but at midday Hideyoshi had waiting for them a hearty dinner, with saké to wash it down, and declared himself amazed at their noble efforts. The men, considerably embarrassed by this amiability, knowing well they had not made any undue efforts, from sheer shame that afternoon showed some advancement in the rate of the work. At nightfall their diplomatic overseer again fed them liberally, but urged them not to make too much exertion lest they injure their health, promising that if the third day showed the fortifications complete the bonus should be double. The workmen, beginning to see the quality of this jest, in high good humour took hold of the job so earnestly that Hideyoshi was able to present himself before his Lord at the close of the period mentioned and announce that his promise had been kept. Nobunaga rewarded him with a handsome largesse, all of which Hideyoshi used in keeping his promise of the extra wages and bonus for the labourers. Though himself still in debt for the money borrowed to make the feasts for the workmen, he was not depressed by these obligations, since more than ever Nobunaga trusted him with power and with the means of enlarging his fortune.

Being now a man of substance, with his future practically assured, Hideyoshi bethought himself of taking a wife. This time he had no intention of permitting others to bungle his love affairs. The social code forbade the principals to meddle in matchmaking. Monkey-Face had small respect for codes and sublime confidence in his ability to manage his own business. Against all the proprieties he started a secret courtship, conducting it so successfully that the clever, attractive girl he had chosen forgot his humble origin and his simian countenance. He fascinated her by his wit and his gaiety, and, more discerning than Kiku, she believed his prophecies of future greatness.

Her father had other plans for his daughter, but Hideyoshi, by one of his usual turns of skill, got rid of his rival and secured for himself the hand of this intelligent young woman. Though, after the fashion of the time, he made several other connections later, the devoted wife never resented them and all his life was his wise and indulgent counsellor and aid. Even after his death Yae endeavoured to protect the child she had never been able to give him and whom he owed to a later marriage.

Within the daimiates, where he was now supreme, Nobunaga by Hideyoshi's advice put down with an iron hand the banditry which the disturbed conditions had rendered so common. He constructed roads, primarily as aids to his military power, but equally valuable to the agriculture and commerce of the country, more especially as the roads were made safe from the highwaymen who had so long preyed upon the merchants and farmers. These measures ensured the loyalty of the lower classes, who found, too, that while Nobunaga was exacting as to taxes these were not levied according to mere greed and need, after the manner of the other warring nobles, but followed a system which permitted them to count upon the ratio of tithes in advance. The spectacle of this more orderly administration aided Hidyoshi in his various missions to the other powerful barons, and gradually he allied many of them to the Lord of Owari.

Among these was Ieyasu Tokugawa, the boy whom Hideyoshi had envied that night when the young prince's retainers had kicked him out of their path. This boy, now grown to a man's estate, was known for his unusual abilities and the power he wielded. Nobunaga and his assistant, Hideyoshi, strained every nerve to attach Tokugawa as an ally and confederate in their purposes, rejoicing when this very desirable recruit, after much deliberation, decided on affiliating himself with their politics.

Thus at last these three remarkable men, so various in personality, and destined to mould so profoundly the nation's history, were brought together. Ieyasu Tokugawa was one of the greatest men of Japanese history, essentially unlike the violent and bloody Oda, and more deeply wise than the gifted parvenu and adventurer, Hideyoshi. A scion of the powerful clan of the Minamoto, he was in character a typical Japanese patrician, grave, proud, and deliberate, never forcing events, but far-seeing as to the future and quietly ready not only to avail himself of opportunity but to mould both men and events towards its development. The two others laid the foundation upon which Tokugawa built one of the noblest political structures ever raised by human wisdom.

The Japanese in that delicate, allusive, symbolic fashion of which they are so fond have summed up the three men in a brief picture. In the forests of Japan there exists a bird call the *hototogisu*, whose shrill voice, heard at unpredictable intervals, is a favourite theme for Japanese poets.

"If the *hototogisu* will not sing when I wish him to, I will kill him," said Nobunaga.

"I will endeavour to persuade the *hototogisu* to sing," said Hideyoshi.

Composedly Tokugawa said: "I will wait until the *hototogisu* wishes to sing." . . .

Feeling himself, with Tokugawa as an ally, sufficiently powerful to advance upon the capital, Nobunaga appeared before it with a great army. There still remained a last feeble representative of the Ashikaga family at Kyoto, with the title of Shogun—without power but clinging to its simulacrum by controlling the Palace and the Emperor who had long since become merely a symbol of government. This empty shell of authority crumbled before Nobunaga's terrible reputation, without a struggle. Appointing himself Shogun, the conqueror installed Hideyoshi as governor of the capital while he went on his way to complete the destruction of those rivals who refused to submit to his overlordship.

Hideyoshi turned with delight to a task according to his own heart. His administration of the affairs of the city displayed his usual wisdom. Nothing escaped his notice, and in rewarding merit and punishing disorder and vice he showed an impartiality very rare at that epoch. Governing his own troops with a rod of iron, he put a stop to the outrages which the soldiery had been accustomed to inflict upon the civilian population, showing no favouritism as between classes, carefully protecting property, and enforcing peace.

The Court, grateful for his justice and protection, bestowed upon him the right to use a crest—the flower and leaves of the Kiri (*Pawlonia Imperialis*) usually permitted only to Princes of the Blood. On his clothes, his armour, and his flag the little monkey-faced wanderer of the roads wore with pride this Imperial design. Upon his war standard he had hung at his first success a gourd, adding another for each military achievement. By the time he received the notable honour of the Kiri, his great standard went before him clattering like castanets with the many proofs of his prowess.

The even-handed justice, the reform of the many abuses which had grown up in the capital during the period of disorder and weak rule, naturally rendered Hideyoshi very unpopular with those accustomed to profit by a loose administration, as well as with those who had gradually encroached in many directions, and who had grown to feel that these abuses were a prerogative. Revolts broke out, which Hideyoshi swiftly put down. Instead, however, of executing the conspirators, as was the habit of that day, he amused himself by playing one of those grave and intricate comedies he so dearly loved. He thoroughly terrified his captives with the fear of the absent Nobunaga's well known bloody vengeance, and persuaded them that by sacrifice of a large part of their possessions, in shape of money, his own influence might succeed in buying their safety. Having thus gathered considerable funds he set the offenders free and turned his attention to repairing the dwelling of the Emperor by means of these bribes, restoring the comforts and luxury of the monarch—comforts dwindled to absolute hardship under the feeble and wasteful administration of the Ashikaga Shoguns. Such use of money exacted by a conqueror was so unusual that not only the court but the people at large were as astonished as they were delighted.

It was at this time that the vexed question of foreign missionaries loomed upon the Japanese horizon. The Jesuits, already active in the far East, had found a foothold in the Southern part of the country. There the nobles, restive under the control of Kyoto—shadowy enough at best—lent a kindly ear to the insidious suggestions of the new comers that the Southern rulers should throw off the yoke of the central government and use the foreigners' aid in manufacturing more deadly arms than those which their enemies could command. The Jesuits brought with them patterns of firearms and the secret of the manufacture of cannon and gunpowder. All they asked in return was the acceptance of their new religion, which in outward form and ritual was not greatly unlike the Buddhism they strove to supplant. Whole provinces were converted *en masse* to the new religion at the orders of their overlords.

Nobunaga, who had a covetous eye upon the enormous wealth of the monasteries, saw in this new foreign element a weapon against the ancient faith which he so much detested. The Jesuits were invited to Kyoto and given many privileges which, after their usual intolerant fashion, they used to crush wherever they could the power of the priests of the native church.

Upon one of the mountains encircling that verdant bowl which holds Kyoto was the great monastery of Hiei-san, from which Hideyoshi's great-grandfather had come. It had been established by the priest Saicho in the eighth century as a small shrine and temple of the Tendai sect. Saicho had made a journey to China to study the doctrines of Gautama, the Buddha, and through his teachings Buddhism soon became popular. Many of Saicho's followers took the tonsure, and around the small temple of Hiei-san the monastery gradually arose.

Now, like the other great religious centres of the time, it had grown rich and powerful. It had many branches spread throughout the country and was itself more like a huge fortress or town than a monastery, being well prepared for defense with arms when necessary.

Throughout the world it was an age of faith. Life everywhere was so uncertain, so liable to sudden disaster that men's minds turned longingly to any promise which seemed to offer, even after death, the security and repose of which they had so little experience in this existence. To ensure this eventual peace they would give freely of their goods. The same thing happened here which was taking place at that period in Europe. Turbulent and plundering nobles dreaded lest the Heavenly Powers might exact after death a *quid pro quo* for their crimes during life, and cannily thought to buy off punishment by sharing their loot with those who had influence at that invisible court. Great legacies were left to the monasteries, and the smaller people sought the same support by their mites. Naturally, their immunity from attack and their ever growing wealth tended to make these congregations haughty and insolent.

Nobunaga, at length feeling himself all-powerful, determined to try conclusions with the monastery of Hiei-san, that seven-hundred-year-old centre of independence. An army was made ready, and in order to quiet uneasiness at the idea of the blasphemy of an attack upon this famous seat of learning and reputed piety, Nobunaga issued a proclamation accusing the Tendai sect of being a centre of anarchy and rebellion, such as he had set himself to suppress everywhere throughout the Empire.

"If I do not take away their power," he said, "this great trouble will be everlasting. Moreover these priests violate their vows and never unroll the sacred books. How can they be vigilant against evil or maintain the right? Surround their walls and suffer none within them to live."

The priests, alarmed, offered a ransom. When this was refused they endeavoured to dispute every foot of the way to their eyrie three thousand feet above the city, but the grim wave of Nobunaga's forces swept them back step by step; the final assault ended in the extermination of every occupant of the hundreds of buildings which had studded the mountain top. Thousands were put to the sword. The torch swept from existence unreckonable treasures of learning and beauty, which during the centuries had accumulated on that lofty plateau, known as the Blue Sky Mountain, from which the inhabitants of Hiei-san had so long looked down upon all the charms of the lovely land which lay at their feet.

The dark seeds of insanity had from the first been developing in the sombre ferocious soul of Nobunaga. His restless violence and wild vices were signs of a nervous disorder within, and this bloody and fiery destruction of Hiei-san was both a symptom and an aggravation of the mounting flood of his madness. His own soul may have quivered in terror before the blasphemy in which he intoxicated himself. From this time onward his life and his vices grew steadily more wild and reckless, though his genius towered ever more startlingly as he went on his course of destruction. Money was thrown about furiously in the gratification of insensate luxury. He erected a gilded figure of himself in mockery of the statues of Buddha, and with shouts of malignant merriment obliged even priests to worship it. Meantime the Jesuit missionaries were caressed one day and repulsed the next, were for a few months allowed to undertake busily the conversion of the population, and then ordered to abandon all propaganda upon pain of exile. His followers began to whisper that some steps must be taken to curb him, but an insolent jest was the final cause of his downfall.

Hideyoshi, always cool and watchful, saw the inevitable end, but continued his unwavering fidelity even in the face of what he recognized as approaching disaster. At times, however, he took it upon himself to attenuate some of his lord's wild orders and for this incurred on one occasion the violent anger of Nobunaga, who commanded him to retire in disgrace to the seclusion of his own castle at Nagahama. This rebuff alarmed the wiser of Lord Oda's followers. They were apprehensive that the proud, and now powerful, soldier would not willingly submit to an undeserved punishment; that a furious dissension between him and his master must entail another of those long civil wars of which the country had grown so weary—a proof of how inadequately they understood the character and intelligence, as well as the patriotism, of the man.

Cheerfully accepting the orders which everyone supposed would fill him with rage, Hideyoshi threw himself into amusement and gaiety with all the energy of his nature. Rising early, he rode, hunted, practised with bow and lance, and discovered each day some new method of diverting himself and his companions. At night he feasted, surrounded by actors and dancers, even joining personally in these comic and diverting spectacles, thereby shocking the more aristocratic of his companions, who looked upon such impersonations as quite beneath the dignity of a soldier. Hideyoshi, however, only laughed at their remonstrances, declaring that he was sufficiently a plebeian to amuse himself as he pleased regardless of aristocratic etiquette. The whole period of his occultation passed in a whirl of activity and laughter, with even a considerable indulgence in saké, a dissipation he usually sternly abjured. Two of his followers undertook to make serious remonstrance, considering that were reports of his behaviour to come to the ears of Nobunaga, this demonstration that his reproof had produced so little impression would anger the despot to the point that he might either cancel all Hideyoshi's honours and sequestrate his property or order him to commit suicide.

"Your having incurred the displeasure of your master," they said, "is a subject for sincere regret and calls for the exercise of great circumspection on your part. But you seem utterly callous as to what has happened. You spend your time in riotous pleasures. Your manner of living is so entirely out of harmony with your ordinary behaviour and so contrary to the usual bent of your mind we are apprehensive that it must be the work of some evil spirit. If you were to show a certain amount of regret for what has occurred—a degree of self-control, Nobunaga would most probably feel sorry for having ordered your seclusion and you would soon be restored."

"You look at things in the wrong light," replied Hideyoshi. "From the first time that I entered Nobunaga's service till now, I have never known a day's rest. Morning, noon, and night I have toiled. Days and nights have I spent in the saddle. Without doffing my armour I have proceeded from battle to battle, from exploit to exploit. The conquest of Mino was followed by that of Omi, and this again by that of Echizen, which was crowned by the annexation of the five provinces that surround Kyoto, and the provinces of Isé. Not for myself" he continued, "but for Nobunaga have all these exploits been performed. After years of toil I have at last found time to rest—thanks to the kindness of the master I serve. This is the return that he makes to me for all I have accomplished. That I now have an opportunity of dispelling the gloom which years of toil have inflicted, is a source of deep gratification to me. For getting rid of melancholy there is nothing like saké. Saké is the broom that brushes away the dust of sorrow from the breast. But to drink by one's self is lonely work. Consequently it is well to gather together as many confirmed saké drinkers as possible; and they should drink till they are dead-drunk—till there is nothing that they fear and nothing that they are anxious about—till to them heaven and earth no longer seem vast, and fire and flood no longer terrible—till they drop to sleep and snore louder than thunder—this is the highest bliss of the drunkard's world. Since I am so much like a monkey, surely my dancing ought not to cause surprise. Ah, 'tis a fine thing to feel drunk! This Hideyoshi is now forty-one years old and never yet has known the delight of getting tipsy."

Hideyoshi's wise wife, Yae, regarded his performances with a smile and declined to let his retainers inspire her with anxiety. She knew him well enough to realize that he did nothing without a reason, and no doubt he had explained to her the wisdom of not appearing either sullen or disturbed, lest Nobunaga might suspect him of planning a revenge for his disgrace.

Hearing one day that one of the beaten nobles had raised the flag of rebellion against the Taira chieftain, Hideyoshi instantly swept away all frivolity and organized his followers to take the field, his preparation being justified by an order from Nobunaga to come at once to his aid as the revolt threatened to be serious. Setting off instantly he arrived at Kyoto long before his master could naturally expect him and at once took everything into his own hands, as if he had not been absent for a day. Aware that he had not misbehaved himself, he never dreamed of appearing humbled by the treatment he had received and promptly proceeded to deal with the revolt as efficiently as always.

Undoubtedly the rumours of Nobunaga's increasing wildness of behaviour had penetrated to the various provinces whose lords hoped to regain their old power and freedom, for Hideyoshi and Tokugawa were kept busy repressing outbreaks in various quarters. One of these, of a serious nature, obliged both of these commanders to march with their forces to the scene of the disturbance. Nobunaga, promising to join them later, was left in the capital with a mere handful of his soldiers. A more considerable body, to serve as his escort when he marched, was encamped outside the city under the command of Mitsuhide, whom his leader had bitterly insulted very recently during one of his wild bouts of drinking.

Mitsuhide had many and dreadful reasons for anger against his commander. At the siege of the castle of one of the rebellious Lords two brothers who were friends of Mitsuhide, though in the opposing forces, surrendered themselves upon his promise that their lives should be spared. Nobunaga, growing always more mad and ruthless, was so infuriated by this piece of chivalry on the part of his follower that not only did he refuse to permit the promise to be kept, but to show his anger burned the two young men alive.

Ordinarily a Samurai, when he was unable to keep his word, expressed his indignation by self slaughter, but Mitsuhide, so deep was his horror at this shame, resolved to take vengeance, instead, upon the man who had placed him in this disgraceful situation. To carry out his intention he affected submission, waiting for the opportunity to cleanse his honour in a more terrible way when opportunity offered. Nobunaga must have been aware that the pretended submission concealed more desperate intention, for the laws of chivalry were the one rule to which all men held in those turbulent days. Yet such was his infatuation that he added to this injury a bitter insult, knowing well that to those haughty soldiers a personal indignity was even more unpardonable than the deadliest injury. Before the forces marched away, Nobunaga, at a drinking party, caught Mitsuhide about the neck and, using his iron war fan as a drumstick, pretended to play a tune upon the proud gentleman's head, declaring it to be as empty as a drum, containing neither ideas or emotions. Mitsuhide still affected a smile but carefully arranged that he should be put in charge of the escort left behind to accompany Nobunaga.

The main forces of the army with their banners and music, bearing the standards of Hideyoshi and Tokugawa, topped the hills and disappeared behind them in the twilight. Still Mitsuhide waited while the hours of the night rolled by. All aid for his intended victim should be far removed that he might have freedom to wipe out in blood the stains that burned into his spirit like an acid.

At the first grey of dawn, rousing his men and putting them in marching order, he quietly entered the city and surrounded the Honnoji temple where the Lord Oda was spending his last night before setting out to join Hideyoshi. Roused from sleep by a flight of arrows thundering against the outside wooden shutters, Nobunaga flung open the casements to demand who dared be guilty of so incredible an action. The mists of morning rendered the outer world dim and ghostly, but he could discern a cordon of armed men drawn about his dwelling. Mitsuhide on horseback under the window was smiling in deadly rage from beneath his raised visor into the face of the enemy he had met at last unprotected; and even through the vapours of his growing madness Nobunaga realized there was no hope of mercy from the man he had so deeply offended.

At a signal from Mitsuhide's hand a second flight of arrows was discharged, before the casement could be flung to, and Nobunaga was pierced in thigh and shoulder. Both flight and surrender were impossible. Too proud to beg for mercy, the bleeding chieftain dragged himself to an inner room where were the women and children of his household, determined that one last horror should mark the passing of his life smeared and lit with so much blood and flame. Using the shorter of the two swords which all knighthood bore, he stabbed every one of his helpless dependents. Then, with a torch he ran to and fro setting the temple alight so thoroughly that in a few moments the entire building was wrapped in sheets of fire; a fitting and characteristic exit for so fierce a genius of war.

Thus vanished the last great figure of the Dark Age of Japan, and with him was to pass that century of ravin, travail, and sorrow. Yet, as has been said, within the lurid madness of Nobunaga's nature, there seemed to burn some purpose of patriotism to light his bloody career. Not a mere condottiere, his aim—and in this he succeeded—was to break the power of the great feudal nobles who were tearing the empire into fragments between them, and to establish again a national and centralized power. Perhaps one less violent and less ruthless than himself could not have accomplished this difficult task, nor made the powerful monasteries submit themselves to the government. When his generals had remonstrated against the massacres at Hiei-san he had answered:

"I wish to give peace to the Empire; to reëstablish the authority of the Mikado. For that end I risk my life every day and never know a moment of repose. I will force even the priests to submit."

He died as he had lived, furiously, before he had reached his fiftieth year, but his great work, and the only work he could do, having such a nature, was completed. His philosophy of life was expressed in the brief poem of which he was most fond.

> "Life is short; for the idle it is a mere dream,
> Only the foolish fear death since all living soon or late must die.
> A man can die but once.
> His only hope should be that his death may be swift and glorious."

THE DELIGHTFUL PARVENU

The rumour of the tragedy flew on swift wings after Hideyoshi, not yet far away. Swinging his troops about-face by a forced march he reached the capital before Mitsuhide could organize any defense, though he had time to attack Nobunaga's son at the Nijo palace and force him in despair to die by his own hand.

Knowing that his time of immunity would be short, Mitsuhide sent out several small parties to ambush and capture Hideyoshi. Almost they succeeded, for aware of the need of haste and abandoning his usual caution, Hideyoshi pushed on ahead of his troops. Suddenly finding himself surrounded by armed men, the Old Fox—as he had come affectionately to be known in place of Nobunaga's half contemptuous title, Monkey-Face—spurred his horse along a narrow footpath, such as lay through the rice fields for the convenience of the cultivators. These paths were so narrow that hardly could a horseman pass between the flooded miry paddies on either hand, and Hideyoshi was well aware that his enemies could follow him only one by one along such a route. Unfortunately for him the path led around a temple and ended abruptly on the edge of a deep river. Quick thinking, however, is the eminent characteristic of the fox mind. Dismounting as he approached the temple, he turned his horse about and, pricking him in the flank with his dagger, drove the maddened animal kicking and snorting upon the single file of pursuing soldiers, who were obliged to throw themselves into the water to escape the frightened animal. Before they could regain the dry land, cumbered as they were by their armour, Hideyoshi dashed into the temple, stripped himself of all his accoutrements, hid them behind a sliding door, and passed naked into the bath where a dozen priests were steaming themselves and the barber was shaving their heads. He submitted himself at once to the barber's ministrations, and when the soldiers arrived they failed to recognize this naked man whose head was covered with lather. Searching the temple in vain for their prey they concluded Hideyoshi had swum the river and escaped. By the time it took them to return to the highway, Hideyoshi's followers had arrived in force and made short work of the baffled assassins. Later, Hideyoshi, with all his hair sacrificed, rejoined his troops and continued his march toward the capital.

Mitsuhide, realizing he lacked strength to maintain himself in Kyoto, threw himself into the castle of Yodo and sent messengers summoning some of Nobunaga's enemies to assist him. Swiftly collecting a considerable force he attempted to give battle to Hideyoshi, who followed him relentlessly. His hastily gathered adherents, no match for the compact and disciplined troops of the Old Fox, were soon routed, and he himself was slain while endeavouring to escape. After the fashion of the time the soldiers cut off his head, bearing it in triumph to their commander, who upon his return to the city offered that bloody and sorrowful trophy of a deeply wronged man to the manes of the insolent despot who had thumped it with his war fan.

Apparently Hideyoshi did not yet feel himself strong enough to claim the succession of the lost leader. The nobles never forgot his humble origin, and they themselves were ambitious to take the dominant place. To settle the question a council was called, which plunged at once into a bitter and stormy session. Nobunaga had left two sons, the children of concubines, and about both rose parties of supporters to urge their separate claims. Hideyoshi, subtle and supple as always, waited until the two parties had come close to blows and then interposed with the suggestion that the real purpose of the meeting was not to argue in favour of special views but to perform a duty to the State. In his opinion, so he said, the only proper successor to Nobunaga was the grandson, the one descendant left in the legitimate line; and since this grandson was a child, a council could be appointed as guardian to administer the affairs of the Empire. Both parties combined to attack this idea, declaring that Hideyoshi was planning to seize the succession. Calmly Hideyoshi replied:

"You speak of my presumption in being the first to attack Mitsuhide and take upon myself the office of vengeance. I am one who, owing to the patronage of Nobunaga, has risen from obscurity, and I acted as I did because I thought it dangerous to allow Mitsuhide to gather strength. Even were I planning for what you are accusing me of, there are other members of the Council who could easily checkmate any plot of mine."

There seemed no answer to this, and it was finally agreed that the four leading generals of Nobunaga's party should form the Council, taking turns in administering the realm, each residing in Kyoto for a certain number of months.

Japanese histories relate that Shibata, the same noble who twenty years before had attempted to rouse Hideyoshi's anger by ordering him to give him massage, invited all the Council to a final banquet, saying with deliberate insolence to Hideyoshi: "You will remember that on one occasion you gave me an excellent treatment of massage. I wonder whether you still remember the art. I should like to have you try it again."

The other guests, gasping at this outrageous insult, expected an immediate clash of swords, but Hideyoshi with his usual placidity smilingly replied: "Not having practised such things since I last treated you I am not sure that I can do it to your satisfaction, but as the request comes from one so great I will try my best."

At once cheerfully tying back his sleeves, he began to knead Shibata's muscles. The latter, embarrassed at the failure of his attempt to find an excuse for slaughtering his opponent, pretended to fall asleep, whereupon Morimasa, annoyed at the failure to stir Hideyoshi's anger, exclaimed: "I am astonished that a man holding your position should lower himself to doing such work. I should rather have my body cut into little bits than submit to such ignominy."

To this Hideyoshi's bland comment was:

"Is it not recorded that the wife of the Emperor Shomu washed the body of a leper? Compared to that what I have done is a mere trifle. I am not only ready to do this but to go much further, and all for the sake of saving the house of Oda from ruin. Are we not surrounded by enemies? There is Mori in the West, who though he has made peace with us is not to be trusted; Hojo in the East; Uesugi in the North, and Chosokabe in the South. All these are rejoicing over the death of Nobunaga, and are waiting for an opportunity to recover their lost territory. What is it that restrains them if not the presence of such men as Shibata, Niwa, Ikeda, and my unworthy self? If we commence to quarrel among ourselves, our late master's cause will be irretrievably ruined. That is my reason for putting up with affronts."

He who laughs last, however, has the best amusement, as Shibata finally discovered. Hideyoshi returning to the capital undertook to gather up the burned bones of his late master in order to honour him with a magnificent funeral ceremony, in the meantime obtaining from the Emperor the title of Shosho, equivalent to Major General. All the nobles and followers of the late Shogun were summoned to the capital to participate in the funeral, for which the colourful and splendid preparations had been unstinted. Quietly at the same time Hideyoshi had placed his forces in such fashion as to command every avenue and point of vantage. At the moment when, according to usage, the nearest relative or representative of the dead should offer incense, the other generals pressed forward the two sons of Oda to claim this privilege, but suddenly in every direction Hideyoshi's troops showed themselves, and the Shosho came forward dressed like a court noble carrying the grandson in his arms and followed by the body of his armed guards. Waving the others back he said: "While the successor of Lord Oda has not yet paid homage to his spirit let none other approach." Overawed by the show of force the lords gave way angrily, permitting Hideyoshi to demonstrate to the great multitude that he himself represented the power of the late Shogun.

The malcontent barons, agreeing that for the moment they were not in a position to contest the assumption of control by their rival, withdrew to their own dominions, planning that in the spring they would undertake an expedition against him.

The winter was spent by the two opposing parties in strengthening their resources, Shibata endeavouring to call to his aid all the discontented victims of Nobunaga's attack on feudalism; Hideyoshi, in his usual diplomatic manner, tied to himself those who longed for an end to the weary chaos.

Shibata, at last thinking himself strong enough, broke into open hostilities and, being overwhelmed upon the field, fled to his castle and prepared for a siege. Hopeless of success, he refused to consider submitting himself to the man he had so often insulted. Hideyoshi promptly surrounded the stronghold and summoned it to surrender. Shibata kept his gates closed but called his few remaining followers about him and drinking a pledge to each gave them leave to seek their safety in any way they deemed best, declaring that he himself would never fall alive into the hands of "that Monkey-Face." His wife, a sister of Nobunaga, he also urged to surrender herself with her children, knowing that Hideyoshi would treat her with all respect. The children she sent to the conqueror's camp with the attendants, but for herself she decided to stay and die with her husband. It was typical of the Japanese age of chivalry that these two remained quietly together through the night composing verses and calmly talking of days gone by, and that in the early dawn they set fire to the castle and committed suicide.

Hideyoshi received the three daughters with all honour, treated them with generous respect, and years afterwards married the eldest, who became the mother of his only son. He also ordered that Shibata's head should not be brought to him, as was the gory custom of the time, but, issuing orders that an honourable funeral be given to his defeated enemy and the heroic wife, he turned swiftly about to meet those who were still unsubdued. Among these were a fortified monastery which had been allied to the famous Hiei-san, and also Tokugawa who had been drawn into the conspiracy against Hideyoshi.

Of the monastery he made short work, but facing Tokugawa he met the only serious defeat he ever experienced. Wisely he came to terms with the great Minamoto, assigning to him all that Northeast territory which Tokugawa coveted, and to which he withdrew. There Tokugawa built the city of Yedo, which afterwards became the nation's capital under the name of Tokio.

At last the little simian-faced wanderer of the fields had become the greatest power in Japan. Persuading the Emperor to bestow upon him the title of Kwampaku, Prime Minister, he appointed a Council of Five to assist in administering the affairs of state. Among the instructions which he drew up for the guidance of his Council the following characteristic paragraph occurs: "Things that are important should be settled in full conference; minor matters may be decided by a conference of two or three. Let nothing be unduly postponed. Receive no bribes. Let there be no partiality. Let there be no friends or enemies. Favour not the rich; despise not the poor."

All his state papers were equally sententious and significant. Caring little for personal riches—though he had grown wealthy with the spoils of those he had conquered—shortly after assuming the premiership he distributed among the assembled populace, from a platform erected in one of the open spaces of the capital, the greater part of all he had acquired. One of his historians describes him at this time:

"Thus did the 'Child of Destiny,' whose life we are considering, move on with calmness and self-possession to the zenith of his power;—self-denying, self-postponing, sacrificing everything to his aim. Never allowing incidents to govern policy; never hurried away from his course by an unlooked-for event; blending and concentrating everything so that it should conduce to the attainment of his one grand purpose, and refusing to admit that any obstacle was too formidable for his genius. 'There shall be no Alps,' was the motto of his life. Like Napoleon he had no real belief in Heaven's help, but—like the French hero—he was fond of attributing his success to supernatural sources for the sake of inspiring awe among his contemporaries. Though he had never studied the universe scientifically, he was as sure as the most advanced scientist of modern days that in his time no supernatural power interfered with the working of natural laws; that events and achievements which the vulgar attributed to Divine intervention were all explicable by, and traceable to, the operation of these laws; that his success depended on the nicety of combinations. His thorough knowledge of men enabled him to make the most accurate calculations as to the manner in which they would act under given circumstances, and to adjust his plans accordingly with astonishing skill and minuteness."

Hideyoshi was never a man of war. His real genius was that of the statesman. When the need could be met only by arms, he could be swift and violent; efficient in this as in other things. Better, however, he loved the brilliant and intricate intellectual combinations by which matters could be adjusted without bloodshed, for above all things he admired order and beauty and the graces of life. Tradition treasures a tale that reveals the real nature of the man:

After the last and greatest of his battles, having finally overcome all really serious opposition, he rode a short way from the field across which he had furiously and successfully led his forces. Dismounting from his wearied horse he sat himself down in his armour upon the grass, calmly announcing to his immediate attendants that he desired to divert himself by making a flower-arrangement. The astonished retainers explained that there were none of the appurtenances at hand for the practice of that delicate art. Hideyoshi, pointing out that a horse bucket was close at hand filled with water, directed them to take from his horse's mouth the bit, one ring of which he hung over the single handle of the bucket and then proceeded with his still bloody sword to cut off various grasses and wild flowers which bloomed near his seat. Using the dependent part of the bit as a flower-holder, he spent an hour in composing one of those subtle and delicate combinations of blossoms and foliage which his people have always so much loved. In memory of this, the most famous Flower-Arrangement School of Japan still uses a bamboo vase shaped like the one-handled horse bucket, and hangs upon this handle a flower-holder in the form of a horse's bit.

It is difficult to imagine such an episode in the life of a Western soldier, but the underlying purpose of the flower-arrangement is to purify and abstract the mind from all violence and material consideration, to calm the spirit and cleanse it of evil.

Hideyoshi explained that he knew he should have to judge and deal with those he had conquered, and that after he had spent so many violent hours in combat, he felt himself in no condition to be either kind or wise until he had entirely cooled the fury and disorder of his emotions by exercising this delicate and exquisite art.

Free at last from the domination of others, Hideyoshi turned his attention to the reconstruction of the Empire. His first effort was to finish the work of suppressing banditry. The roads which he set about rebuilding and rebridging, became safe for trade. This made possible the revival of agriculture, so depressed during the long period of disorder that no man could be certain of reaping the fruits of his labour. The farmers were given every encouragement, and order soon showed its effects in the increase of the national revenue.

While keeping the army trained and disciplined, Hideyoshi employed the soldiers in works of repair and reconstruction, knowing well that idleness breeds discontent and loose living. Lightening as far as possible the burden of taxation upon the farmers and traders, he repressed with a heavy hand any undue exactions by the nobles.

Like all great rulers he was fond of building. At Osaka he took over the ruined temple of the Hongwanji to reconstruct it in the form of a mighty castle, which he always regarded with special pride until it was wrecked by a great earthquake—a heavy blow to his delight in his magnificent creation. Shortly before his death he composed the last of his many poems lamenting this beloved work:

> "Like the dew I fall.
> Like the dew I will quickly vanish,

And even the fortress of Osaka
Becomes but a dream in a dream."

Not only did he concern himself with the restoration of trade, but his mind turned actively toward developing external commerce. This had been in the past valuable and extensive. Japanese ships had traded all through the Southern seas as far as Siam, and the traders had commanded vessels larger and swifter of sail than the caravels in which Columbus crossed the Atlantic. The long period of disorder had practically put an end to this merchant marine. Hideyoshi restored and improved the harbour of Nagasaki, dug a network of canals about Osaka to permit the ships to penetrate well into the land, affording them excellent wharfage for the discharge and loading of their cargoes. Nagoya also, at the head of Atsuta Bay, was developed, and its old-time trade restored.

Unluckily a new difficulty arose to interrupt the reorganization and readjustment of the Empire which Hideyoshi had set about with so much interest and activity.

The old rumour of the enormous riches of Japan which had set Columbus forth upon his great Western voyage also fired the cupidity of others. The Portuguese, envious of the Spanish wealth drawn from the Americas, cast an eye toward those fabled roofs of gold of which Marco Polo had brought report. Already Portugal was established on the coast of China at Macao, and, after the usual fashion, it was determined to send a small party of missionaries under Francis Xavier to spy out the land. This was in 1549, and Xavier, disappointed at discovering a country rent and impoverished by long disorders and finding that the golden roofs were a myth, quitted it almost immediately. Feeling nevertheless that such a situation might lend itself to a chance for propaganda of his faith, he shortly returned with a small body of Jesuits.

Landing in the South he devoted himself to an attempt to convert Otomo, one of the princes of the Satsuma clan. This great clan, always one of the most powerful in the Empire, its princes acknowledging but a shadowy vassalship to the Emperor, held themselves to all intents and purposes independent sovereigns. So distant was their province from the capital that little interference with their rule was ever attempted by the central power. Even Nobunaga had made no effort to bring them under his sway, and Hideyoshi diplomatically had followed that example.

The Jesuits found in the subjects of Otomo a ready soil for their teaching, which tended in the direction of the suggestion of complete independence. No violent wrench was needed to accept the new faith, for the Buddhist ceremonials had become, in the course of centuries, very similar to those developed in Christian lands. So many were the points of resemblance that the Jesuits were inclined to imagine some of their own faith must have preceded them, this similarity being due only to the tendency of human beings to develop independently along the same lines.

Otomo permitted himself to be baptized, receiving the title of Don Francis, by which he is known in the Jesuit annals. Following the orders of Prince Otomo, large numbers of his subjects embraced the new faith. Conversion might have progressed peacefully had not the Jesuits become aggressive, violently attacking the native priests and continually insulting them. Nobunaga, then in

THE DELIGHTFUL PARVENU 237

power, had so intense a dislike for the powerful Buddhist hierarchy that as plaintiffs they received small comfort at his hands. Seeing in the newcomers a possible weapon against his ecclesiastical enemies, he invited the Jesuits to the capital, gave them land, permitted them to build churches, and used them to humiliate the rulers of the great temples and monasteries.

Intoxicated with their success, the Jesuits believed that the conversion of the entire country was merely a matter of time and sent home such flourishing accounts of their progress that the Franciscans in Spain, always the enemies of the Order of Jesus, grew jealous and, with Spanish encouragement, sent their own missionaries to contest the field. Nobunaga thereupon, finding himself complicated by the disputes of the two orders and realizing he had but introduced a new element of unrest, withdrew his favour and forbade further propaganda, which thereafter could be conducted only under cover.

Meantime the persecution in the South under the christianized princes increased in violence and ferocity. Don Francis boasted of having burned three thousand Buddhist temples and convents, as well as having slaughtered their inmates. He sent, under Jesuit escort, an embassy to the Vatican to make his submission to the Pope, receiving in turn permission to hold himself entirely independent of the Japanese government.

Hideyoshi, too much occupied at first after Nobunaga's death to deal actively with the situation, was interested in the fact that the Jesuits were teaching the Southern princes how to manufacture gunpowder and cast cannon, and, through his emissaries, made himself familiar with the methods of constructing these new arms. His interest in commerce had also led him to see the value and superiority of the Spanish ships. He suggested to the Jesuits that they should teach his people the art of constructing these vessels, offering to purchase such of the Spanish ships as had reached the Japanese shore. The Jesuits continually promised but carefully refrained from carrying out his wishes. Determined, however, to learn their methods, Hideyoshi himself went to inspect a Spanish ship which had been wrecked on the coast. Closely examining it, he made many inquires as to the manners, laws, and history of Spain, asking the Spanish captain how it was that little countries like Spain and Portugal had been able to conquer such enormous territories in the two worlds. The reply reveals the real cause of the failure of Rome's enterprises in Japan. The captain indiscreetly explained: "We owe it to the missionaries. When Holy Fathers have conquered the hearts and souls of a barbarous people, our king easily takes possession of their bodies and their country."

Hideyoshi offered no comment but stored away the pregnant suggestion in his intelligent mind. Already he was disturbed that the Southern princes should be sending forth embassies without his authority, and that they should be developing a commerce with the Spanish and Portuguese colonies independent of all control by the central government. It is said, too, that having recently taken as one of his secondary wives Shibata's daughter, an ardent Buddhist and a beautiful and intelligent woman, to whom he was greatly devoted, he was much influenced by her in his slowly growing determination to bring the South under his control and put a stop to the persecution of the Emperor's Buddhist subjects.

THE DELIGHTFUL PARVENU 239

Don Francis declined to submit himself to any orders from Kyoto. Therefore the Kwampaku decided to take the field to enforce his authority; but the Satsuma were famous warriors, the terrain was difficult, and for some time the event was in doubt. The Jesuits always insisted that their final defeat was due to the treachery of the priests of the Shin sect, who persuaded such part of the troops as were Buddhists to break, before the last battle, the points from their arrows and secretly withdraw the balls from their muskets.

Once Hideyoshi felt himself supreme he put out his first edict against the Jesuits:

"We are informed by the Lords of our Council that certain missionaries of strange countries have established themselves in our land to preach a religion contrary to our laws and our institutions. In their blindness they have destroyed the shrines and temples of Buddha. These acts merit severe punishment, but in our clemency, we only command them to leave Japan within 20 days, under pain of death. During that time it is not allowed to molest them; but if, after this delay, they are still here it will be our will and our pleasure to arrest them and torture them as for a crime of high treason. As for the Portuguese merchants, we allow them to stay and to traffic in our sea harbours, until further notice; but it is strongly forbidden to bring with them monks or nuns from their country. In case of contravention all their ships and goods will be confiscated."

Hideyoshi, unlike Nobunaga, was always indulgent to his enemies once they submitted. He contented himself with changing some of the rebellious princes from one fief to another in order to break their hold upon their followers. He concentrated all commerce into the Bay of Nagasaki and, in order that the state might control it, forbade its being carried on elsewhere. He also left in the conquered provinces two representatives to see that his rules against persecution should be obeyed. The Jesuits assembled their converts in a conference where it was decided that, though they had by force to obey the rule of Hideyoshi, this ordinance of his against persecution was a direct contravention of Divine Law. Hideyoshi, so long as they did obey, was content and allowed the Jesuits to remain as long as they refrained from violence against Buddhism.

The country being at peace and its condition rapidly improving under his wise administration, he turned his attention to restoring the dignity of the Emperor, a dignity which had been so ignored and abased during the long period of anarchy that when the Jesuits wrote reports to their superiors they had no idea of his existence, supposing Nobunaga and Hideyoshi the real sovereigns of the country.

The restoration of the Emperor's palaces was completed. For one of the Imperial princes there was built on the Western bank of the river Katsura a palace still admired as one of the most beautiful of the royal residences. At Hideyoshi's command this was surrounded with gardens laid out by Kobori-Enshu, a famous master of gardening and tea ceremony. Before beginning his work Enshu persuaded Hideyoshi to agree to three conditions: never to come to inspect the work before completion, never to look at the expense of the labour, and never to fix a time for the work to be completed, to all of which conditions the Kwampaku smilingly

THE DELIGHTFUL PARVENU 241

agreed. Within the limits of these ninety acres Enshu expended every resource of his genius, planning it so well that the centuries have only added to its suggestive and intricate charm, and Hideyoshi during his lifetime visited it constantly with a never failing delight.

At Momo-Yama, or Peach Hill, so named for the forest of flowering peach trees which grew on its slopes, Hideyoshi built on the crest of the eminence his own home. This he named the Peace Palace in honour of the tranquillity he had at last succeeded in imposing upon his war-torn country. It looked down upon a lovely landscape rosy with blossoms in the spring, tapestried with glowing tints of maples in the autumn, and commanding a superb view across the historic Yamato Plain and over the winding Uji river. Upon this was spent six million yen—an enormous sum at that time—and upon it was lavished every beauty of which the skilled hands of the Japanese artists and artificers were capable. Hideyoshi, a man of the people, less reserved in his tastes than the nobles, heretofore the patrons of art, filled this famous palace full of pomp and colour. The luxury of its decoration was sumptuous, its sculpture of the greatest richness.

The Kwampaku's dream of splendour was created for him by the famous artists Motonobu and Yeitoko. Abandoning the simplicity and tender shades which the Japanese of the Ashikaga period had so loved, they experimented with suggestions gathered from the more modern schools of painting in China and produced scenes crowded with gorgeous figures and jewelled hues. Yeitoko, breaking away from the old method of laying on colour, obtained his effects by using dark tones and a glaze of transparent tone upon this dark base, thus achieving a tempera much like the European painting in oil. By this means he obtained for his massed pigments an effect of great power and brilliancy. His greens deepened into olive, his blue into lapis-lazuli, his orange and reds into carmine and cochineal; the whole forming a glowing mosaic. The famous Hidari Jingoro, the left-handed carver, added wonderful lace-like sculptures of wood, which also glowed with gold and a thousand colours.

Among the treasures with which the great Parvenu adorned his home were a hundred sets of those folding screens with which the Japanese reduce and enlarge the size of a chamber according to their will. Decorated by Yeitoko, Motonobu, and other artists of renown, these screens were vivid with colourful processions and battle scenes, with landscapes, flowers, and birds, usually upon a golden background. Hideyoshi used these screens for the first time to line the road by which the Emperor made his progress from his palace in Kyoto to visit the "Little Monkey-Face" of the past, now the ruler, in fact, of the whole Empire. It was a glowing moment for the Old Fox, for the Mikado still remained—despite all the humiliation the Imperial line had suffered—the revered and mysterious figure toward which every Japanese heart turned with tenderness and respect as the centre and source of the race, the living proof of their descent from the Gods. Not since the time of Yoshimitsu had the sovereign visited one of his subjects, and few were acquainted with the proper ceremonies to be observed. Many were the investigations and searchings of old records to insure that all should be done after the ancient fashion and no jot of the elaborate traditional ceremonies neglected. The preparations for the pageant occupied three months. When all was ready Hideyoshi with the officers of the State waited at the door of his Palace to accompany his Imperial master.

The month was April; Momo-Yama was flushed with the glories of the peach and cherry blossoms. The Emperor had with him the Empress and the whole royal family, beside a multitude of attendants. The splendid screens walled the way to hide the sacred Sovereigns from the gaze of the populace. Behind them the nobles in their glittering armour stood at attention with their troops. The Emperor made the progress alone in his great lacquered car drawn by black bulls from the Imperial herd. The other royalties were borne in gilded and tasseled palanquins upon the shoulders of white-clad bearers; while the vast multitude of the populace knelt along the whole route with bowed heads, as if a God passed by. To them indeed this was the direct descendant of Amaterasu, Goddess of the Sun. No such spectacle had been seen in Japan for a hundred years.

The Emperor entered first into Hideyoshi's house, as if it were his own, remaining for five days, and being entertained with every device of luxury and beauty which the Prime Minister could command. At the end of the visit he was escorted home, laden with gifts from the Kwampaku and all the chief nobles of the land, whom Hideyoshi had assembled to swear allegiance to the Emperor and his Prime Minister. They agreed that anyone breaking this oath should be punished by his fellow barons and, after the manner of the time, they pronounced curses on the perjured one in the name of all the gods of the sixty-six provinces of the Empire.

The little ragamuffin runner of the roads had attained at last the supreme glory possible to a Japanese subject. He had given peace and order to the realm and had restored to the sacred head of the race all his lost dignity and splendour.

During these years of Hideyoshi's slow rise to power he had not been wanting in filial piety. A man so typical of the ideal of the Japanese would be in full accord with their conception of life as an unending cord, upon which the individual was as a bead strung for the moment. After his first successes he had visited his mother and made arrangement for her comfort and protection. As he rose to high position he more and more surrounded her with honour and agreeable conditions.

Being for long without offspring of his own he had adopted his sister's sons, encouraging them in the hope of becoming heirs to his wealth and power. His family, as is invariably the case with relations of successful adventurers, accustomed themselves to living in almost royal state, but he never permitted either them or himself to forget their humble origin. In public speeches and state papers he cheerfully referred to his being a parvenu. Being stamped, however, with the civilization of his race, all his tastes were for refinement and beauty. He practised assiduously the art of flower arrangement and of the tea ceremony. He covered with honours and constantly employed the famous Tea Master Rikyu, to lay out his gardens and teach him those four cardinal virtues supposed to be inculcated by the Tea Cult: urbanity, courtesy, purity, and imperturbability. "The tendency of the Cult," says Brinkley, "is to combine aesthetic eclecticism of the most fastidious nature with the severest canons of simplicity and austerity."

Even in camp he frequently relaxed himself with this diversion. In the old book, *Toyo-Kagami*, written by one of his associates, it is recorded:

"The temple of Hakosaki, facing the western sea, augustly guards the shore against any invasion of foreigners. The pine woods extend as far as Kakata along the clean sandy beach, where the breeze among the branches harmonized with the sound of the waves. It was the latter part of June (by the old calendar), so toward evening, after a hot day, they strolled to the pine woods, looked out upon the waters, and imagined China was not so far away.

"Hideyoshi told the attendants to compose poems on the subject of 'coolness,' and he himself composed several poems.

"Far into the evening we enjoyed ourselves, talking and drinking."

Three poems the writer of *Toyo-Kagami* includes in the story, verses in the style known as *uta*, composed of thirty-one syllables. The first person writes the first three lines and his companion concludes it with the last two; the fashion of the time was to weave a portion of this first verse into the second one, or third, if the diversion continued.

The Japanese poem is difficult to render into English. Its method is to use a sort of shorthand of language in which the idea is only suggested to the intelligence. This presupposes, in the most flattering manner, that the reader's perception is so exquisite, that a mere suggestive touch will arouse in his mind an answer of delicate and multiple reverberations drawn from all his stored sentiments, longings, and memories. To us, with our more verbose and defined modes of expression, these verses seem but mere broken fragments of vague sensibility. But to the Japanese his morsels of prosody are like grains of musk and myrrh perfuming the whole mind with a pervasive fragrance of emotion.

The first of these poems may be phrased as follows:

"On the bay softly moves the evening breeze.
Cool, cool, sound the long, languid waves."

Already Hideyoshi was considering an expedition to China, and his companions, aware of this, pick up the word which was the keynote of the preceding poem and, perhaps half in warning, reply:

"Will it be so cool as this in the land of Cathay?
Fain would I ask of the wind passing over the waves of the Western Sea."

The diplomatic Kwampaku administers in his answering verse a delicate snub:

"I have become oblivious to the thought of heat and of having to go home.
Only I think of the soft beauty of the twilight sea."

Rikyu, the Tea Master, sometimes came to camp or joined Hideyoshi in country excursions, and on these occasions the friends amused themselves by improvising little ceremonial tea rooms among the pine trees. There still remains at Hakosaki a pine tree called "Rikyu Kama Kake Matsu" (Rikyu's Kettle-Hanging Pine), to a branch of which the Tea Master hung his kettle. Making use of dried pine needles for fuel, he boiled water and offered tea to Hideyoshi. This event is chronicled in the book of *Toyo-Kagami*, which says:

"Kwampaku Dono gave a party on the shore; there was drinking of saké, singing of *utai* (classical songs in *No* plays), and composing of poems. Night came on and before we parted he ordered us to write a poem upon the pine trees. Regretting to part with them I said:

THE DELIGHTFUL PARVENU 247

Matsubara ni tomari karasu no koe o sai
Urayama re nuru kaeru so no michi.

(The voices of the crows settling for the night in those perfumed branches fill me with envy and yearning.)"

Apparently Hideyoshi never affected with his companions the haughtiness of the beggar on horseback. The intimate records of his friends picture him always gay and witty, full of the good fellowship of his earlier and humbler days. He could, when opposed, be angry and sometimes cruel. These were, however, but passing flashes of temper. An amusing story is told of a report made to him of a soldier's criticism of his actions during one of his campaigns. Infuriated, the Kwampaku sent for the soldier's immediate superior and ordered that the man should be crucified. It may be mentioned in passing that the Japanese crucifixion was not a lingering torture. The victim was simply tied to a cross-piece of wood and immediately slain by having his heart pierced with a lance. The dread of this punishment was based on the feeling that it was an especially ignominious form of death. The officer to whom the order was given, reluctant to inflict this punishment, said he knew the man to be an admirable soldier whose one fault was his outspokenness. Departing slowly to carry out his unhappy mission he had not gone far, before Hideyoshi recalled him to say:

"After all this man did not make his criticisms to my face and you may content yourself with simple decapitation."

Again before he had passed out of sight, the officer was summoned to the General's presence. Hideyoshi said he had been considering the argument the officer had urged, that the condemned man was an admirable soldier, and had concluded to allow him to commit suicide—considered by all Japanese as a most honourable form of meeting the end. A third time the officer was arrested in his progress, and Hideyoshi said a little shamefacedly:

"I have been thinking over these criticisms, and considered the man's ignorance of my real plans. The actions of which he disapproves he was unaware were meant to give a false impression to the enemy. I realize that he was not much to blame. Indeed I am inclined to think he must be a person of real abilities since he was so interested in our success that he resented the movements which he considered likely to delay it. You had better send for him and ask him to join my immediate suite, and I think very shortly, when he sees what is achieved by the things he disapproved of, he will be the first to regret what he has said."

Taken into Hideyoshi's attendance this soldier became his fanatically devoted admirer.

Illustrative of the hearty geniality and hospitality of the little parvenu was his famous tea party at Kitano, near Kyoto. Unlike the extremely private and reserved diversions loved by the aristocracy, Hideyoshi determined upon a really democratic garden party to celebrate the solidifying of the Empire. To make merry with people and to share his pleasures with everyone was his delight. He ordered the following notice to be written on tablets and distributed throughout the neighbourhood:

"On the first day of the coming October, at the pine fields of Jitano, will be held a Tea Ceremony.

THE DELIGHTFUL PARVENU

Without distinction of rich or poor, high and low in rank, all are invited to partake of this pleasure. Gorgeousness is forbidden and simplicity is the rule in the performance. Various tea things of my collection will be exhibited there for everyone desirous to see. Anyone who has taste for the Tea Ceremony, no matter what he is—Samurai, citizen, common farmer, or servant—is welcome to the party."

Probably this famous tea party was the happiest moment of Hideyoshi's career, giving him a deeper satisfaction than even the visit of the Emperor. For fundamentally, in spite of the dizzy eminence to which he had risen, he remained essentially a man of the people, loving jollity and feasting and the warm heartiness of good fellowship. Among the nobles and in the Court he remained always the new-comer, the parvenu, but to the multitude he was a hero, the saviour of the land, one of their own, equal to the greatest.

Enormous crowds of all classes accepted his invitation, for people of rank thought it wise to attend, and all the smaller folk were flattered at being entertained by the great man. Those unfamiliar with the Japanese people before they began to adapt themselves to the manners of the West, would imagine that such a mixed party might degenerate into vulgarity, unaware how innate were the social graces of the Island people in every order of society, how deeply ingrained was the code of manners, and how instinctively the Japanese loved fineness of behaviour. Even so late as the coronation of the Emperor Hirohito in 1915 more than a million people disported themselves on the night of the Emperor's crowning in Kyoto as lightly and gaily, as beautifully and gracefully as a revel of butterflies, without one incident of violence or vulgarity, and with a thousand beautiful fantasies. So Hideyoshi's garden party was a charming episode.

The time being October, when the maples and chrysanthemums were in their glory, nature had furnished a deep-tinted and perfumed tapestry as a background for the colourful costuming of the people who moved amid all this beauty. The picture must have been as rich as those upon the splendid screens which lined the Emperor's path on his route to Fushimi. There were pageants, such as the Japanese so well know how to improvise into loveliness with the slenderest material. Everywhere tea ceremonies, and flower arrangements, verse making, songs and dances. As night came down innumerable tinted lanterns, swung from long bamboos, moved like floating bubbles of light—streams of faintly coloured luminosity that met and wound and flowed, like shimmering rivers in fairyland.

Not always did the Prime Minister divert himself on so large a scale. He retired at times, as do all his people, from the world of affairs to bathe his spirit in the cool silences and reticences of nature. One of his favourite retreats was the old Buddhist temple which looked down into the glen of Takao Yama. Here at the season when autumn flushes the maples with rich dim hues of purple and smouldering crimsons, he hid himself for a day or two from the cares of state, loving to watch the wreaths of mist float through the gorge like drifting smoke above those fires of glowing foliage, and to find, in this noiseless lapse of the hours, refreshment and peace.

One of his refuges from the stress of his strenuous life was the Daigoji, a temple in the Uji district, southeast of Kyoto. This temple had been founded in the middle of the ninth century by the celebrated priest Rigen-Daishi, a royal prince. Successive emperors had lavished upon it gifts and adorned it with priceless paintings and carvings.

At one time, in the height of its glory, there were twenty-seven temples in upper Daigoji, sixty-five in the lower, including an imposing five-storied pagoda. Like so many of the great Buddhist establishments, this, too, had fallen into decay and disrepair during the long century of anarchy and under Nobunaga's persecution of the Buddhist faith, but what remained was still a treasure of beauty. Hideyoshi, with his joy in all things fine and noble, spent largely in repairing and adorning what remained. The wall pictures and sliding screens were painted by Kano-Sanraku with that gracious simplicity characteristic of the best periods of the national art. Its shrine contained the most beautiful image of Buddha in all Japan—an image free from the heaviness which, in so many cases, is repugnant to the Western eye, a convention inherited from the early Buddhist images brought from China and Korea. The golden head and limbs of this lovely statue are as supple and graceful as those of an Indian God. The eyes, under their half-closed lids, made of some nacreous material, shine with a living light, and the delicate face has some quality of supernatural divinity which stirs in the beholder a deep tenderness of emotion. This is especially true when the shoji are drawn back, and from the garden pool near by green reflections from the giant trees light the shining countenance with a strange ghostly radiance. Hideyoshi, with the aid of Rikyu, restored the delicious garden into a place of verdant silence and peace, lit by the mirrors of its small still lakes whose glaucous reflections tinge all its shadowy ways. It was here that the weary statesman came whenever his soul was deeply disturbed; it was here in this quietude, face to face with the Buddha—that noble aureate vision of repose and remoteness from all the fret and fever of living—he found again his courage and self-control.

At Daigoji, a few months before his death in his sixty-third year, he gave the last of his famous Tea Drinkings, known in history as Hideyoshi's "Daigo-no-hana-no-en," meaning "Hideyoshi's Flower Banquet at Daigo." To celebrate this spring festival he ordered early in the year that seven hundred large cherry trees should be planted from the entrance of the temple on both sides of the road all the way to Yari Yama, so that when he was ready to welcome his guests they came to him through an archway of rosy boughs meeting over their heads.

Another of his special pleasures was to go some night between the tenth and the fifteenth of June to see the "Battle of the Fire Flies." Here through all the centuries a strange phenomenon has taken place. Untold myriads of these flitting, shining creatures assemble for a few nights every year for their nuptial mating. Floating in his own barge down the small swift river, he could see the wooded hills rising steeply from either side in the darkness, quivering from the water's edge to their peaks with innumerable pale sparks like trembling diadems of jewels. Back and forth across the water streamed comet-like trails of the luminous insects, wheeling and circling against the velvety background of the night or gathering into knots to drop and break upon the surface of the current and drift glittering away, so that the Japanese speak of the river at this

THE DELIGHTFUL PARVENU 253

time as the "River of Heaven," or the "Milky Way."

Still another of his joys was the "Lotus Breakfast" of July. Early in the grey dawn he went with a few companions to a platform raised in the centre of a wide, shallow, marshy lake. At this season its entire surface is covered with the jade-coloured leaves and faintly rosy blossoms of the lotus. With the first touch of the level rays of the rising sun, the lotus opens its delicate beauty to the day and emits its intoxicating perfume. Here little Monkey-Face, who had smelled of human blood on so many a stricken field, loved to sit in the freshness of the dawn and feed upon these pure and sacred fragrances.

The whole year at Kyoto is marked by flower festivals: the plum blossoms in February, the peach in March, the cherry in April; and May is crowded with the azaleas, peonies, wisteria, and kerria. June brings the iris, July the lotus, August the lilies, September and October the chrysanthemums, and November the maples, and even December and January have their flowers of the snow. Every one of them is celebrated by special festivals and "flower-viewings." Each and every one this typical Japanese loved and snatched time from his duties to taste.

Not only a lover of all the charms of nature, he also delighted in the work of man's hands, when that work was beautiful. The painters found in him a magnificent patron; the builders and architects were given commissions to express all their proudest and loveliest ideas in the erection and restoration of castles, palaces, and temples.

Japan has perhaps the most remarkable tradition of sculpture of all the peoples of whom there is record. From the earliest introduction of Buddhism in the beginning of the seventh century—which produced a sudden and splendid development of the plastic art—an unbroken series of masterpieces in wood and in bronze has proved Japanese eminence in this form of art, not alone on the grand scale, but with equal skill and genius in the most miniature forms. Other countries, such as Greece, Egypt, and Italy, have had their great periods which exhausted the impulse of the producers, and which decayed eventually into weakness and banality. But Japan's sculptural capacity seems never to have exhausted itself. For twelve centuries she has constantly produced, in endlessly varying development, an unbroken series of noble creations.

So rich and profuse has been her production that despite those two great enemies of her art, fire and seismic disturbances, the student may trace even yet her whole splendid plastic history through a line of continuously noble achievements. Such an example alone is the famous wooden statue of the Chinese priest, Ganjin, who, come to teach Buddhism, was shipwrecked on his way, and, though rescued, was blinded by the salt water. He founded a temple at Nara, and there his statue is kept in a sealed godown forbidden even to the head priest, who cannot show it without written instructions from the governor of Nara, so valuable is it considered. One well known critic writes rapturously of the image:

"This supreme masterpiece is preserved in a niche enclosed by curtains of old silk. When they are drawn aside, the spectator is face to face with a startling apparition. He is seated with clasped hands, his thumbs pressed together; his robe is crossed in two large black and red folds upon his breast; his shaven forehead is deeply wrinkled, and under the closed eyelids the pupils are suggested with extraordinary vivacity and sensibility. He was blind and the veiled eyes are evidently those of a being whose whole life was internal, and who, in the obscurity of this mysterious retreat, placidly prolonged the unfathomable dream. There is a strange calm on the face, which no earthly emotion seems ever to have ruffled. One has a sense of uneasy shame at having laid a profane hand upon the curtains of the shrine, disturbing by an indiscreet curiosity the touching and eternal reverie of the sage."

Though the period of Hideyoshi's rule at Kyoto was not the most eminent in the Island history of sculpture, still he vigourously encouraged all the best plastic artists of his day, especially those whose carvings added to the beauty and grace of his buildings, and he gave generous patronage to the weavers and dyers whose textiles have ranked but little lower in beauty, imagination, and splendour than the work of the great painters. The lacquerers, too, found in him an intelligent patron, as well as the great makers of the famous bells whose musical murmurs sweetened with their golden resonance all the echoes of Kyoto from its thousand temples. Especially he loved and encouraged the famous swordsmiths whose blades are still the treasures of the modern collector.

Hideyoshi restored and nourished all the abounding art impulses of the country—impulses which had suffered so lamentably during the period of disorder—so that when the long era of peace under the Tokugawas supervened, the arts were found vigourously flourishing and ready to flower forth in that magnificent period of calm and political order which continued for more than two and a half centuries, during which period Japan never heard the bruit of war.

So multitudinous were these activities of the Taiko (as Hideyoshi was now known) in the cultivation of beauty that the ordinary individual might have been excused had he neglected somewhat the affairs of state; Hideyoshi was far, however, from being an ordinary person. A French writer says of him:

"By an extraordinary mixture of force, of ruse, of patience and persuasion, he substituted for anarchy an order durable and pleasant, and centralized in his own hand the government of a pacified country. He thoroughly organized the army, and administration, developed agriculture, industry and commerce. He was the creator of the first Japanese navy. He encouraged especially commercial adventures by sea, which carried Japanese commerce through all the southern islands of Malaysia and as far as Siam. At home, meanwhile, he intensively exploited the native mines, and drew from them enormous resources."

The same author says of Hideyoshi's beloved and regretted castle of Osaka: "It was one of the most colossal works of which man has dreamed; its Cyclopean remains even yet arouse astonishment."

Very naturally Hideyoshi hoped to found a dynasty to succeed him. That is an immortality for which all great men long, not alone, as cynics suggest, through egotism, but for the reason that one who has created is loath to see his labours wasted

THE DELIGHTFUL PARVENU

and his work destroyed. Because of this desire, as his wife Yae had given him no children, he took—with the consent of that patient and devoted helpmate—five concubines. According to the laws and customs of the land this was no impropriety. Since the lack of lineal successors in any household was considered the worst of misfortunes, the wife who could not continue the line accepted patiently that these concubines should be taken into the household, where they were treated with respect and dignity and were considered legitimate members of the family. One of these "associate wives" finally gave him a son upon whom Hideyoshi doted and in whom he placed all his hopes, but the child's career was short, and the Taiko was for a time after the son's death overwhelmed with despair.

In the numerous histories of Hideyoshi's life written by the Japanese, there are a mass of legends and tales concerning him, many of which seem to have no foundation in fact and to be but the irresponsible gossip which invariably gathers about the lives and doings of famous folk. While he has remained always a national hero, some of these historians have not hesitated to attribute to him many lamentable qualities, many vulgar tendencies, and outbursts of unpardonable cruelty. The most distressing of these stories is that in his later years he became attracted by the daughter of the Tea Master, Rikyu, and demanded that she enter his household as one of his concubines. According to this tale Rikyu greatly objected to what, in spite of custom, he considered an ignominy, offering as excuse that she was a young widow, devoted to her husband's memory and unwilling to form any new connection. Hideyoshi, it is said, fell into a fury at this denial and made threats that he would seize the young woman by force. When his emissaries arrived they found that the Tea Artist and his proud daughter had committed suicide to escape the fate intended for her. There seems to be no proof of the truth of this other than mere tradition, and liberty may be taken to doubt it, considering Hideyoshi's character and his long affectionate intimacy with Rikyu. What seems undeniable is that unlimited power gradually affected the cool judgment and discretion of the little parvenu, as is evident in his illusion that it was possible to conquer Korea and China, and combine three empires into one under the Japanese crown.

Korea, ever since its conquest by the Empress Jingo, had been considered by the Island Emperor as a tributary state. Tribute had certainly been paid by the Koreans for many centuries. This revenue from the continent had fallen into abeyance during the period of disorder, the Koreans being well aware that a power so shattered by dissension was unable to enforce its claims. Hideyoshi not only determined that tribute should be resumed, but was made anxious for the safety of his own country by rumours that China proposed to extend complete sovereignty over Korea and said openly that having once accomplished this, the conquest of the Japanese Islands might follow.

The Land of Morning Calm has ever been as sensitive a question to the Island Empire as Belgium has been to England. The narrowness of the seas at that point continually made it a matter of concern that no inimical force should be established on the Korean coast. Hideyoshi was ignorant of the enormous extent and the latent power of China, and to his mind it may have seemed possible, once having seized Korea, to make himself master of the

THE DELIGHTFUL PARVENU 259

Chinese people. He sent a haughty message to the Korean court demanding that the long overdue payments should be resumed, and when his delegates returned with unsatisfactory and shuffling answers he set about active preparation for enforcing his claim. Some historians suggest that this expedition really arose out of the need for finding occupation for his restless nobles, so long accustomed to warfare that tranquillity overwhelmed them with ennui and gave opportunity for dangerous conspiracies. It was not the first nor the only time a ruler has considered a foreign war a lesser risk than discontent at home.

Enormous preparations for the expedition were set on foot. The exact number of troops transported across the Straits is unknown; certainly not less than a hundred and eighty thousand men, and the movement by sea of so large a force casts an interesting light upon the amount of Japanese shipping at that date. Each province was requisitioned for a certain number of troops led by their own overlords. For months the shores of Japan heard the trampling of horses and clang of armour and saw the fluttering of banners and standards emblazoned with the flower crests of great and petty chieftains. Unfortunately the clattering gourd standard was not at their head. Had Hideyoshi led the expedition in person, the result might have been far more decisive. His genius for war was unquestionable, the proof of which is that the plan of campaign, which he personally devised, was almost exactly the same as that used by the Japanese commanders in 1900 in their successful invasion of Korea, when they met, and defeated, the great power of Russia.

Several considerations persuaded him to trust the enterprise to others. His Council felt that his absence from the islands—politically still heaving with the ground swell of the long storm of nearly a century's confusion—was too great a risk to incur. No one could foresee what might arise were the magic of his name and personality removed to a distance which, in that age of slow transportation, seemed very great. He was growing an old man. Three hundred years ago an individual in the late fifties had generally outlived the bulk of his contemporaries and was looked upon as an aged person, so much shorter was the average span of human life at that era. Another and still more personal reason for his regretful decision to delegate the command was the approaching end of his mother, for whom he had a passionate affection. She entreated him not to leave her, reminding him of his long years of absence during his youth and of the many terrors and anxieties she had suffered on his account. The combination of all these considerations induced him, much against his will and judgment, to trust the invasion to others. The result justified his doubts.

Had he been present, his relentless firmness and impetuosity, combined with his quick-witted method of seizing upon political opportunity, would have made impossible the long delays in the completion of the campaign. The Koreans, never a very warlike people, were unable to offer a really vigourous opposition. As in all wars of the epoch, a well defined commissariat was unknown. An invading army lived upon the land of the invaded, a clumsy and wasteful mode of sustaining troops. Those whose land is attacked naturally fall into great confusion and cease to produce an adequate amount to sustain the enormous inflow of consumers, and waste and burn their crops rather than that they should fall into the hands of the invader. Drastic measures for collection only increase the disorder and unite the people in their opposition.

The Korean court upon news of the invasion had sent embassies to China to beg for assistance. While this was freely promised and many lofty and orotund edicts were emitted, as usual in China practical aid was slow to arrive and never proved of any considerable efficiency. The Japanese troops found no great difficulty in dealing with the Chinese forces. The real enemy was within the ranks of the Japanese themselves. Jealousies among the leaders made it difficult to wield effectively that huge weapon which Hideyoshi had provided. One of the commanders, the Christian convert known as Don Austin, was said to have carried his jealousy so far as to have deliberately on occasions taken measures to render his associates' strategy futile.

One story told of this campaign shows how much the expedition lost through the absence of the Taiko. He had made his headquarters at Nagoya, where he drilled recruits and endeavoured to meet the constant pleas for supplies. His commanders complained that the troops were starving in the devastated country. Hideyoshi by tremendous effort got together three million kokus of rice and managed to assemble sufficient shipping to land it at the ports of Korea. The envoy from the army protested that too many men would have to be detached from the troops to guard these prodigious stores.

"Don't guard it," said Hideyoshi. "Let it fare as it will."

"If we do that, the Koreans will capture it all," objected the envoy and was astounded when the Taiko asked:

"Well, is it not what we want?"

"But if we lose our provisions we shall be in trouble."

"It is a case of three million kokus. Such a quantity of rice is not to be carried off in a hurry, nor can it be consumed in a short time."

"But the Koreans will carry it inland."

To this Hideyoshi replied sharply:

"Nothing could suit us better. You have been complaining of the lack of land transportation. To get the enemy to do your transport for you is a good idea. They can't consume any great amount of it on the road, and as you need it you can fall upon them, and take it away. By adopting this plan our troops will always find provisions waiting for them as they advance into the country."

For lack of this ingenious and original thinking the expedition suffered.

The campaign dragged on for several years, and finally the Koreans sued for peace. It is not quite certain whether the Koreans or the Chinese suggested the offer which was laid before the Japanese chiefs. It may have been merely one of those supple and skillful feats of Chinese diplomacy by which it has so often hoodwinked its opponents. The Japanese conquerors were led to believe that a sealed letter to Hideyoshi from the Chinese Emperor contained an acceptance of Japanese suzerainty. Accompanied by the Korean ambassadors and the Chinese envoy bearing the letter and what he claimed were the Chinese royal robes and imperial insignia, the Japanese forces reëmbarked for their own country leaving some garrisons behind them.

Hideyoshi was intoxicated with this news, brought to him by an avant-courier. At last it seemed his career was to be crowned by a complete and dazzling triumph. He saw himself the ruler of the greater part of Asia and believed that he, the little wanderer of the road, had brought his country to the pinnacle of power. Only his ignorance of the real nature and extent of the Chinese Empire, the disintegration wrought by his years, and the heady draughts of continued success could have so bemused the erstwhile shrewd, clear-eyed realist.

A magnificent festival was prepared at the capital to welcome the returning troops and to accept the submission of Korea and China. All the nobles were assembled, before whom Hideyoshi appeared clad in the robes brought by the Chinese envoy. The submission of Korea was accepted. A priest was commanded to break the seals of the Chinese letter and read its contents. Astonishment and rage were universal when, after all the honourific titles of the Chinese Emperor were recited, the document continued in these words:

"We therefore specially invest you with the dignity of Japan, and to that intent issue this our commission. Treasure it up carefully. Over the sea we send you a crown and a robe, so that you may follow our ancient custom as respects dress. Faithfully defend the frontier of the Empire; let it be your study to act worthily of your position as our minister; practise moderation and self restraint; cherish gratitude for the Imperial favour so bountifully bestowed upon you: change not your fidelity; be humbly guided by our admonitions; continue always to follow our instructions. Respect this!"

The Taiko, dashed by this bland insolence from the lofty position he supposed himself to have reached, became inebriated with fury. He flung the Chinese diadem to the ground, tore off the robes, and snatching the document from the hand of the startled priest, rent it into fragments crying: "Had I desired to become the Emperor of this country, I needed no permission from a Chinese barbarian."

The meeting broke up in disorder. The Chinese envoy was ordered to leave within the hour and tell his master that Hideyoshi would answer his impertinence with arms in his hands.

At once he set about collecting men for another expedition, and this time he determined to lead it himself, convinced that only his own presence would insure the real punishment of China. Possibly this rage and disappointment affected his health. Very possibly the public rebuff he had received had somewhat shaken the blind confidence with which his hitherto unbroken success had inspired his followers. All his advisers urged him to be content with the submission of Korea to his demands, and those who had led the previous expedition had indubitably gathered some sense of how vast an undertaking the conquest of China would mean. Refusing to listen to any counsels of circumspection, he threw himself with all his youthful energy and audacity into the preparation for his revenge. The cautious, cool-witted adventurer was changed by humiliation into a rash and angry old man.

The expedition finally sailed in the month of February, 1597. The Koreans, having had their lesson, offered little open opposition, but the Japanese, though they met and defeated the Chinese army, found themselves always further from the source of supplies, with a hostile country in their rear. At the final moment Hideyoshi's health had made it impossible for him to cross the seas, and his last days were darkened by the growing sense that he had done a foolish thing in sacrificing the lives of his countrymen merely to vindicate his own pride.

The one light upon his darkening path was the birth of a son, the child of Shibata's daughter. Again his hopes rose of founding a house and passing on to one of his own blood the rule of the Empire which he had rescued and organized.

Looking about him for someone he felt he could trust to guard the infant after he had passed away, he could see but one pair of hands strong enough to control the realm and to impose the child as his successor. Ieyasu Tokugawa he had always feared and respected, perhaps a little envied, and not wholly understood. The cold poise and long patience of that magnificent aristocrat were always somewhat daunting to the plebeian. Always he felt that had Tokugawa cared to try conclusions with him the outcome would have been highly doubtful. He knew him to be a warrior with gifts as great as his own, a far-seeing statesman and able administrator, and he suspected him of a steady ambition. Yet time and again when the aristocrat by taking sides against him might easily have reduced him to extremity, Tokugawa had held his hand and, standing aside, had watched his work and permitted him to overcome his opponents. There could be but one explanation of such conduct—that the man was sincerely a patriot, holding above his own ambition desire for the good of his country.

Tokugawa had quietly accepted Hideyoshi's dictum that he should abandon his inherited lands and take in exchange territory to the North and East. There he had vigourously set about enlarging the little village of Edo into a walled town to which he gave the name of Yedo, building himself a powerful fortress-castle defended by great moats, organizing and ruling his new domain so well that the territory, which had been wild and sparsely settled, largely increased its population and became flourishing and orderly.

Hideyoshi hoped by intermarriage between his own kinsfolk and members of the Tokugawa family to tie this powerful clan of Minamoto to his interests. This is a curious illusion, examples of which history constantly recounts in all lands. Yet the shuffling about of the female relations of ambitious men, like pawns in a game, has never succeeded in restraining any aspiring individual from grasping at power whenever the temptation became great. The poor pawns meanwhile, having invariably been trampled upon, are swept from the board whenever masculine blood grows hot.

Hideyoshi, during the long period when he had given up hope of a direct descendant, had adopted his nephew as his heir and had promised him the reversion of power. The appearance of his longed-for son immediately produced complications. Always preferring the diplomatic method when possible, he endeavoured to persuade the nephew to adopt the new-born child. The disappointed heir, having sons of his own, refused to set them aside in the succession for this newcomer and took up arms to settle the question. The Taiko made short work of this outburst, and realizing that the little Hideyori would soon be supplanted when his father was no longer there to protect him, married the boy to a granddaughter of Tokugawa, hoping that the great clansman, satisfied to see his own blood in the place of dominance, would protect the little couple, so helpless without him. Tokugawa, content as always in his relations with the great Parvenu to bide his time, accepted the alliance and also the appointment as head of a council which was to rule after Hideyoshi's death until this child, allied to his house, could assume the reins of power.

Feeling that his end was approaching, and that he had prepared the way for his child, the Adventurer set himself to face the last great adventure into the Unknown. Summoning Tokugawa to his bedside, he urged him to recall the Japanese troops from Korea, foreseeing it possible, once his strong hand had become mere clay, that disorder in the Empire might once again wreck the land. He felt that foreign enterprises at such a time were unwise; Tokugawa must have all the forces of the government close at hand. With vision cleared by coming death he realized that the whole undertaking had been unworthy of him.

On the fifteenth day of September, 1598, the wanderer of the roads came to the end of his path—a path which had led through wild and violent places, amid cruel jealousies and confusion, where he had trod firmly and high-heartedly, making his way skillfully between all obstacles, with undaunted vision fixed upon a lofty goal—the goal of a united revivified Fatherland—in mind and spirit the complete Japanese.

A Jesuit annalist says that the nobles "were very much relieved when Hideyoshi passed to the number of their dead gods instead of counting among the living men of this earth." With the people, however, mourning was universal. They had resented the waste of their sons and brothers in the Korean expedition, but death draws a tender mantle over the faults and mistakes of one who has earned love and loyalty by his great deeds. They remembered only that Hideyoshi ended the long anarchy which had rent the land and had borne so hardly upon the simpler folk. More especially did they love him because he was one of their own, yet had made himself master of all the powerful and warlike patricians. The good measures of his administration were recalled: his order, his even-handed justice, his wise development of the nation's resources. Most of all they delighted to recount his human characteristics: his courage, his abounding good temper, his mocking and merry wit, his magnificent hospitalities, and his fond affection for all those pleasures which were typical of Japanese life. A thousand anecdotes passed from mouth to mouth picturing his many charming qualities. He took his place as a national hero, the pattern of all that was lovable and admirable in the race.

The Emperor, who had owed to the Parvenu his restoration to dignity, issued an order placing him among the national divinities with the honourific title of Toyo-kounikdai-mio-zin (great luminous genius of the prosperity of the country), and a temple was consecrated to his spirit near Mount Hiei-san.

Hideyoshi's story is not closed by his death. To understand his accomplishment, the deeds of his successor must be added to the chronicle. Had he been so unhappy as to leave no successor capable of completing his work, all would have been lost in renewed disorder and disaster.

The Japanese say, somewhat cynically, "Nobunaga made the fire, Hideyoshi cooked the dinner, Tokugawa ate it.". . .

Which is to reason too narrowly. Humanity is wont to impute to pure selfishness the measures making for a statesman's own advantage. Ieyasu

THE DELIGHTFUL PARVENU 269

Tokugawa knew that a long regency would endanger the still unsolidified structure of the newly centralized government. That his assumption of personal power was satisfying to his own desires may scarcely be doubted; yet it was also true that the nation's larger aims and general happiness were more adequately achieved by setting Hideyoshi's infant son aside for the dominance of his own family. Patriotism was probably an equal element with personal ambition in persuading him to this decision—a decision questionable only from the point of view of his private honour, and even from such an angle it might be urged that Tokugawa had no special obligation to the dead leader. A patrician himself and a man of eminent gifts, he had always held his hand when he might have asserted his own claims. Allowing the plebeian to control events and take the lead in the nation's affairs; judging that the needs of the government might be better met by his great contemporary—all this seems to prove that the good of his country meant more to Tokugawa than his own dominance. Hideyoshi gone, these considerations were no longer powerful. Public affairs still demanded a strong hand and a single will. A council was unable to function with the directness and cohesion which the situation required, and his long patience and self effacement were concluded.

Assumption of control proceeded deliberately. The Council was not called upon for consultation, and measures were taken to insure his sole administration. Yae, a woman of marked intelligence, counselled the restless and ambitious mother of the little Hideyori to accept these conditions, but in vain. A cabal was formed as the centre of all the discontented elements, and before long this had broken into an open revolt which Tokugawa, as able in the field as in affairs of state, put down ruthlessly. The young heir and his aspiring mother were segregated in a confinement which, while firm, was without hardships, and the new ruler proceeded to organize the government according to his own wise ideas. The centre of power was removed from Kyoto to his own city of Yedo. Local administration was left to the provinces, but lest the nobles abuse their delegated authority, each daimyo was required to spend six months of every year in the new capital directly under the eye of the Shogun, leaving his territory in his absence to be administered by a chancellor. The code of laws was carefully formulated and relentlessly administered. The religious orders were allowed great freedom in all spiritual matters, but not permitted to keep armed retainers, though the Shogun himself endowed them liberally for all purely religious purposes.

One element, however, this far-seeing statesman dealt with drastically. The Jesuit and Franciscan missionaries still remained in the country and were carrying on their propaganda in spite of the interdiction of Hideyoshi. Absorbed by his Korean expeditions the Taiko had paid them but scant attention, indulgently acceding to their pleas to be allowed to continue their residence in the country, his reply being: "I will willingly permit it if you will abstain from preaching."

It is interesting to note the Franciscan report of this matter: "As we had decided to take no count of this restriction we said not a word but made a profound salute." It is not to be supposed that Hideyoshi was fooled, because he remarked later: "If they do not show commonsense they will soon learn

THE DELIGHTFUL PARVENU 271

that they cannot play with me with impunity."

Immediately upon the Taiko's death both parties among the missionaries, supposing themselves at last free from all interference, became open in their proselytism, and violent quarrels broke out between the two orders.

During his long period of quiet waiting, it is obvious that Tokugawa had been active in informing himself of everything concerning the Empire and the course of events in Asia resulting from the Western intrusions. He had doubtless been told by Hideyoshi of the menacing suggestions of the Spanish sea captain. As Japan was at that time active commercially upon the sea, he had means of learning the results in the neighbouring countries of the religious and military activities of the Western people. He saw that everywhere the Asiatic races were being dominated by the Europeans. The Asian methods of defense were too feeble to protect them from the higher organization of Europe, and he determined that the Empire should not succumb to these intruders. The decision at which he arrived was startling and unprecedented, but genius never waits for precedent. At one stroke he undertook to cut off all communication with the outer world, even at the cost of destroying all the commerce that Hideyoshi had been carefully fostering and of the complete sacrifice of Japan's use of the sea. He expelled every foreigner, and when the missionaries fomented rebellion among their converts, he relentlessly wiped out those who preferred their new religion to their patriotism. All Japanese subjects were forbidden to leave the Empire upon any excuse whatever, and no foreigner was allowed to set foot upon the mainland. The only exception made was the setting aside of a small island where the

Dutch traders were allowed to come twice during the year to meet with Japanese merchants. The Hollanders were chosen for this privilege because they had made no attempt to change the faith or allegiance of the Japanese but had been content merely to take and to offer such goods as were needed. The Shogun wished, too, to keep a small window open upon the outer world through which he might learn what was happening in other lands.

The sacrifice was enormous and astonishing, but the results justified this amazing man in his bold step. No doubt Hideyoshi's expedition into Korea had been valuable in impressing the Western world with the military prowess of the Island Empire. While expeditions were encroaching everywhere upon Eastern territory, none of the Western powers thought well of trying conclusions with these self-made hermits. Another element conducing to the security which Tokugawa sought was the missionaries' reports of the absence of gold or portable wealth. Had Japan been unlucky enough to possess India's riches, even her stern and warlike manhood might not have been able to save her from the depredations of those ravenous flocks of Western eagles which were feeding upon Asia elsewhere.

Thus the great Minamoto chieftain slammed the door in the face of the world and devoted his life to creating in his islands the type of civilization he deemed best suited to his people. So wisely did he work that for two hundred and fifty years he gave to his race complete peace, an experience unexampled in the history of the world. Not only did no invader attempt an intrusion, but within the Empire itself order was maintained and content unbroken. Elsewhere, long periods of quietude have resulted in loosening and enfeebling the fibres of the people, but so ably did Ieyasu Tokugawa plan his political structure that effeminacy never softened the quality of his subjects. When at last the West forced open Japan's closed doors, they found a race capable, both mentally and physically, of protecting, within a short period, its place among the great powers of the world.

A modern writer summing up the state Hideyoshi and Tokugawa created says:

"Ever since the sixteenth century Japan has enjoyed one of the most perfectly organized governments on record. For two centuries and a half this government, the work of two superlative statesmen, maintained unity and order with a minimum of tyranny and corruption, establishing the traditions of discipline and obedience to central authority which have since rendered such remarkable service. Though reluctant to come out of her seclusion, she emerged with herself perfectly in hand and ready for the crisis."

It was part of the wisdom which he never failed to exhibit in matters of state that Ieyasu abdicated in 1605 in favour of his son Hidetada while retaining in his own hand much of the power and direction of affairs. By this means he made sure that his successor would be thoroughly trained in his duties before he himself disappeared from the scene. From his quiet little retreat in Shidzuoka he continued to develop and perfect his organization. He left it only when Hideyori, now become fifteen years of age, attempted once more to arouse a revolt. This he put down, but again, in 1615, the smouldering embers of long repressed disorder broke into flame. The aged Shogun, now in his seventy-fourth year, took the field to put an end to the attempt of the discontented to renew the old anarchy. In this last of his wars he was wounded in the groin by the thrust of a lance, and though he succeeded in stamping out the final spark of the old fire, he never recovered from his wound but died nine months after in April, 1616. The wife and the son of his great predecessor had perished together in the castle of Osaka set on fire during the war, and at last the Tokugawas had no further rival.

In his retreat in Shidzuoka, Ieyasu had completed the text of the House-law laid down as a rule for his successors. Perhaps no abler state document has ever been drawn than this, which concludes:

"Life is like unto a long journey with a heavy load. Let thy steps be slow and steady that thou stumble not. Persuade thyself that privations are the natural lot of mortals and there will be no room for discontent, neither for despair. When ambitious desires rise in thy heart recall the days of extremity thou hast passed through. Forbearance is the root of quietness and assurance forever. Look upon wrath as thy enemy. Find fault with thyself rather than with others. Better the less than the more." In these closing words he summed up the rules by which he had lived.

Iyemitsu, the third and powerful Shogun, created for the ashes of his grandsire one of the most beautiful resting places ever conceived. His remains were carried to the green and lofty heights of Nikko, a place of mountains belted with forests of splendid conifers, down whose ravines were heard the voices of a thousand crystal streams. A great double avenue of cryptomeria was planted for forty miles to shade his approach. Across the river he passed to his tomb over the sacred red-lacquered bridge built to commemorate a miracle: A saint desiring to reach the other side prayed to the gods for aid and immediately found two red dragons stretching from shore to shore to offer him a pathway.

Through gateways and shrines adorned with every sumptuous glory his way passed up a long stone stairway to the crest of a peak, where his ashes were at last enclosed in a simple bronze urn standing alone amid a girdle of mighty evergreens.

Shah Jahan and Chien Lung were unhappy in that they were succeeded by men of inferior ability who brought their work to naught. The Great Parvenu, fortunate in many things, was peculiarly so in that the labours he had but half finished were taken up by hands even more skillful than his own. Could he have known the results, so entire was his patriotism that he would doubtless have been content to see his son set aside to make way for the genius which was to bestow upon his country such inestimable blessings. Japan herself was fortunate in having produced in rapid succession three such sons: Nobunaga, a blind and resistless force to crush the bloody and selfish provincialism of the warring chieftains; Hideyoshi to lay the foundation of a vigourous and centralized government; and Ieyasu Tokugawa to build upon that foundation a political structure so solid and enduring.

www.ingramcontent.com/pod-product-compliance
Lightning Source LLC
Chambersburg PA
CBHW021120300426
44113CB00006B/221